MY YEARS IN GERMANY

Duncan M. Graham
Hamilton

76
76

Cor

6SP

MY YEARS IN GERMANY

by

MARTHA DODD

LONDON
VICTOR GOLLANCZ LTD
1939

First published April 1939
Second impression April 1939

For

MY FATHER AND MOTHER

PRINTED IN GREAT BRITAIN BY PURNELL AND SONS, LTD. (T.U.)
PAULTON (SOMERSET) AND LONDON

CONTENTS

I

TO BEGIN WITH

Before 1933 my life was rooted in America, in her earth and cities, people and attitudes. Except for a brief trip to the Far West and a year in Europe which left me, as it does most Americans, with a permanent desire to see and learn more of the ways of different lands and national traditions, my experience was centred around the life we led in Chicago and in Virginia. When I was a child my father had bought a farm in Virginia, my native state, and we went there every summer to rest from the strenuous atmosphere of Chicago.

It was a beautiful spot, this dairy farm of a few hundred acres, with a simple and ancient farmhouse on it, tucked away among magnificent old trees and shrubbery, in the foothills of the Blue Ridge mountains, only fifty miles from the capital of the nation. We had long quiet summers there, with soft nights of fragrance and cool mountain breeze, days of reading, resting, physical exercise. We always came closer together as a family group in these surroundings, seeing one another constantly, discussing plans and dreams, studying the life about us, among the Negro and poor white workers. My father in those days believed that children should combine physical exercise with productive work. So instead of playing tennis, golf, and swimming, we picked peaches and apples, sorted them for the commercial market, tended the garden; my father and brother often ploughed the field, threshing the wheat, and in general working by the side of the farm labourers. In a month or two we were refreshed and the strain was eased, so that we could go back to Chicago and intellectual work with eagerness and anticipation, all of us feeling the harmony of love and common interests.

In these summers, when I was between thirteen and fifteen, I came upon the Russian writers whose works I read devotedly and passionately and who had a great influence on my early life. I was already, in my own mind, a budding writer and poet, an ambition which remained through my high school and university careers. Also at this time I came across Nietzsche's "Anti-Christ" with an introduction by H. L. Mencken, both of which impressed me tremendously. I started a correspondence with Mencken shortly after, which lasted several years. It was a stimulating experience and helped to encourage a critical sense.

In a life of unbroken admiration for my father I remember only two habits of his which bored and distressed me. One was his passionate concern for history and economics, and the other, his persistent effort over a period of several years to introduce my brother and me to the literary beauties of the Bible. Time and again I would slip away from the dining-room table, where most of the conversations of the family continued after the meal was over, rather than hear these complicated discussions and long readings. I think my mother sympathized with my attitude toward the Bible, since she herself had been through a strict religious training in her youth. But she did deplore my lack of interest in politics, which was even then an absorbing interest of hers.

This unawareness of political and economic issues, large social problems, stayed with me throughout my three and a half years at the University of Chicago. I specialized in English and managed to go through a great university with excellent marks but without the knowledge that should have been the basis for them. I narrowed my interests down to literature and art, and though I attended economy, philosophy, and science courses, I immediately forgot them, to return with a little clique of so-called intellectuals to elaborate arguments and discussions of literary ideas and techniques, of poetry and painting.

I went to a progressive University High School which was called "U High," or by some rival schools "Jew High." Nevertheless until I entered the University I had not the faintest idea of anti-Semitism, in either its mild or vicious forms. When Loeb and Leopold committed their tragic crime I was less aware that one of them had attended the same high school and were both Jews than of the fact that they were bored, over-brilliant, and sophisticated sons of rich men.

The subtle and undercurrent propaganda among the undergraduates, those socially and financially prominent as well as some of the more conscious intellectuals, made me aware for the first time that there was such hostility toward Jews. When I was interested in a young Jew I began to realize the extent to which this petty but far-reaching ostracism could go. However, my susceptibility to propaganda went only so far as to make me think that most Jews were rich and close-fisted, brilliant and pushy. Until I went to Germany I had not been subjected to any cleverer propaganda. I was slightly anti-Semitic in this sense: I accepted the attitude that Jews were not as attractive physically as Gentiles and were less socially presentable. The argument that I was to hear a few years later in Germany about their domination of all cultural and economic life, and desire for world power, was too patently absurd for anyone to present seriously in these years and in these surroundings. But I do remember that even many of the college professors resented the brilliance of Jewish colleagues and students.

For several years I had known Robert Morss Lovett who taught English Literature and Composition at the University. The last year I lived in America I saw him more than I did friends of my own age. We used to have long evenings together in which he gave me my first clue to the existence of a world outside the closed and rather arrogant literary one in which I was living. His provocative questions and pointed analyses of books and events began to open a mind that had been closed. He told me of war and working conditions, of inequality and injustice, of economic persecution, of the impossibility for anyone to live or work in isolation from these things; all of which at that time only touched the surface of my mind. I tried stupidly to refute him. I argued, what does it matter to writers and artists, how and why does this concern me when I am reviewing books and writing love stories. He would answer quietly, persuasively, patiently, with the warm sympathy of a restrained but highly emotional nature and the cold clarity of his mind. With the exception of my father and another older teacher and friend, he meant more to me in this period of my development than anyone else. I loved him as a friend, I was grateful to him as a teacher, for he was the first to encourage me deeply in my writing. As a socially functioning human being I was to learn his significance and courage later, in the climate of Nazi Germany where the seeds he planted were to grow.

Two other experiences in this last year made a deep impression on me; unconsciously, they must have meant much more than I realized at that time, because I recall them now with such vividness as I seek to choose the significant details in my pre-Nazi life. I saw a protest strike outside my window in the Chicago *Tribune* office, in which several policemen on horses rode through the peacefully marching, harmlessly placarded group, brutally clubbing many men to the ground. When shots were fired I knew that the police were responsible. Someone said that the covered objects in the *Tribune* lobby were machine-guns. Even if it were not true, I wondered why people would say they were there at this time, and what they could be used for. Going home that night and dining with my family at a faculty club, I described indignantly what I had seen. Someone in the group turned laughingly to me and said: "Well, well, you seem to have turned into a Bolshevik, standing up for those strikers so ardently." I didn't see what connection this had with my attitude and I resented being called a Bolshevik; I was merely sympathetic with people who expressed their ideas bravely.

The other incident concerned a book I was told to review for the *Tribune*. I had left the university after three and a half years to take the job of Assistant Literary Editor of this newspaper. I received one morning Ella Winter's "Red Virtue." Perhaps it is not an important book. I have not reread it since, but it made a vivid impression on me then. It had freshness and vitality, a stimulating point of view which

I had never heard before. I reviewed it with high praise and discussed it with my father. Russia had only been a name to me and Bolshevik a term of heavy, if somewhat vague, opprobrium. My father listened sympathetically to my description of the book and then said quietly: "There may be some good points in the system you mention, apparently the author thinks so; but I can't believe that any form of government which oppresses the freedom and initiative of the individual can be anything but dangerous to the human soul in the long run." I was to see and learn later for myself. In the meantime I held very close to my heart a book that told of the economic and moral emancipation of women, not thinking or caring in what country or under what system it occurred.

Another important friendship developed in the last year and a half of my residence in America, which in some ways both supplemented and enlarged the influence of Robert Morss Lovett. I had known Carl Sandburg since I was fifteen years old and he had always been a dear friend of my parents, but it was not until I was twenty-three that I began to feel the genius and uniqueness of his personality. Here again was an infinitely wise and warm man, much older than myself, who tried to release what creative energy I had and to broaden and deepen an almost negligible social consciousness. He told me to write everything I felt, to pour it out regardless of what shame I might later feel about exaggerated lyricism, overwriting, and sentimentality. He told me to see life, to open myself to all new adventures of the mind and spirit, to be reckless and yet contained, to identify myself with the struggles and emotions around me. He revealed the profoundest contempt for the aloof, the objective spirit.

Partially in reaction, also because I knew deep in me that he was right in showing me things I had closed my life away from, I fought against his ideas, reviled radicals and their ilk, and resented the emphasis he put upon the simple man. Faint stirrings came nevertheless and, though I denied that I would ever feel the indignation against society which he said all men and women worth their salt felt and acted upon sometime in their lives, I responded to the challenge and felt my circumscribed little world shaken by his great wrath and belief.

These two friendships began the process, in the last year of my life in America before my residence in Germany, of opening my life and heart in a way that was to change my life's pattern and direction.

AN UNCONVENTIONAL APPOINTMENT

SHORTLY AFTER FRANKLIN DELANO ROOSEVELT was elected President, my father was taking a vacation in the beloved hills of Virginia. He came back to Chicago with reports of the excitement and enthusiasm about the new President, whom he had known personally many years before in Wilson's cabinet. We had all been eager Roosevelt partisans and I voted for the first time in 1932. My father was greatly satisfied with Roosevelt's election, the first Democratic and progressive President since Wilson.

Soon, however, we settled down after the feeling of tenseness and victory, into our normal ways of life, always keenly aware that new things were happening, and even more in store, in Washington.

I was still working on the *Tribune*, filling a routine not entirely pleasing to me but satisfying in a smaller sense, because I was earning my own living. In my spare time, usually at night from eight until one, I wrote short stories, hoping that in a few months or years I might be able to give up my job and become a full-time writer. I did not like having to review from four to six books in one column. The editor of the paper was cutting down on literary space and I felt strongly that I couldn't be fair to important books in such short space.

One morning in June my mother called me up at the office and without warning me at all, said excitedly: "Your father has just received a telephone call from President Roosevelt asking him to accept the post of Ambassador to Germany!" She cautioned me not to tell anyone, since my father had not made his decision.

That day was a hard one to pull through. I had to go through my usual routine as if nothing had happened. It was particularly difficult for me as I love to share excitement and problems with friends. During that day I didn't tell anyone of the event and didn't for a moment think of going to Germany with my parents. I knew I was old enough to live an independent life; I had a job and the beginning of a writing career; I didn't want to pull up roots at this stage of my life. But I also dreaded the thought of being separated from my family from whom I had never been separated before.

I tried to visualize the Germany my parents would be living in, to recall all I knew and had heard about the new developments. I remembered Hitler as a clown who looked like Charlie Chaplin, who burned books and against all the prophecies of mature and trained people had set up a dictatorship. But this is as far as my penetration of international politics led me at that time. I couldn't quite place, in my mind's eye, my father in such an atmosphere. Still I knew that the offer of the post was a great honour, rarely refused, and would be a crowning achievement to his life of selfless devotion to history and his country's democratic tradition.

I felt it was a great decision for my father and mother and I knew they would be as torn in the making of it as I was in thinking about it for them. Yet I knew that if my father thought he could render a service to his country, he would do it at no matter what cost to his personal life. He wanted to finish his long history of the Old South, and he was rooted in his quiet and productive life of scholarship and teaching.

The pure distraction and strain of that day finally came to an end. My hands were cold, my cheeks flaming and the secret heavy on my heart. I rushed home at five o'clock, eager to know the developments of the day.

President Roosevelt had called my father and urged him to accept the position, saying he could render great service to his Government. He finally, after consulting my mother and carefully weighing his future and his hopes, called back to the White House, and accepted the appointment, with the stipulation that he intended to, and must, live on his salary.

The President agreed heartily to this and indicated his personal approval of modest living and expenditure.

The appointment was an astounding one and we spent the evening discussing the possible motives for it. There had been many names suggested for the post, names representing fortune and political contribution. Though my father had been active in a small way behind the scenes for many years in the Democratic Party, particularly during Wilson's administration, he had made no real contribution to the party's funds and held no official position. We concluded that he was appointed because of his knowledge of Germany's history, language, and culture—he had spent three years there as a young man and had received a doctor's degree at Leipzig University. We also suspected that a friend of ours, Daniel C. Roper, Secretary of Commerce, had urged and supported the appointment. Could it have been, we asked ourselves privately, that President Roosevelt wanted to register his belief in the democratic system by sending a representative as unconnected with Fascism as any human could be?—a man who had been loyal and unwavering in his support of democratic ideals, modest, scholarly, incorruptible politically and financially, a student of the old Germany where freedom was still not an empty slogan?

In any case, as the days went by and pressure was put upon me to go along at least for a year, we discovered that my father felt an elation and enthusiasm that his restrained manner could not hide from those closest to him. He admitted shyly that as a young student he had dreamed of going back to the Germany he loved, as a Consul or minor diplomatic official, to represent his own country. He believed, despite the monarchical and autocratic rule of the Kaiser that had existed so long in Germany, the German people were essentially a democratic-minded, highly educated and liberty-loving nation. He had defended Germany after the War when it was almost treason in this country to do so. He had deplored the Versailles Treaty and had ultimately found some flowering of his own political ideals in the Republic and the Weimar Constitution. More than that, there was an almost sentimental nostalgia for the Germany of his youth, the country that had opened up the tremendous cultural horizons to him, softened his heart by the kindness and generosity of its people, both simple and educated.

These days were flooded with remembrances. Was this professor still teaching, was that friend still alive; could he recapture his former mastery of the strangely beautiful and brutal tongue? Did we know this opera and that, which he attended in Berlin or in some other city? Did we remember the poetry of Schiller and Goethe? Wouldn't we like to hear something about the countryside and the philosophers? Did we know that a German girl had once put violets in his room every day?—this was drawn from him by my mother, who had the teasing gaiety of a young girl.

I recall various dinners given in our honour before we left, when my father would haltingly try out his German on German friends or professors of the language. He tried to sharpen his memory of all things German. He read books, talked evocatively about friends, scenes, history, until my mother and I began to feel the enchantment and power of the distant land he felt so close to.

I had several long talks with both my parents as to the advisability of leaving America. They answered all my arguments wisely and with sympathy. I would repeat: "What if I lose my job, now after I am beginning to do real work, and can't get another next year? Suppose I cannot write over there?" They replied that an experience of this sort would far outweigh these considerations. And they said if I felt my work to be that urgent I could certainly return when I wanted to and resume it, perhaps in the same place and with even better advantages. My mother was especially eager to have me with her in an experience which she felt intuitively would be a difficult one for her. They argued that I would see history in the making, would broaden as a person and a writer after contact with a different people and a different set of traditions. I realized they were right and would feel much happier if both their children would be with them in the sharing of this new experience. My father also pointed out that the study and mastery of a new language and literature could only have a beneficial effect on any intellectually curious and ambitious person.

My brother, to whom I was deeply devoted, was teaching in Washington, D.C., at the time of the appointment. Since his graduation from college he had been studying for a master's degree and teaching in various universities—Rutgers College University of North Carolina, and now American University in the capital.

He was three and a half years older than I, though most people thought he was younger. Youthful, eager, naïve and talented, his interests, hopes, and activities were almost identical with mine. Therefore we were closer than most brothers and sisters. Our dream was one day to have an apartment together and live useful and productive lives. Neither of us wanted to marry—especially I who had been married for a short period unhappily. Our family ties were abnormally close and dear to us. And we really felt we would not be grown up enough to live without the exciting, tender, and constructive companionship of our family.

When we wired Bill he seemed to accept as a matter of course that we would all go together. He was anxious to get his doctor's degree, and it appealed to him to have a German university degree—as his father had. He, too, apparently did not realize the significance of living in Nazi Germany. He did not think of the residence there as a lark however— rather as an invaluable experience in the stream of living history. He urged that I go with the family and influenced me. We decided to meet him in Virginia in two weeks.

It was fortunate for both of us, devoted friends and confidants as we were, that we observed Nazi Germany together. His critical intelligence and his opportunities to see many places I was unable to see helped me tremendously to understand the whole scene. And we were able constantly to compare notes, to exchange views, reactions, emotions with each other as well as with our parents.

So we decided that I should go with them for a year. I announced my decision in a few days to the literary editor.

Bᴏ

She understood and was herself excited by the news which by this time was in the papers. I remember she and I discussed one day what I should buy for my stay there, clothes and so forth. She commented: "Well, you won't need many dresses and certainly not formal ones because, since the Court life has been destroyed and the Nazis have come to power, there must be no social life." Her picture of the primitivism and the reversion to an almost stark simplicity of living was about on a par with mine—and equally false.

Until we left for Virginia, two or three weeks after the appointment, we were deluged with telephone calls, telegrams, reporters and photographers, invitations. It was all very confusing, a strange intrusion and imposition on hitherto strictly private lives. We didn't know how to handle the newspapermen or what to do about their desire for special scoops and stories. We didn't like to confirm the appointment until it had been passed on by the Senate. And I am sure we began to make a series of blunders that were to continue, to our friends' and our own amusement, for several months. But it was thrilling for all of us, nevertheless.

To show how unconscious I was of the political implications and significance of the Nazi regime, I do not remember any of us being especially disturbed at the thought of living under a dictatorship. Yet now I know my father must have spent many anguished moments thinking of it and anticipating his personal discomfort in such an atmosphere. He did say several times, he wondered how the Germans as they now were could accept his book on Wilson and his general liberal political philosophy. We discovered later that when his name had been presented to the German Government, the officials scarcely knew who he was and when they found out, were not too eager at the prospect. They could not refuse him, however, without offending a foreign State.

His continual repetition and emphasis upon the impermanence of our stay should have given me pause. He said: "Don't take your household things. Leave most of the furniture and belongings here, because we will be back in a year." I am sure now, after having watched him as a functioning diplomat for over four years, that he must have then thought he could have some influence in moderating the policies of the Nazi regime in its internal and foreign problems, a chance to bring them back to reason, to recall forcefully to them their recent democratic past. He must not have known—and how could anyone?—how inexorably determined they were to impose their system on the nation and even the world, or perish in the attempt. He probably imagined that they would not last very long, as many people did in those days; or that, if they did, the excesses of their seizure of power would be modified as they became more experienced in governing. In any case, the reservation, constantly repeated, that a year would be enough for us, indicated that my father contemplated returning to America if he could not be effective or constructive as a diplomat and idealist.

At the farewell dinner given to us by the German groups, the German-American societies, and the German Consulate, I sat at a table between Carl Sandburg and Thornton Wilder. All my other friends had given me flippant advice as to how to act in diplomatic society, taught me amusing phrases to say to Adolph Hitler when I met him, scared my mother and me to death about the pretentious and magnificent displays and the financial output necessary to become successful representatives of our country. But Thornton Wilder, friendly, eager, and charming as usual, and Harriet Monroe gave a sound counsel to learn the language and mingle with the Germans rather than with the foreign groups.

Carl Sandburg talked in his best manner—inimitable and characteristic: "Find out what this man Hitler is made of, what makes his brain go round, what his bones and blood are made of. Before your eyes will pass the greatest pageant of crooks and gangsters, idealists, statesmen, criminals, diplomats, and geniuses. You will see every nationality in the world. Watch them, study them, dissect them. Don't be frightened or diffident, don't let them or your experiences spoil you or your eagerness for life. Be brave and truthful, keep your poetry and integrity."

We left Chicago in a flurry of flowers and friends, under a nervous strain which we thought unbearable but which was only the beginning and a poor approximation of what we were to know of gnawing nerves, raw and exposed sensitiveness, and grief. We took a train for Virginia where we hoped to have a few days of rest from packers, well-wishers, sudden-appearing snobs and social climbers who out of a clear sky had "known, loved, and respected us all these years," confusions and steady streaming admonitions.

We spent a week on the farm, the fragrant southern daytime heat and cool clear mountain nights, the smell and beauty of earth and quiet, restoring some sense of reality and perspective. My father was having conferences with President Roosevelt and the State Department, was spending perspiring tedious days among confidential papers and documents, learning more of the situation in Germany and what was expected of him as America's representative.

Driving to New York in our Chevrolet which we decided to take over with us, we arrived on a hot summer day and were once more flooded with telephone calls, telegrams, invitations, and demands of all sorts. We escaped as politely as possible and finally sailed on the *Washington* with more flowers and gifts and good wishes than we knew what to do with, and a disproportionate amount of sadness and foreboding.

For the first day or two I wept copiously and sentimentally for the things and people I was giving up—I thought for only a year. America and my life there seemed inestimably precious when I found myself finally faced with the reality of a foreign land and a sphere of experience completely unknown to me.

The sea was calm and beautiful and we had time and quiet to discuss the new era that lay ahead of us. My father was very serious and, behind his habitual reserve, rather nervous. Before the boat had sailed the newspapermen had urged him and my mother to extend their arms in a good-bye salute to America. Both parents complied in what was to be interpreted later in the press as a Fascist salute—a greeting we were scarcely aware of then.

The voyage on the whole was both a thoughtful and a gay one. My father spoke earnestly of the necessity for us children to learn the language and try to understand the culture of the people. He would insist that we all stay in his stateroom for an hour or so a day and listen to him read German—from a history book, if I remember—to familiarize ourselves with the sound of the tongue. He taught us the few essentials of the pronunciation and manners of speech. The accent in any language has always been comparatively simple for me so I didn't have much trouble at first. He read E. A. Mowrer's book, "Germany Puts the Clock Back," which someone had sent him on the boat.

The second youngest son of the President was on board, a charming, intelligent, gangling boy on a vacation after graduation. We had fun dancing and drinking champagne. I remember we compared passports and were amused at the comparative simplicity of his which read: "Franklin Roosevelt, Jr., is the son of the President of the United States of America." Mine, a diplomatic one, was much more pretentious . . . "a daughter of William E. Dodd, Ambassador Extraordinary and Plenipotentiary of the United States of America to Germany."

We touched, or at least came near to touching, Ireland, a sight for which we stayed up all night; a beautiful and entrancing vision of brilliant green hills, soft and wild in the dawn light. I have passed this island seven or eight times and still feel the magic and wonder of it, even from the boat's distance in the Irish Sea, and have promised myself each time that here is one place I shall not miss before my travelling days are over. We stayed for some time in Havre and I got off to see the Roosevelt boy and his party onto the train for Paris. So anxious was I to touch French soil, which I had known and loved before, that I looked far and wide for a stretch of earth on which to put my toe. I finally had to scratch up a bit of gravel between the railroad ties and touch the tip of my toe to the earth beneath. I was satisfied.

The rest of the trip to Hamburg was very dull indeed after the liveliness of the last days on board. Most of the passengers had gotten off at either Southampton or Havre. We had a slow sail up the Elbe and finally docked at Hamburg. Germany was here at last, with all of its profound meaning, the new future only guessed at and begun, to which my father gave all the idealism of his deeply emotional and disciplined life, with which he expected to co-operate and which he hoped to benefit. I was moved by the eagerness, which he unconsciously expressed in returning in one of the highest positions our country can offer to its citizens, to the country he had so well loved, understood, and defended. For us, his children, here was a new adventure breaking into our middle youth, not sought after, not really fully appreciated; it was not an end or a beginning for us—or so we thought—but an episode occurring in the security of circumstance and love. It was not recklessness for us; it was our parents' gift of an experience which could open or close or mean nothing in our lives. We greeted Germany with excited hearts, taking the future in our stride with the uncapturable nonchalance of youth, ready for anything or for nothing.

2

We must have presented one of the most amazing spectacles in the history of diplomatic arrivals, though, of course, we were completely unconscious of it at the time. My father had misread a telegram sent by the counsellor of the Embassy. He thought that the tickets to Berlin, the private car, etc., had all been arranged, so we didn't bother about arranging for them on board, and in the confusion of disembarking forgot to get our necessary cards. Until the last moment he was busy with interviewers and newspapermen. One of the journalists was a correspondent of a Jewish newspaper in Hamburg. He wrote an article saying that my father had been sent over to solve the Jewish problem. Later we heard about it, and realized how badly garbled the account was. The German papers were very polite to us, but took the occasion to point out that this was the way of Jews.

My brother had planned to drive our Chevrolet to Berlin, but had done nothing about the red tape of getting it off the ship, with the permits and licences, and so on, that it involved.

The Counsellor, the adviser to the Ambassador and next in

rank to him, a gentleman of the most extreme Protocol[1] (we hadn't yet heard this word) school, with grey-white hair and moustache which looked curled, elegant dress, gloves, stick and proper hat, a complexion of flaming hue, clipped, polite, and definitely condescending accent, was so horrified at our informality that his rage almost—not quite—transcended the bounds allowed by his rigid code of behaviour. We had no pretentious car, we had no chauffeur; valets, secretaries, and personal maids were ominously missing—in fact, we looked like simple ordinary human beings the like of which he had not permitted himself to mingle with for perhaps most of his adult life.

Finally, everything was put in order, my brother driving the modest car and the rest of us going by a regular train to Berlin (we should have at least taken the "Flying Hamburger," the fastest and most expensive special). My father sat in one compartment talking over the political developments of Germany with the Counsellor, who was attempting in the most polished manner he could summon, to hint that my father was no longer a simple professor, but a great diplomat, and his habits and ways of life should be altered accordingly. But the honest and subtle, gentle and slightly nervous scholar was to remain as firm in his integrity of character as if there had been no change in his environment or position. I didn't realize how futile all admonitions were, and I am sure my father was as supremely indifferent to them then as he was to be later when great pressure from all sources was applied to effect the desired transformation.

My mother and I were in another compartment, she uneasy and heavy of heart at the thought of the duties and change in life-patterns confronting her; and I sound asleep on her shoulder, both of us shrouded in expensive flowers.

The train stopped suddenly and I had just time enough to rub my eyes, jam on my hat and step onto the platform, a little dazed and very embarrassed. Before me was a large gathering of excited people; newspapermen crowding around

[1] A word which in most languages means a set of rigid social and diplomatic rules of etiquette and conduct.

us, and the ever-watchful Counsellor attempting to keep them away; Foreign Office representatives, other diplomats, and many Americans, come to look over the strange Ambassador and his family. The flashlights were a steady stream of blinding light and somehow or other I found myself grinning stupidly into the camera with bunches of orchids and other flowers up to my ears. My father took the newspapermen aside and gave them a prepared statement of greeting and we were hustled away.

I was put into a car with a young man who, I soon learned, was our Protocol secretary. I finally got the definition. He was pointing out the sights of Berlin to me. We drove around the Reichstag building, which he duly named. I exclaimed: "Oh, I thought it was burned down! It looks all right to me. Tell me what happened." He leaned over to me, after several such natural but indiscreet questions, and said, 'S-ssh! Young lady, you must learn to be seen and not heard. You mustn't say so much and ask so many questions. This isn't America and you can't say all the things you think." I was astonished, but subdued for the time being. This was my first contact with the reality of Germany under a dictatorship and it took me a long time to take his advice seriously. Long habits of life are hard to change overnight.

We arrived at the Esplanade Hotel and were ushered into the Imperial suite. We gasped at its magnificence and also at what we thought the bill would be. Again the rooms were so filled with flowers that there was scarcely space to move in— orchids and rare scented lilies, flowers of all colours and descriptions. We had two huge high-ceilinged reception rooms lined with satin brocades, decorated with gilt and tapestried furniture and marble tables. Our welcoming friends finally left us to our own devices and my father went to bed with a book. Mother and I sat around, small and awed by the glamour of being the Ambassador's family, receiving cards that began coming in and more baskets of flowers, wondering desperately how all this was to be paid for without mortgaging our souls. We did not know then that the hotel has special rates for visiting "potentates," and had been even more considerate in our case. The Adlon hotel manager had wired us to accept a suite in his hotel free of charge, or at such a low rate that it seemed free, but Ambassadors had had the habit of residing at the Esplanade and we were not allowed to break the precedent.

My father was in magnificent humour at dinner-time. We all went down to the hotel dining-room to order the meal. My father was pouring out his German, teasing the waiters, and asking them questions—most undignified behaviour for an Ambassador. I never heard so many *"Dankeschoens"* and *"Bitteschoens"* in my life in one single evening, and it was my first introduction to the almost obsequious courtesy of German waiters. We had a good but heavy German dinner and I tasted my first German beer.

After we had finished, we decided to walk around a bit near the hotel before going to bed. We walked the length of the Sieges Allee lined on each side with rather ugly and pretentious statues of former rulers of Germany. My father would stop before each one and give us a short historical sketch of his time and character. He was in his element here as he knew German history almost by heart and if he missed out on something, he made a mental note for future study. I am sure this was one of the happiest evenings we spent in Germany. All of us were full of joy and peace. We liked Germany, and I was enchanted by the kindness and simplicity of the people, as far as I had seen them. The streets were dully lit, almost like a small American town late at night; there were no soldiers on the streets; everything was peaceful, romantic, strange, nostalgic. I felt the press had badly maligned the country and I wanted to proclaim the warmth and friendliness of the people, the soft summer night with its fragrance of trees and flowers, the serenity of the streets.

I was laid up in bed for the next few days with a bad cold. Sigrid Schultz came to see me. She is the correspondent for the Chicago *Tribune* and has been in Germany for over ten years. Small, a little pudgy, with blue eyes and an abundance of golden hair, she was very friendly and intelligent, with a mind alert if not always accurate, and a great news-hound. She had known the Germany of the past and she was sick at heart now.

She told me many stories about the Nazis and their brutalities, the Secret Police before whom she was regularly summoned for the critical reports she wrote. I didn't believe all her stories. I thought she was exaggerating and a bit hysterical, but I liked her personally and was interested to get a line on some of the people I was going to be associated with—diplomats and journalists.

I had a letter to the already quite famous American newspaperman H. R. Knickerbocker from Alexander Woollcott which I soon sent by post. He called up and asked me for a tea date. He was a small, slender man with red hair and warm, bright brown eyes, and a mobile mouth. We danced—which he does beautifully—and he asked me if I knew German or Germany, or anything about the Nazis. After revealing to him what must have seemed like appalling ignorance, he talked a bit about the Nazi leaders and soon shifted to other things. I wasn't interested in politics or economics and was mainly concerned in getting the "feel" of the people. I was delighted by them and still remember my joy that afternoon at the Eden Hotel, watching their funny stiff dancing, listening to their incomprehensible and guttural tongue, and watching their simple gestures, natural behaviour and childlike eagerness for life.

During this first month we were receiving calls from Germans and Americans, listening to all sorts of points of view to which I did not respond very deeply, being so utterly absorbed in understanding the temper and heart of a foreign people. Unconsciously, I began to compare them, as we went around to reasonable or cheap restaurants—not at all in the accepted fashion of diplomats—to the French. The Germans seemed much more genuine and honest, even in the merchant class. I was pleased that they did not try to cheat us when it was so clear that we were foreigners, that they were very solemn and sympathetic when we first started to speak our pathetic German. They weren't thieves, they weren't selfish, they weren't impatient or cold and hard; qualities I began to find stood out in my mind as characteristic of the French. We joked a lot, and I think only my father took seriously the warnings that the servants were apt to be spies and that dictaphones and eavesdroppers were encircling us.

Among the various newspapermen I met at this time was Quentin Reynolds, the Hearst correspondent. He was a big hulk of a man, with curly hair, humorous eyes and a broad beaming face. Sharp and tough and unsentimental, I thought him an excellent newspaperman. He had been in Germany a few months and was picking up the language rapidly. He knew intimately such legendary figures as Ernst ("Putzi") Hanfstaengl, and arranged for us to meet at a party given by an English journalist. It was a lavish and fairly drunken affair with an interesting mixture of Germans and foreigners. Putzi came in late in a sensational manner, a huge man in height and build, towering over everyone present. His face was heavy and dark, rather underslung and concave in shape. He had a soft, ingratiating manner, a beautiful voice which he used with conscious artistry, sometimes whispering low and soft, the next minute bellowing and shattering the room. He was supposed to be the artist among the Nazis, erratic and interesting, the personal clown and musician to Hitler himself. He usually dominated every group he was in by the commanding quality of his powerful physical presence, or by the tirelessness of his indomitable energy and never-ending talk. He could exhaust anyone and, from sheer perseverance, out-shout or out-whisper the strongest man in Berlin. I was fascinated and intrigued by my first contact with a Nazi high up in official circles, so blatantly proclaiming his charm and talent. Bavarian and American blood produced this strange phenomenon. He could never have been a Prussian and he was proud of it.

III

FIRST IMPRESSIONS OF GERMANY

QUENTIN REYNOLDS SUGGESTED to my brother and me that we take our Chevrolet and make a trip with him through Southern Germany and Austria. With a little persuasion my parents thought it would be a good way for us to study Germany.

So the three of us set out in August, a little over a month after our arrival, and made for the south. It was an exciting trip and the lack of German gave us some amusing moments in asking directions and ordering food. We stopped off at Wittenberg and saw the ninety-seven theses of Luther nailed, in bronze, on the church door, and went on to Leipzig, my father's old university town. There, of course, we drank many steins of beer in the old Auerbach Keller in honour of the meeting of Faust and Mephistopheles. All along the roads and in the towns we saw the Nazi banner, with the red background, the white circle in the centre emblazoned with the mystic crooked cross. Driving in and out of towns we saw large banners strung across the road on which I recognized the word "Jude." We realized this was anti-Semitic propaganda, but we didn't—at least I didn't—take it too seriously. Furthermore, I couldn't read the German well enough to have a full understanding of the words, and I must confess the Nazi spirit of intolerance had not yet dawned on me in its complete significance.

Enthusiasm was wild—or so it seemed on the surface. When people looked at our car and saw the low number, they "Heiled" energetically, probably thinking we were an official family from the great capital. We saw a lot of marching men, in brown uniforms, singing and shouting and waving their flags. These were the now-famous Brown-Shirt Storm Troopers, through whose loyalty and terroristic methods Hitler seized power. The excitement of the people was contagious, and I "Heiled" as vigorously as any Nazi. Quentin and my brother frowned on me and made sarcastic remarks about my adolescence, but I was enjoying everything fully and it was difficult for me to restrain my natural sympathy for the Germans. I felt like a child, ebullient and careless, the intoxication of the new regime working like wine in me.

We stopped in Nürnberg for the night and, after having reserved attractive and cheap rooms, went out to roam over the town and get a bite to eat. As we were coming out of the hotel we saw a crowd gathering and gesticulating in the middle of the street. We stopped to find out what it was all about. There was a street-car in the centre of the road from which a young girl was being brutally pushed and shoved. We moved closer and saw the tragic and tortured face, the colour of diluted absinthe. She looked ghastly. Her head had been shaved clean of hair and she was wearing a placard across her breast. We followed her for a moment, watching the crowd insult and jibe and drive her. Quentin and my brother asked several people around us, what was the matter. We understood from their German that she was a Gentile who had been consorting with a Jew. The placard said: "I have Offered Myself to a Jew." I wanted to follow but my two companions were so repelled that they pulled me away. Quentin, I remember, unfeeling and hard-boiled as I thought he was, was so shaken by the whole scene that he said the only thing he could do was to get drunk, to forget it—which we all did on red champagne.

I felt nervous and cold, the mood of exhilaration vanished completely. I tried in a self-conscious way to justify the action of the Nazis, to insist that we should not condemn without knowing the whole story. But here was something that darkened my picture of a happy, carefree Germany. The ugly, bared brutality I thought would make only a superficial impression on me, but as time went on I thought more and more of the pitiful, broken creature, a victim of mass-insanity.

I urged Quentin not to write up the story. It would make a sensation because of our presence—the new Ambassador's children. It was an isolated case. It was not really important,

would create a bad impression, did not reveal actually what
was going on in Germany, overshadowed the constructive
work they were doing. I presented many foolish and contradictory arguments. He decided not to cable the story, but only
because he said there had been so many atrocity stories lately
that people were no longer interested in them; he would write
it as a news-story when he returned. But when we got back
to Berlin we discovered that another journalist had been in the
town and had cabled the story immediately and that all the
press everywhere had headlined it, and also commented on
our being witnesses.

The next morning we headed south. My brother was trying
to make Innsbruck to see a girl of his, so we sped through the
country, stopping only long enough to get food and gasoline
and have a drink or two. We drove to Bayreuth but we were
too late for the opera so we only visited the opera-house for a
moment and in the dark, and hurried on. Quentin took the
wheel and we sped over mountains and hills and curves at a
mad rate. Little south-German villages, beautiful solid white
houses, flying by us on each side, looking ancient and ghostly
and lonely as our headlights flashed over them for a second.

We finally got to Innsbruck, tired but miraculously alive,
and soon went to bed. The next morning we looked around
the town, one of the most beautiful spots in Europe. The
scenery was magnificent and the people even more helpful and
friendly than in other places—but, of course, it was not a Nazi
town.

From there, farther into Austria: Vienna and Salzburg. We
stayed a few days, heard an opera and an indoor production of
Everyman, walked through the lovely old streets, visited the
Castle, drove out to lakes on the outskirts of the town, beautiful
blue pools in the midst of high mountains, drove and walked
through the suburbs, and agreed that this was the most perfect
place we had yet seen. Salzburg is a town of music. The
atmosphere is alive yet soft, people speak in subdued but
vibrant tones, music is written on their faces and in their
movements. They walk more gracefully, think, speak, and act
as if life had become fuller and deeper from their experience.

One night at a famous wine-cellar we ordered several bottles of the sweet, fresh, intoxicating wine of the district. The wine-garden nestled under the magnificent sheer cliff on the top of which the Castle loomed. The bells of the cathedral started singing in rich, throaty, and pure tones, the sound meeting with the cold, sheer rock above us and soaring into the dark heavens. People were silent and awed, listening to the ringing air, rhythm swinging through the night, melting and mounting in soft tonal waves to the cool, starred space above. We came out a little dazed and drunken with sound and music. In the square, people were loitering casually, talking in modulated undertones yet with a curious swelling gaiety, as if their mood was following the magic and ecstatic flight of the cathedral bells. Then we heard slowly, because our ears were still so full, the echo of another music, another symphony—an orchestra was playing in a building on the far side of the square, the tones fluid and clear in the thronging of the huge, vibrant dying bells.

I have never seen anyone drunk in Salzburg. Something in the atmosphere of the town forbids it. One can be intoxicated, quiet and light-hearted at the same time, but never drunk.

We finally left Austria, with its grace and charm, softened careless speech, and went back to Germany, having only once received a Nazi salute as we were nearing the border. It was strange returning to Germany, the music and poetry we had been so full of seemed ominously absent. Again as we travelled north along the Rhine, we saw the flags and the marching men, the brown uniforms, the martial character of the nation beginning to impress itself. It didn't seem as spontaneous in the Rhine country as in other parts and we were wondering as we drove along and tried to talk with the people, what reservations they were making. The Nazi emblems and symbolism seemed grafted on to this dark and vivacious people.

We stared, in the usual fashion of tourists, at the famous Lorelei Rock, dark and mysterious above the murky, slow-moving Rhine, stared in wonder at the ancient ruins, evocative and beautiful, isolated and majestic on the tops of wild mountains. We drank more than the usual portion of golden wine, like liquid sun caught in a glass. Finally, the time was up and we drove quickly towards Berlin, passing through the dark and deeply-wooded Harz, memories of the myths, legends, and fairy stories in our minds.

Back in Berlin again, feeling already as if it were home, and rested and fresh from the exhilaration of travel, we began to open our eyes to things about us, to contrast the Germany we had been travelling through with the Prussia we resided in.

Quentin called to say that his home office was annoyed that he had missed the story in Nürnberg. The Foreign Office called at our home, seemingly very much perturbed; regretted and apologized for the incident of isolated brutality which they assured me was rare and would be punished.

2

For several weeks before I had left on the trip, my mother and I had been looking around for suitable houses. I was amazed at the magnificence of some of them and at their comparatively low rent. I learned they belong to Jews who either were seeking protection through diplomatic tenants or were planning to leave Germany. I began to realize then how tragic were Hitler's measures against the Jews, even the wealthy class. Despite the grandeur of these houses most of them seemed pretty antiquated to us, with their gaudy but valuable furniture, tapestried walls, old-fashioned plumbing, kitchen-and-servant accommodation. Since we hadn't brought over our furniture, and to furnish an Embassy in the proper style would have cost us a sum far beyond our means, we had to find a furnished place.

After much delay and anxiety we located a beautiful place, on Tiergarten Strasse, off the main street and with a large garden in the back.

American Ambassadors in Germany have always had difficulty in finding houses. Several years ago our Government had bought a tremendous palace on Pariser Platz, inside the Brandenburger Tor, and furnished it lavishly, the purchase-price and remodelling costing several million dollars. On the eve of the Ambassador's occupation a serious fire burned out most of the interior of the building. Since that time our Government has done nothing to rehabilitate this palace, or to sell it and buy a new one. An American company bought the place some years ago at the ridiculously low sum of $150,000 and sold it to the American Government at $1,700,000—a profit of $1,550,000—more than ten times its original price. The company was then so completely dissolved that to this day no one knows the original promoters—at least in Berlin. There may be men elsewhere who not only knew the company's directors, but, also its inner workings. But perhaps their positions are too important for them to reveal their knowledge.

The situation was a continual disgrace and one which my father determinedly and regularly tried to remedy. He wrote repeatedly to the State Department to try to have them take some action on it, one way or another. The magnificent building stood idle and gutted while very large sums were being spent annually in rent for all the branches of the United States Government represented in Berlin. Investigating committees, committees of estimate and so forth came over yearly supposedly for the sole purpose of solving the Palais riddle. My father, furious with the inaction—if not more—of certain officials, suggested it be exchanged for another building. But nothing was ever done. Congress would not appropriate the necessary sum, it was reported, and the house problem was to continue.

It would be important and I think revealing to have a congressional investigation of this whole Blücher Palais matter. What company bought it, who were the men who made the profit, why did my father's blunt and honest inquiries meet with no result? Maybe it was really because the American Government could not "afford" to restore the buildings, even though it was building and renovating at the same time many other Embassies elsewhere. Perhaps, on the other hand, there are more complications than we yet realize.[1]

As a matter of fact, we were very pleased with the house we found, and my father was especially delighted since it was in

[1] Since this writing the American Government has agreed to restore the Blücher Palais to be ready in the spring of 1939—at the approximate cost of $1,000,000.

such a quiet location, with a garden and trees, and just near enough to the Embassy for a brisk walk every morning. Downstairs were the servants' quarters, the porter's rooms, the entrance hall with *garderobes* (check rooms), and the kitchen, which alone was about twice the size of an average New York apartment. Upstairs we had a large reception hall, a beautiful oval-shaped ballroom with a wonderful floor and woodwork, a library with red damask walls and hundreds of priceless books, bric-à-brac, a fireplace and Gothic and Early Renaissance woodwork; two other reception-rooms, one with dark green, the other with pink satin, damask walls; a dining-room with red tapestried walls and furniture, that seated twenty-five people; and a charming bright sunroom and stone terraces that led in a winding stone stairway down into the perfectly planned garden. It was a luxurious house, too pretentious for our family tastes, but serving more than adequately for an Embassy since all the rooms opened on to one another in a large semicircular design, for receptions and large parties. We felt that the furniture was too heavy and the bric-à-brac too cluttering, but no German villa on this scale was any different. This was the taste of the people and we found it invariably the same. The room that we lived in most and which I liked the best was the library, lined with countless books, and one section of which was cosy, warm, and friendly, with a glowing fire.

As is the case also in most German homes, the bedrooms and sitting-rooms on the third floor were pretty grim affairs. We had a nice sitting-room and a strange, gaudy bedroom with a bath, the size of a reception-room, entirely done in gold and coloured mosaics, the bath tub on a sort of dais. For weeks I roared with laughter whenever I saw the bathroom and occasionally as a lark would take my friends up to see it, when my father was away. The rest of the rooms we had to furnish ourselves.

So this was to be the home for the American Embassy. After we put up the plaque with the American eagle on it outside the second iron gate, we tried to settle down to normal diplomatic and family life.

My mother, brother, and I had a German teacher right away. He was a funny little moustached gentleman with a few teeth missing, imbued with strange Eastern lore. We tried to make him talk about the Nazis, but he firmly refused. He taught the Berlitz system, had infinite patience and a slightly tragic manner. We teased him unmercifully, said the most outlandish things we could think of, but only succeeded, during the entire time we had him, in getting one, or at the most, two laughs. He must have had the most superhuman control of his facial muscles, and if he feared one was about to twitch he would gaze intently at the ceiling as if studying some infinitely important message there.

We grew very fond of him and his eccentricities. When he came into the room he would take our hands and hold them at arm's length, bowing deeply from the waist, so that we could see all the way down his neck and spine, raise himself suddenly and say, "*Guten Morgen, Excellence ; wie geht es ihnen.*" After several repetitions of this, he would turn to other things. He always stood up, was infinitely embarrassed, and flushed easily when we offered him a chair. At the end of the lesson he would gently indicate that he was on the point of departure, go through the same entrance-rigmarole and back himself out of the room. To him we were always the "Excellences and their family," no matter what wrong we did; we were of a class so untouchable that he would even stream out curious stumbling sentences of apology when we paid the bill.

My brother soon matriculated in the university and I went along to courses of English poetry and of philosophy, in German, to learn the rhythm of the language. My mother was busy with the tremendous job of learning to manage a house with six or seven servants, which she found infinitely more difficult than managing with one; learning the Protocol and the impeccable manners and inviolable customs of the diplomatic corps. We did not begin entertaining until October, so she had a chance to feel her way around, make innumerable and expected calls, and be invited out every night.

My father presented his credentials to Hindenburg as soon as he returned from his estate in East Prussia—Neudeck,

which had been given to him by the Government and which
he had put in his son's name, to avoid inheritance and other
taxes. But my father was impressed with the old gentleman
and came away with the feeling that he was hostile to Hitler
and was a fairly learned and liberal person.

During all this time my father was in the uncomfortable
position of having to protest every few days against the treatment of Americans. He would come home for lunch depressed
and alarmed at the never-ending brutality of the Storm
Troopers, who were beating up everyone who did not salute the
Nazi flag. There were terrible, murderous incidents of Jews—
both foreign and German—who were beaten because of failure
to see the flag or even simply because they looked Jewish. I was,
of course, shocked, but still I closed my eyes to the real picture,
obviously because I had little understanding yet of social,
economic or racial conditions and motives. I was trying to find
excuses for their excesses, and my father would look at me a
bit stonily if tolerantly, and both in private and in public
gently label me a young Nazi. That put me on the defensive
for some time and I became temporarily an ardent defender
of everything going on. I would repeat the old arguments
of the enthusiasms of the youth, their glowing and inspiring
faith in Hitler, the good that was being done for the unem-
ployed. I felt there was something noble in the fresh, vigorous,
strong young faces I saw everywhere, and would say so
combatively every chance I got. I remember writing letters
home, and telling visitors that I thought there was a rebirth
in Germany as exciting as anything I had ever witnessed, and
that the press reports and atrocity stories were isolated examples
exaggerated by bitter, closed-minded people.

One day an American girl I had met, who was studying
social conditions in Germany, called up and asked if I wanted
to see a labour camp and a concentration camp. I was eager
to see both. She arranged for it immediately. Two men and
my friend called for me one morning and we drove out to an
Arbeitsdienstlager a few hours from Berlin. She sat in front with
a representative from the Propaganda Ministry and I in the
rumble-seat with a young Foreign Office attaché. The man

in front was carrying on a vivacious conversation with my friend, who translated for me. He revealed the wildest enthusiasm. When I indicated, to the man sitting by me, my complete concurrence, he frowned and tried to moderate the propaganda of the other one. I scorned his efforts to disillusion me and felt blissfully happy that a less cynical person was with us.

We went into the shacks out on the marshes and were shown around the sleeping-quarters, library, recreation hall, and dining-room of the labour camp. The girl was busy interrogating everyone she saw, and taking pictures. The boss of the camp asked us to sample the food. We sat down to an abominable meal of coldish mush and prunes, but even that didn't dampen my spirits. We walked for hours in the hot sun, watching the men at their task of digging ditches to reclaim the marshes. Everything seemed very nice and orderly and there were no military parades and exercises, as I had been told by my "venomous" friends. I was anxious to report and say, "I told you so!" My white summer shoes were being ruined, and I was tired and, I must admit, quite bored. I asked to go home, pleading an engagement. On the way back, several miles from the camp, my friend spotted a group of men in strange positions in an open field. She insisted on stopping and rushed over to the spot with her camera. I could see that the men were doing military exercises, lying flat on their stomachs and then jumping up and dashing across the field. There was also rifle practice. She took me aside very cautiously for a second and said: "You see, this is what they really do. The camp we have just been in was forewarned that we were coming, so we saw nothing but the most innocent and constructive activity. We ran on this one accidentally and you can see the difference!" I pooh-poohed her hysterical estimate of things and thought: she is, of course, an enemy trying to find the worst things in the nation. But I paused a moment in astonishment as I saw the strange and irritated look on the face of the Propaganda representative.

The invitation to the concentration camp never materialized and by the time I could have seen one with very little difficulty—that is, after I made the acquaintance of Diels, the Chief of the Secret Police—I was too depressed to continue my investigation of model German camps, labour or other-wise.

The assaults on Americans were getting so violent and so numerous that my father had finally to protest to Hitler him-self. He had already made representations to the Foreign Office and was seriously assured each time that such things would never happen again. After the interview, we tried to get an articulated picture of Hitler from him. But he was very reserved and curiously quiet and would say little, except that he looked like his photographs, could be charming in manner, was excitable of nature, and had promised to end the attacks. As a matter of fact, these incidents did stop shortly after the interview.

Edgar Ansel Mowrer was having serious trouble with the Nazi authorities at this time. He was president of the Press Association and did not conceal his hostility to the Govern-ment. One day he was advised that the Government could not feel itself responsible for the behaviour of its unruly Storm Troopers, and advised him to leave the country immediately. He refused to do so. Shortly after, he was told that his safety was in question and that he must get out in three days. He came to my father early one evening, to ask his advice. My father was lying down, so Mowrer was ushered into the "master bedroom." Slender, stoop-shouldered, with a dark, gaunt, early-Christian-martyr face and fine voice, he revealed an intensity and passion I had not seen before in Germany. He presented his case in cold, clear terms, and my father, weighing the facts, and drawing conclusions, I suppose, from the experience of other Americans faced with Nazi antagonism, advised him to leave. Mowrer never quite forgave my father for this advice. I have seen him many times since and he still thinks a test-case should have been made of this ultimatum, with the backing of the Embassy. His is a mind irrevocably and logically opposed to Fascism and his sensitivity and gentle nature received wounds he can never forget. He has a cold but burning love for humanity, and he felt that all the decencies had been violated in Germany, the soul crippled and distorted. I was inclined to think him Jewish—which I later learned was not true—and considered his animus to be prompted only by his racial self-consciousness. In a few days he and his wife had packed up hurriedly and left.

One of our first diplomatic dinners was given to us by the staff at the beautiful home of the Counsellor. It was very formal and, I thought, very silly. We went into the dining-room quite pompously, each member of the staff assigned to take in a woman on his arm and seat her according to the most rigorous Protocol. There was no interesting conversation of any sort, only banter and superficialities and platitudes—not at all the kind of thing we had been accustomed to. My father attempted to give a serious tone to the evening, but, of course, desisted when he felt the lack of response. He soon resorted to foot-tapping and distant looks, an old, and clearly unconscious habit of his.

Another dinner was given us by the Belgian Minister and his wife, Count and Countess de Kerkove. Both were very large and very impressive-looking people, with that curious blank, hard stare that becomes habitual on the face of a diplomat long in the service; by the time we arrived through a path of liveried servants, all the other guests were there standing in line to receive us. All the women were covered with diamonds or other precious stones—I had never seen such a lavish display of wealth. With my father's usual courtesy he let my mother and me go first, introducing us informally. So unobservant was I of manners of this type that it was almost a year before I realized that daughters of diplomats are not supposed to linger long with their parents, but to disappear quietly among men and women of lower rank. But I, on the contrary, stayed by the side of my mother and father most of the time, and took part in conversations which they had with people around them. I was used to being treated like an adult and having my opinions at least listened to. And, not being in search of romance, I was much more interested in the ideas of my elders than in the polite advances of my contemporaries.

There was a very elaborate dinner; most of the dishes I was scarcely on eating-terms with, either because I hadn't seen them before or because I was so overwhelmed by the way and form in which they were served that I didn't know how to manage them, and I cast desperate looks at my mother in the centre of the huge table, who seemed to be managing nicely. Afterwards we went into another elegant reception-room for coffee and drinks. Standing around for an hour or two, talking a lot and saying nothing, my father made the move to go, at ten-thirty. There was a good deal of genteel raising of eyebrows, but we braved the storm and went home. No diplomat is supposed to leave before eleven at the very earliest.

At one of these dinners—and they were innumerable and all on about the same scale—I met a young Frenchman, a secretary in the Embassy. He began calling on me, taking me out to movies and so forth, after having asked my parents' permission. I suppose I practised a great deception on the diplomatic corps by not indicating that I was a married woman at that time. But I must admit I rather enjoyed being treated like a maiden of eighteen knowing all the while my dark secret. I didn't care about doing anything about it and I was trusting they didn't either. I felt, too, not having a divorce gave me a sort of protection against rash behaviour with these "irresistible" foreigners!

The Frenchman was a charming young man of about thirty. He was an intimate friend of François-Ponçet (who treated him like a well-loved foster son), and a brilliant and unusual diplomat in every way. He was honest, almost blunt, and excitable. The Germans began telling me that he was a spy of Ponçet's, that he was the head of the French Secret Service in Berlin. I repeated jestingly everything I heard, to him. I didn't know whether it was true or not—I don't to this day—but I soon realized that he was a trusted friend of the Ambassador, and because of this had many enemies within his own Embassy and elsewhere. The German men I had met were extremely unfriendly to him and made no attempt to conceal it. They feared that I would be subjected to anti-Nazi propaganda. But he became one of the few loyal and interesting friends I had throughout my four and a half years in Berlin.

When I knew him then I was in my most violent pro-Nazi period. I accepted ideas and what I felt were necessities of action that many Nazis refused to accept themselves. Consequently, I was anti-French. Nothing French pleased me. I even reviled the language, saying that it was brittle, nasal, and hideous. I compared the warm, open-hearted friendliness of the German people, with the exploiting, mannered character of the superficial French.

But I was, in spite of myself, attracted to the tall boy, romantic and perfect of feature, and to the clarity and logic of his brain. We drove long hours in the beautiful hilly lake-country outside Berlin and had even longer talks. He began to explain militarism to me and the way the Germans had used it to solve temporarily the economic crisis. He would point out military camps, air-fields, that were sprouting up all over the country; we would pass by concentration camps in the car; huge transport trucks with war material would get tied up in traffic, because of the innumerable military parades. Slowly but surely, though I fought against it and teased him, making fun of his most serious observations, I began to think a little. Still I was not greatly concerned by the rearmament that was going on before our eyes, against the Treaty of Versailles. I was simply a little more critical and ready at least to open an ear that had been closed to other than National Socialists.

A young Frenchman I had known when I was in Paris five years before, came to Berlin for a few days. Armand and I took him around town and I was anxious to have him see that the Germans were not so dangerous as they thought in France. I put *their* best foot foremost, but the boy would come to me, after having talked with other friends of his in Berlin, with the most hair-raising tales of atrocities and military activities. I told him his mind was being poisoned and reprimanded him for not seeing that the only peace in Europe worth having would be a peace based on Franco-German understanding. "Every Frenchman who comes here should

be shown the best qualities of the German people," I said.
I must have seemed very impertinent and stupid to my new
French friend who had studied and lived in Germany for
seven years; and our friendship almost broke up several times
because of my arrogance.

I had a birthday party in October, three months after our
arrival, and when I felt I knew enough about managing social
events to try my hand. My mother and father did not appear,
which was shocking to most of the people invited, since young
girls are not supposed to entertain on their own in these
circles. I had invited some of the people I had met, whom I
thought attractive. Young Prince Friedrich, the youngest son
of the Crown Prince, came exactly on time, with a precise
little bouquet of carnations in his hand and a polite bow from
the waist. I considered him charming, with his almost perfect
"arrow-collar ad." features, the blond hair and air of shy
innocence and guilelessness. He certainly, in the time I knew
him, never said a word out of order or did an unconventional
thing. If he had a mind at all unique or interesting, I was
never privileged to see it—and I think my experience was not
uncommon. But I had never seen a Prince before, and certainly never a handsome, blushing one.

Another of my guests was a notorious Princess—at least, she
had become one through marriage—but I didn't know about
her then. She was bored to death and the only thing that held
her was the promise of Hanfstaengl's appearance. A few
Reichswehr officers, young, heel-clicking, courteous almost to
the point of absurdity; an S.A. man and a few others. It was
certainly a mixed gathering and I remember I only served
beer and punch, when whiskey and champagne were the
usual thing. A Greek girl, the daughter of a diplomat whom
I was to see a great deal of in all sorts of curious circumstances,
entertained the crowd with her sharp, pungent, and *risqué*
wit and heavy, dark beauty. She was studying to be an actress
and, had she not been the daughter of a diplomat, her habits
of speech would never have been tolerated by Berlin society.
As it was, they thought she was a sort of acceptable freak.
She was and remains the only articulately intelligent woman

I met among the diplomatic corps, despite her curious self-consciousness, Nazi-mystic leanings, and slightly psychopathic inclination to shock people.

Hanfstaengl came roaring in after midnight, met the bored Princess going home and lured her back for a moment. He had a drink, was persuaded to go to the piano, where he tore out several exciting and flamboyant songs. He always left the piano crumpled and exhausted, not to mention himself and his listeners, and the rooms of the Embassy reverberated with sound for days afterwards. After this splurge of not-entirely-real dynamic energy he left, gesticulating profusely and shouting his adoration of everyone and everything in the house, including "Papa" Dodd, as he called him; this was the soothing personality whom Hitler so thoughtfully kept by his side in moments, and long evenings, of stress and strain. Whatever you thought of him in your most secret heart of hearts, Hanfstaengl was at least someone you could remember in the endless pallid days of innocuous diplomats and their parties. Or so I thought, and so I still think, though one develops an immunity to the insane social life and is disproportionately thankful for small bits and rays of originality, no matter how dull they might seem in another milieu.

IV

INCREASING ACQUAINTANCE

OUR HOUSE WAS always full of people; young Germans, students, Foreign Office attachés, Government officials, newspapermen, and officers in the S.A., or S.S., or Reichswehr.[1] The pro-Nazi and the anti-Nazi feelings almost balanced each other. The students and intellectuals, artists and professional people, the aristocracy, all expressed, in varying degrees of passion and caution, their distrust of Hitler and the new regime, though at the same time they were ardent patriots and revealed the special mystic German attitude toward the Fatherland. Many of the aristocrats, those nearest the Royalty, were anti-Hitler mainly for reasons of birth and breeding. They were expecting, from day to day, month to month, year to year, that Hitler would keep his promise and restore Royalty and therefore their own class. It is amazing how tenaciously they clung to this fantastic idea. Even in the autumn of 1937, they were still giving tentative and half-hearted support to the regime, with these hopes in mind. Most business men and industrialists were well aware that Hitler's socialist slogans were only slogans and would in no way affect their domination of economic life. Their factories were working full-time again and there was no need to worry about strikes, trade unions, and independent labour movements.

Most people who had travelled a lot in the outside world, had lived in foreign countries, whether they were Nazis or not, felt that Hitler's methods were dangerous and might cause Germany to lose prestige and sympathy in international affairs.

[1] The S.A. are known as the Storm Troopers (Sturmabteilung)—the large brown-shirted army which formed the nucleus of Nazis who helped Hitler to power. Their ranks were later decimated by the Purge. The S.S. were the picked Hitler troops—chosen as a special guard to protect the Leader—consummate in their mastery of propaganda and Secret Service work and their loyalty to Nazi principles and noted for their height and handsomeness. The Reichswehr is the official German army.

Among the Stahlhelm organization, an army of stubborn, proud war veterans, there were many hard-bitten men who loathed Hitler and had a contempt for him I had seen nowhere else in Germany. Within a year after his seizure of power, the Stahlhelms were liquidated.

I knew a young S.A. boy who had been in the Hitler movement for several years. He had a curious name which indicated his Slav origin (around the Spreewald section in North Germany there still exists quite a large population, direct descendants of the early Slavonic invasion of Germany, with their own language, customs and costumes, religion and folk-lore), had a beautiful broad, child-like face and no more than an average brain. He was a great Nazi enthusiast and believed that Hitler really meant something with his socialist slogans. He hated the Communists like poison, though at one time he had known and been in sympathetic contact with a few; his hatred was deliberately encouraged and developed by the propaganda he was subjected to. He thought, like millions of others, that within the framework of law and order and general capitalist principles, justice could be done to mankind. He believed, with the same millions of others, that the Fatherland had been mortally crippled by the Treaty of the Allied Powers and he put his faith in Hitler to restore Germany and bring prosperity to the simple man.

He would have long arguments with me about the domination of Jews in cultural, scientific, professional, and economic life. He would corroborate these views by sending me innumerable pamphlets of statistics on Jewish monopoly of German life. Arguing passionately, with flaming eyes and dramatic gestures, he tried to convince me. The house was flooded with the proofs of his arguments and I spent a lot of useless hours listening to violent abuse of Jews and Communists. The only good effect this friendship had in increasing my understanding of Germany, was to challenge me into thinking through clearly my own point of view, which was beginning to develop at this time. I drove into the country with him, took long walks on Sundays as is the custom with the Germans, swam, went to movies and night clubs, enjoyed

the gentle courtesy of flowers and notes, and learned more
and more about German ways and beliefs. He was and remains
the norm of German life—the middle bourgeois trying to find
some beauty and faith to replace crumbling structures of
behaviour. I felt the pathos of his clinging to Hitler despite
his instinctive distaste of the methods employed, and I was to
feel more acutely the tragedy of his personal position, in June
of the same year.

The young Reichswehr officers I knew at the time expressed
a more moderate view of the new regime. They definitely
distrusted the Leader and didn't like what they considered
"socialism" in the programme. However, they were very
guarded in their language and indicated that as long as Hitler
left their Army alone, as an autonomous unit in the German
nation, and gave them the chance, economically and otherwise,
to develop and become more efficient, they would be content.
They wanted their own freedom, their own leaders, their
non-political nature. Many of them were royalists, many of
them were purely and simply soldiers, happy in their work
and the economic security it brought them; but they wanted
to remain the unique and aristocratic clique they have always
been in Germany. These young soldiers were extremely
pleasant, handsome, courteous, and uninteresting—they were
infinitely less symptomatic of the new Germany than their
confrères in the S.A., and S.S. At almost any time, under
almost any system, they would have had the same attitudes.

In general there was quite a lack of caution in the expression of views at divergence with Hitler's. Or this may have
been caused, even at this early stage, by an attempt to sound
out the new Ambassador's family. In any case I met several
young men in the Foreign Office who pretended to be critical
of Nazi Germany. Flowers and attentions came from many,
arguments and statement of cases along with them. "Of course,
this is intellectually untenable." "This method is incredible
and unwise." "How can such lack of foresight be endured?"
But always, despite appeals they made to their listeners'
reason, and their own mental reservations, they would very
subtly point out that, after all, Hitler is doing thus and so,

eliminating unemployment, giving the Germans a sense of national pride again. These were attitudes most difficult to combat, particularly if one had an instinctive feeling of sympathy for the German people and a sense of indignation at their treatment after the War.

One young man, whom I later heard had been at this time studying methods of propaganda and learning discipline in the Secret Police department while ostensibly being attached to the Foreign Office, was particularly assiduous in his attentions and subtle arguments. As always, he was handsome, blond, innocent, and enthusiastic, with a slightly more devious and trained mind than the S.A. man. Another one, in the Foreign Office, had married into an extremely rich family, closely connected, personally if not otherwise, with Goebbels and Hitler. Both of them were S.S. men, a fact which meant little to me until I got to know them. The Washington diplomat was one of the slickest and, in some ways, most unattractive men I had met thus far. At first, I thought him handsome— there seemed to be an influx of blond Aryan wholesome-looking talent. But on second glance, he had a broad, sly, brutal face, and I found him a man of easily acquired mannerisms—for instance, though he knew very little about America, he had acquired the slang and accent to an almost perfect degree— with a superficial and probing intellect, if one could call it that, and a curiously brash, and at the same time conciliatory, pattern of speech and behaviour.

He was a man whom I could not and did not trust, with a capacity for ugly fanaticism and polished trickery. Ambitious, brazen, and impertinent, he was one of the first disillusions I had in German official life. By the very fact that he would support a certain point of view, a sensitive person would almost instinctively take the opposite, no matter on what subject.

I went out with him several times and he was always eager to know what my father thought of this and that development. I knew by this time that whatever I might repeat of my father's attitude to such men, would go immediately to the Propaganda Ministry or to the Secret Police, in both cases finding its way very quickly to higher circles, Foreign Office and Governmental.

A young correspondent in London of the *Deutsche Allgemeine Zeitung*, was called to Berlin to take over the editorship of that paper. I met him shortly thereafter—at a party given by newspaper people. It was rumoured that he was Jewish, which, of course, he vociferously denied. He was another type of German for whom I had no particular sympathy. Definitely opportunistic and a bit obsequious, he and his English wife frequented our house more than almost anyone else, for several months.

During my four and a half years in Germany I found only one excuse for the interminable social season (in which, during the winter months, most people got in two to four teas a day and a lunch or dinner—dull beyond belief, with the distasteful fake glitter of high society), and that was the opportunity to meet interesting people whom you could arrange to talk to later in more informal and congenial circumstances.

At one of these dinners or receptions I met Rolf Diels, then Chief of the Secret Police under Goering. He had been with Severing, a Socialist Prussian State Secretary in the days of the Republic, and was supposed to have betrayed his chief. Though his career was mildly social-democratic he fell easy prey, through his ambitious and unscrupulous nature, to the Nazis. I didn't, of course, know any of these things until a year or two later. The best things I can say about Diels I should say at first. He, while he was in his job, was always attempting to appease American anger and indignation. He co-operated almost invariably with our Consulate and Embassy. He released several Americans, and, with some small risk of incurring Nazi enmity, tried in several instances to conform to or put through our demands for our own citizens, those wrongfully assaulted, arrested or imprisoned. He was sensitive, of course, to American public opinion and felt more concern about it than some of the high officials at that time. This was not done out of the kindness of his heart, I know, but rather from his unusual intelligence and political opportunism. He definitely wanted the Embassy to be friendly, not only to

Nazism but to him. I am also equally convinced that he was, and is, no more of a Nazi than many of the others who give lip-service to it for their various personal or political reasons.

I have talked to several men and women who have come out of concentration camps, who say that at least twelve people a day were killed while Diels was Chief of the Secret Police. He had under his own control the horrible Columbia House, one of the most ghastly prisons in Germany, a political prison in the city of Berlin. When he walked into a room, or rather, crept on cat's feet, he created a nervousness and tension that no other man possibly could, even when people did not know his identity. Tall and slender, with jet-black luxuriant hair, he had the most sinister, scar-torn face I have ever seen. His mouth was twisted from early sword-wounds and his cheeks had livid lines of scar tissue. His eyes were black, cruel and penetrating. He came from the soft and gay Rhine country.

He took a vicious joy in his Mephistophelian manners and always wanted to create a hush by his melodramatic entrance. He has been to our house many times, often on purely formal occasions, and gave the lasting impression of being the only man who got by our efficient butler without being announced. The parties would be going full-swing, people talking, drinking, dancing, or eating. Then suddenly, late in the evening (he always came late) you would almost feel a chill in the room, and Diels would appear at your elbow in all his dark and horrible glamour! This impression is not an isolated or individual one—I have checked it with many friends and though some of them say that when you got to know him he was quite gay and informal and charming, they all acknowledge the sinister quality of every meeting with him.

He belonged to the S.S., but claimed that they hated him and that he received his real support from the S.A. men. I certainly doubt the latter. He described to me many times the intrigues and inner-party struggles and hatreds. He liked and trusted no one (though he gave, seemingly, his loyalty to Goering), and no one liked or trusted him. No matter how fine and innocent a character might originally be—and his

Dg

certainly was not ever—a job of the nature of his would invariably and inevitably corrode the character. Towards the end of his career in this post, he became more neurotic and full of obsessions than anyone I knew in Germany—even those whom he persecuted. But that story must wait.

I am sure Goering himself was distrustful of him, but I felt, either from watching the two together or hearing Diels talk, that Goering was afraid of him.

I was intrigued and fascinated by this human monster of sensitive face and cruel, broken beauty. We went out quite a lot, dancing and driving. I went to his office once and saw dictaphones on the desk in an unpretentious, large, and somewhat bare room. He gave me the first indication that spying was done not only by the Secret Police Department but by every department. He indicated that Goebbels spied on Goering and Goering on Goebbels, both on the Secret Police staff, and the Secret Police section on both of them. There began to appear before my romantic eyes—yet not so romantic after all, since these are authenticated facts—a vast and complicated network of espionage, terror, sadism and hate, from which no one, official or private, could escape.

I began to realize that the diplomatic corps itself was not immune, that all diplomats were analyzed in files that kept growing, their activities and points of view watched and reported. He convinced me through indirection or otherwise, that our Embassy office and residence were wired for dictaphones, either in the walls or in the telephone. I soon learned not to say a thing over the telephone which I did not want recorded somewhere in the innumerable places for such things. Murderous stories began to circulate, to which I lent more and more of an ear as I became wiser to the ways and methods of dictatorship. Cars had driven up in the middle of the night, S.S. men had jumped out and in a moment had come down from a house or an apartment, with a man or woman who was never seen again. Such cases actually occurred thousands of times, but they began to take on definite reality, and when friends of friends of mine were the victims, I was sobered and silenced.

So, during the year I knew Diels fairly well, I myself got into a nervous state that almost bordered on the hysterical. If I had been with people who had been brave or reckless enough to talk in opposition to Hitler, I spent sleepless nights wondering if a dictaphone or a telephone had registered the conversation, or if men had followed and overheard. I had terrible nightmares. My room was on the second floor of the Embassy, a large, many windowed room, looking out on the gravel drive to the street. The wall could easily have been scaled. During the autumn and early winter nights, I imagined I heard steps and then long silences, shots, or whispered conversation; I thought I saw moving shadows behind the immense stone pillars of the entrance, all, of course, my imaginative translation of a tyre bursting (or perhaps actually a distant shot), a flurry of dead leaves, the wind rushing over the loose gravel, moonlight through swaying branches. I often felt such terror that occasionally I would wake up my mother and ask her to come and sleep in my room.

I feared all the time that, by some subtle probing, Diels would draw out information from me about my German friends, which would cause their death. His mind was brilliant, complex, and dangerously accurate. He was a perfect man for his job, even though he looked the part a bit too obviously. As I came to know more and more about the technique of terror and Fascism, to be more aware of what was going on, receive confidence of official Germans and diplomats, I desperately regretted that my memory could not be destroyed. I did not trust myself in the mental hands of an arch-conspirator, as well I might not! Of course, I saw less of him in the following three years, but when I did go out with him, even after I had developed a certain cynicism and self-confidence, he always put the fear of the devil in me and without fail caused these nervous spells to recur.

One night we had been out late dancing and he wanted to come up for a drink in the library before going home. He was at this particular moment somewhat uneasy himself—perhaps because some intrigue of his had failed or not met with party approval. In any case, he wanted to talk frankly. I grabbed a pillow from the sofa and made for the telephone. He asked me what I was going to do. I told him. Then a sinister smile crossed his lips and he nodded his head quietly.

From that time on I always covered the telephone with the heaviest soft thing I could get my hands on, before I would let anyone talk freely. I told my father of the incident and he himself was impressed enough to make a little device of his own, a small cardboard box stuffed tightly with cotton, which he put over his telephone when anyone was revealing confidences in his office. Whether technically it was of any use, I don't know. But in any case, there was a chance, indicated by the Chief of the Police to be not too slim, that the sound might be smothered as it registered. And it was a half-humorous, half-serious way of letting the Germans know that the Ambassador had at least heard rumours of their tricks! Now, of course, I know that such instruments can be and are used constantly with telephones, and that furthermore, you can buy a dictaphone, supposedly made by an American company, which when placed against the wall of an adjoining room will register the conversation going on in that room. Whenever we went away for a week or even a few days, we felt that either more dictaphones were being installed or the ones we had were being tested with the collusion of our servants, whom we never trusted after the first few months.

I am sure that part of this atmosphere created by Diels was deliberately manufactured. He wanted, for the satisfaction of his sense of personal power, to frighten even the diplomats. If he had any other purpose in mind, for instance, to spy on us or our friends, or to give an impression of the effectiveness of the Nazi methods, he failed miserably. In the first place, we already knew letters were being tampered with, and suspected that confidential telegrams sent in code (no doubt translated by the Nazis regularly) were read, that even our diplomatic pouch itself was being opened. In the second place, we learned not to talk even about our own opinions. Diels had established in our minds and souls certain incontrovertible facts and attitudes toward Nazi dictatorship that were to lead us to a complete and uncompromising analysis. But it is definitely true, in view of the circumstances that later developed, that Diels himself felt he was constantly facing the muzzle of a gun. Whenever he wanted to talk openly or be himself naturally, he would always drive out into the country and talk while we walked in the woods, or had a coffee at some obscure restaurant. It was the old story of the Frankenstein that turned on its creator and destroyed him. And this was even before the bloody days of June 1934.

2

One day Diels called me and asked if I would like to hear any of the sessions of the Reichstag Trial. I knew very little German at the time, but I thought it was an event which I should not miss, if only to get the drama and colour of the courtroom scenes and the personalities. I didn't know much about the Reichstag Fire. I had heard it rumoured, of course, that the Nazis did it and put it on the Communists. By this technique, the Nazis rode in on the electoral date as the defenders of the precious national monument to a way of government they had constantly vilified and rejected. That seemed rather ironical to me, but I had not followed too closely the developments, nor the comments on them in the foreign press. The Berlin sessions were on, after the Leipzig ones were over. I also had heard from all my newspaper friends that, besides the actual participants, two people whom I knew rather intimately, could give the full details of the treachery and conspiracy: Diels and Hanfstaengl. Naturally I accepted Diels' invitation with alacrity.

My brother and I drove up in our father's official car and entered the tremendous structure which was being repaired (it had not been a serious fire). We found our way to the small room where the Trial was going on, closed to all but newspapermen and a few observers. We sat in a group of about seventy-five people, among whom were all the newspapermen and the daughter of the Police President of Berlin. She kept making unsympathetic comments about the Nazi behaviour. By this time, we were so sceptical of people's motives that we let her criticism pass uncommented upon, fearing that she was only trying to get us to commit ourselves and, if possible, semi-officially, our father.

On the defendants' bench sat Torgler, Van der Lubbe, Popoff, Tanoff, and Dimitroff. Torgler looked ghastly, a greenish-grey prison pallor on his face—one could imagine that his body and clothes gave out a prison odour. He was tense, scared, nerve-racked. The newspapermen insisted that there was very likely a dictaphone under his chair and that he had been subjected to horrible torture. I didn't believe either. The Bulgarians looked wiry, tough, indifferent. Van der Lubbe was one of the most awful sights I have yet seen in human form. Big, bulky, sub-human face and body, he was so repulsive and degenerate that I could scarcely bear to look at him. He sat there, motionless, his head and hands hanging down between his knees, either in a trance or doped. He seemed to be slobbering at the mouth and the only movement he made was when one of the guards would attempt to raise his head and he would let it fall heavily again.

Torgler rose to defend himself. He made a good impression. Though he was always considered a little weak, he seemed to show at this moment a cold, mental self-possession and sharp, objective courage. There was a certain restrained nobility about his bearing and manner. He later remained in prison, then in a concentration camp, and finally was supposed to have recanted. He accepted the Nazi faith, was released under another name, and is living quietly in some small town not far from Berlin. What went on before the conversion, in both concentration camp and prison, is a story that perhaps will never be told. Certainly at the moment I saw him I would never have believed that his intellectual integrity would allow him to accept his persecutors as the saviours of the German race. And I, among thousands of others, would like to hear the full account of what pressures it took to destroy the fibre his life had revealed.

Of course, Diels and Hanfstaengl wanted to know our impression of the trial. I told them both I thought it was an extremely absorbing business, even though I didn't know what the people were saying. I also said I thought Torgler very attractive, self-possessed, and intelligent, that he had made a good impression on the courtroom and the hearers. Hanfstaengl ranted and raged, saying I was crazy and anti-Nazi and emotional and uneducated. Diels was very quiet and made no comment. Never in the time I knew him did he ever indicate by word or deed that he believed the Communists to be guilty. He simply didn't talk about it, except for one time before the June Purge.

I tried to get out of Hanfstaengl something of what he knew about the fire. He said he had been at an official dinner the night of the fire and had gone home rather early, after a pleasant evening. At twelve o'clock he said Goering had called him in a great state of excitement and said the building was on fire. He had rushed to Goering's house and they had conferred as to what should be done. At this point the story would always break off, become confused or incoherent. We all knew that the only secret passage to the building led directly into Goering's home. Diels knew this too, but Diels was too clever to talk at this period.

Diels told me that Goering was going to appear at the trial in a few days and that everything was being prepared, that I shouldn't miss this, by any means; it would be the most dramatic event of the whole proceedings. This time I had a ticket for the floor of the courtroom itself, not in the back with the newspapermen and listeners. Mother and father were terribly excited and eager to know what this session would be like. For some reason, my brother couldn't attend this session. I walked in, my heart in my throat, as I was seated much too close to the front. Goering and Diels were on the side conferring, only a few yards from me.

I suppose there were a lot of preliminaries, but I was so fascinated watching these two men that I didn't take my eyes off them until Goering got up to offer his testimony. He was faced by Dimitroff, a brilliant, attractive, dark man emanating the most amazing vitality and courage I have yet seen in a person under stress. He was alive, he was burning; fire of conviction, indignation, and hatred flamed in his posture, his magnificent voice and face. Some people's faces never come alive, they always look dead, pallid or passive, or have a cold reserved intellectualism like the face of Torgler. But Dimitroff was not only a shrewd dialectician and logician, he was a man, a superb dynamic personality.

I shall never forget his living stillness as he stood there listening to Goering, his face expressing a fiery contempt. It was a real fight, a real struggle. Goering took the stand, huge, paunchy, his stomach protruding swollenly, his face sagging; pompous and yet a little nervous. His voice was uncontrolled, his gestures melodramatic.

Dimitroff interrupted him several times and he flew into a rage. He continued his testimony and Dimitroff got up to answer. What they said to each other is on record, but how they looked is perhaps not. Dimitroff, in superb and impassioned, but controlled oratory, pointed out the flaws and dangerously absurd contradictions of Goering's speech. He made such a case, with deadly sarcasm was beginning to reveal so much, that Goering shouted for him to stop. He screamed at him, hoarse, frightened, his face turning so deep a purple that it seemed the blood would burst forth in a stream; choking, trying to drown out the accusing, brilliant, convicting voice of the other. He finally shouted, "You know what will happen to you if you ever get out of this! I will see to it that you get the justice you deserve!" And by saying this Goering freed Dimitroff from the living death of a Nazi concentration camp. Dimitroff let him continue and then made some insulting remark by which Goering had him evicted for contempt of court. It was a narrow escape for the Nazis.

All the time Goering was speaking, Diels was standing behind him, his elbow on the judge's bench, watching every move and listening to every tone and word coming from his lips. Again one got the impression of a sinister and diabolic presence. He was tense, foreboding, with an almost mesmeric influence on Goering, at this session. Goering occasionally would indicate by a change in movement or posture, or tone of voice, in a slight turn of the body toward Diels, how acutely aware he was of his presence. Diels moved from the judges' bench now and again to stand in other places where he could see Goering better, watch his profile or turned face.

I am utterly convinced that Diels collaborated on, if he did not actually prepare, the speech of Goering; that everything was timed and planned by him and that Goering was aware of Diels' shrewd mastery of the facts and the scene, and that he resented it. I am also convinced that they had it planned that Goering was to fly into a rage if Dimitroff got too close to reality, or if his unwavering logic revealed too much. Goering knew his man, his courage, and his indignation. By going into a rage, hurling insults and calumny at the right moment, he knew that Dimitroff, as a human and as a hater —of a passionate temper, anyway—would respond in much more telling and vicious insults. Then would come his eviction from court in time to save the day. The only slip was when Goering let his wrath master him and he dropped the fatal phrase that he personally would get Dimitroff, if he were released. By assuming he would be acquitted, he consequently assumed he was not guilty of the charges he had hurled at him. Dimitroff was taken out of court between two guards, certainly justified, personally, publicly and legally, that the threat on his life was most damaging evidence against Goering.

Knowing Diels and having been personally present, sensing the demoniac atmosphere and having received the impact of the clash of loathing between Dimitroff and Goering, and knowing something of Nazi methods, it would take much concrete evidence to prove to me that Diels had not managed and designed, with his unfailing cunning, this entire plot. In fact, he did not deny having a hand in the writing or talking-over of what Goering would have to say. And he was especially anxious to have me present on this day, almost as if he were showing off his own craftsmanship.

As everyone knows, Dimitroff was later acquitted and sent out of the country. There were rumours that he was to be shot while crossing the Soviet border. If he had been shot, the outside world would have laid the murder directly at Goering's feet. At this time, and particularly after the furore the whole trial caused in foreign countries, the Nazi officials were not as cynical and arrogant in their proclamation of power. It was, I believe, Goering's blunder, and their concern for outside opinion which forced the Nazis to release the men they had accused.

Van der Lubbe, of course, was executed, but no doctor was allowed to conduct an autopsy and the Nazis refused to send his body home for burial. The Dutchman was certainly a dupe for clever and desperate men, ambitious to seize power in Germany. Whether he was besides a pervert, or a psychopathic degenerate and self-hypnotist, or had been doped, no one knows; very few men are alive who know the entire plot. The Purge took care of most of these. Diels, however, could tell the full story.

3

Hanfstaengl had been calling up and wanting to arrange for me to meet Hitler. Hanfstaengl spluttered and ranted grandiosely: "Hitler needs a woman. Hitler should have an American woman—a lovely woman could change the whole destiny of Europe. Martha, you are the woman!"

As a matter of fact, though this sounded like inflated horse play as did most of Putzi's schemes, I am convinced he knew the violence and danger of Hitler's personality and ambitions, and deceived himself, at least partially, and wished frantically that something could be done about it.

So, for some months, when he was not telling assembled guests that he would like to throw a hand-grenade into the house of the little doctor which was below his apartment, he was trying to find a woman for Hitler. However, I was quite satisfied by the role so generously passed on to me and rather excited by the opportunity that presented itself, to meet this strange leader of men. In fact, I was still at this time, though growing critical of the men around Hitler, their methods and perhaps the system itself, convinced that Hitler was a glamorous and brilliant personality, who must have great power and charm. I looked forward to the meeting Putzi told me he had arranged.

Since I was appointed to change the history of Europe, I decided to dress in my most demure and intriguing best—

which always appeals to the Germans: they want their women to be seen and not heard, and then seen only as appendages of the splendid male they accompany—with a veil and a flower and a pair of very cold hands. We went to the Kaiserhof and met the young Polish singer, Jan Kiepura. The three of us sat talking and drinking tea for a time. Hitler came in with several men, bodyguards and his well-loved chauffeur (who was given almost a State funeral when he died recently). He sat down unostentatiously at the table next to us. After a few minutes Jan Kiepura was taken over to Hitler to talk music to him, and then Putzi left me for a moment, leaned over the Leader's ear, and returned in a great state of nervous agitation. He had consented to be introduced to me. I went over and remained standing as he stood up and took my hand. He kissed it very politely and murmured a few words. I knew very little German, as I have indicated, at the time, so I didn't linger long. I shook hands again and he kissed my hand again, and I went back to the adjoining table with Putzi and stayed for some time listening to the conversation of the two music-lovers and receiving curious, embarrassed stares from time to time from the Leader.

This first glance left me with a picture of a weak, soft face with pouches under the eyes, full lips and very little bony facial structure. The moustache didn't seem as ridiculous as it appeared in pictures—in fact, I scarcely noticed it; but I imagine that is because I was pretty well conditioned to such things by that time. As has often been said, Hitler's eyes were startling and unforgettable—they seemed pale blue in colour, were intense, unwavering, hypnotic.

Certainly the eyes were his only distinctive feature. They could contain fury and fanaticism and cruelty; they could be mystic and tearful and challenging. This particular afternoon he was excessively gentle and modest in his manners. Unobtrusive, communicative, informal, he had a certain quiet charm, almost a tenderness of speech and glance. He talked soberly to Kiepura and seemed very interested and absorbed in meeting both of us. The curious embarrassment he showed in meeting me, his somewhat apologetic, nervous manner, my father tells me—and other diplomats as well—are always present when he meets the diplomatic corps *en masse*. This self-consciousness has created in him a shyness and distaste for meeting people above him in station or wealth. As time went on, Hitler's face and bearing changed noticeably—he began to look and walk more and more like Mussolini. But this peculiar shy strain of character has to this day remained.

When I left the Kaiserhof with the ecstatic and towering jitterbug Putzi, I could lend only half an ear to his extravagant, senseless talk. I was thinking of the meeting with Hitler. It was hard to believe that this man was one of the most powerful men in Europe—even at this time, other nations were afraid of him and his growing "New Germany." He seemed modest, middle class, rather dull and self-conscious—yet with this strange tenderness and appealing helplessness. Only in the mad burning eyes could one see the terrible future of Germany.

When I came home to dinner I described my impression of the "great leader" to my father. He, of course, was greatly amused at my impressionableness, but admitted with indifference that Hitler was not an unattractive man personally. He teased me and urged me not to wash my hands for weeks thereafter—I would certainly want to retain as long as was hygienically possible, the benediction of Hitler's kiss. He said I should remember the exact spot and perhaps, if I *must* wash, could wash carefully round it. I was a little angry and peeved at his irony, but tried to be a good sport about it.

That night I had a small party at my house. Young Stresemann, whom I had met shortly after I arrived in Germany, the musically talented eldest son of the famous statesman, came, as did the Frenchman of whom I was very fond despite my conflict with his political views, and a man named Hans Thomsen, who was in the Kanzlei of the Fuehrer and supposed to be very close to him. Of Danish descent, and with the suavest and gentlest manner I had met among Germans, he was both charming and interesting to me. As time went on he frequented our house with his friend, Miss Rangabe, with clock-like regularity—and never missed a party of mine or my parents for a year to two. He seemed to be an ardent Nazi, approaching the whole problem, I thought, from a reserved and intellectual point of view. There was very little hysteria about him; I thought, as many did who met him, that he might have private and personal reservations, but that on the whole he was one of the best representatives they could have. He was extremely popular with the diplomatic corps as a whole, and his soft, restrained manner made more friends for his party than almost any man in our circle. Diplomats, including my father, would take him aside and consult fairly confidentially with him, describing what they considered were terrible mistakes in policy, internal and foreign; and would make friends with the blond-haired, soft-spoken, subtle and mature diplomat, so that Thomsen enjoyed an "inside" track with the corps, freely and frankly offered, and perhaps as freely made use of by the Germans.

Hanfstaengl came late, as usual, that night and when he arrived was in jubilant spirits. He carried on an animated conversation with young Stresemann about music, and both agreed that Schubert's *Unfinished* was one of the most glorious bits of music ever written. Judge a German by his musical tastes and you have a pretty definite clue to his intellectual position in general. I went to the victrola and put on the Horst Wessel Lied which someone had given me. It is fairly good marching music and when sung by large throngs can be quite stirring—and is the double National Anthem of the Germans. Hanfstaengl was enjoying it, not entirely without humour. Thomsen suddenly got up, went to the victrola, and turned it off abruptly. There was a strange tenseness on his face. I asked innocently why he didn't like it. He answered, very sternly: "That is not the sort of music to be played for mixed gatherings and in a flippant manner. I won't have you play our anthem, with its significance, at a social party." I was startled and annoyed.

Hanfstaengl gave Thomsen a vivid look of amusement tinged with contempt and shrugged his shoulders. He said later: "Yes, there are some people like that among us. People who have blind spots and are humourless—one must be careful not to offend their sensitive souls."

Somehow the evening was spoiled. The guests kept up their lively conversation and discussion, but most of them, not being fanatic Nazis and some definitely anti-Nazi, now knew that Thomsen was not a gay, intelligent, lighthearted, or reasonable friend, but a passionate partisan. They reacted to this in their individual ways and they were all a little self-conscious in his presence.

Unconsciously this may have been the turning-point of my reactions of a simple and more social nature to Nazi dictatorship. Accustomed all my life to the free exchange of views, the atmosphere of this evening shocked me and struck me as a sort of violation of the decencies of human relationship.

4

Another young prince of the Hohenzollern family came into the circle of my friendships about this time. (I had been introduced to his younger brother several months earlier by George Sylvester Viereck, the unattractive American, a Nazi propagandist.) Louis Ferdinand had just returned from America, where he was known in the Ford factory as "Dr. Ferdinand." He had worked four years, in North and South America, first as a simple labourer in the Ford company, and had absorbed to an amazing degree the culture and manners of America. He loved the country passionately, but was called home by his grandfather, the Kaiser, I believe in the hope that Hitler would keep his promise to the Royalty and restore one member of the family.

I first met him at a large diplomatic tea. He seemed strangely uncomfortable and out-of-place—not because of any consciousness of his distinguished birth, but rather from his democratic and natural instincts. Since then he has learned to be quite a diplomat, suave, noncommittal, gracious. But at first he was more American than the Americans—which made him vastly unpopular with the Nazis. He was generous, frank almost to the point of bluntness, affectionate and informal. He drank, danced, thought and acted like many Americans I have known. Tall, slim, beautifully built, he had the darkness and temperament inherited from his mother, the Russian side of the family. His face was interesting, though not handsome in the conventional sense sharply cut, with the long thin nose of his family, the loose mobile mouth, sometimes narrowed to sternness and at other times gentle and full, bright and expressive brown eyes, beautiful hands, fine high forehead and thick dark hair. He looked more like an ordinary person's idea of an artist, erratic and sensitive, than an heir-apparent to the German throne.

I soon learned that his real passion was music. He played the piano very well, not with the roistering, rambunctious technique of his friend Hanfstaengl and, of course, completely without the latter's vulgarity. He touched the keys softly, delicately, almost as if the reverence he felt for the instrument kept him from abusing it. His favourite composer was Chopin— I have never known a man more devoted to the works of this master than the young Prince. He was resuming his music lessons and the study of the Russian language, which he loved.

Though he never said so, I felt that here was a personality completely out of touch with Nazi Germany, a misfit in the society he was forced to accept and live in. In fact, his whole personality was lost in Germany, would have been lost under any rigid system. He was a strange combination of Latin and Slavic virtues and flaws. He would vary from moods of the deepest, almost suicidal depression, to extreme gaiety and exuberance at a moment's notice. Romantic and realistic at the same time, full of joy, and morose, he was one of the most interesting men I was to know in Germany and one of my dearest friends over the long four-and-a-half year period. His temperament, education, experience, and tastes created a nature whose elements were in constant conflict and will always be, no matter what happens to him or where he goes. He would have been a comparatively happy man in a free and democratic society.

We went often to concerts, he always oblivious of his surroundings and transported by music—and took drives in his Ford, of which he was very proud. We lent each other books, discussed art and philosophy and America, felt closer to each other than we did with our other friends—in fact, the feeling of being exiles brought us together. I was invited to the palace of his parents in Potsdam for their annual balls, their birthday parties and family celebrations. I was as thrilled as a school girl when he opened one formal ball at his parents' palace by choosing me—and childishly pleased at the stares and attention we received everywhere.

Louis loved American cigarettes so much that I gave him many cartons which we received very cheaply without tax or duty and he would take great pride in pulling them casually out of his pocket and offering them to friends. Of a very suspicious nature, after a few months in Nazi Germany, he trusted only three people. It must have been a harrowing experience for a naturally open and generous nature to be forced into an attitude and atmosphere of suspicion which didn't even spare his own family.

The first time my brother and I went to dinner with his family group, we were met on the bridge outside Potsdam and accompanied to the palace by Fritz, his younger brother. The house was more like an enormous, rambling, raftered, two-story English country house than a princely mansion. It was set in beautiful grounds and lawns, with terraces rolling down to the lake.

The inside of the house was more pretentious, innumerable large rooms leading on to one another, the main room with a tremendous two-story ceiling and huge stone fireplace. But the whole effect was cozy rather than forbidding and, at Christmas time, with the gigantic tree brilliantly decorated, almost touching the ceiling, with flowers and shrubs and presents around it, it was almost like a glorified living-room of any German family.

My brother and I walked nervously down the long halls until we finally were led into this main room. The Crown Prince, a tall, thin, blond-grey haired man who didn't look his age, had the same long, finely-cut Hohenzollern nose, pale blue, rather close-set eyes, and thin, perpetually smiling mouth, set in a gargoyle grimace of condescending pleasantry. He affected the democratic manner now so popular with ruling heads. He kissed my hand—later, as I got to know him better, also my forehead—and made some intimate jocular remark supposedly to put me at ease.

The Crown Princess was a large, dark woman, dressed in regal violet, with sparkling eyes, a pug nose and abundant brown hair. She seemed very democratic and informal in her manner, but in her character I sensed a much more dominant, ambitious personality than her husband's. She could be very pompous in her graciousness, had a shrewder intellect and was more tenacious in her purpose. She was a driving force behind him in whatever was undertaken.

I shook hands with her and, when she asked me to sit down on the sofa, I immediately did so. I realized later that I should have bowed and waited for her to sit down. But I saw no reason, then, or later, for bowing to her. My instincts against this custom, I suppose, were purely American. I had not met any kings, or kings-to-be, in my life, and if I had, I suppose I would have gasped at them like most Americans and done nothing more articulate. We had several discussions about it later in our family, when we were told we were the only people in the diplomatic corps and among Germans, even the Nazis, who didn't curtsey to her Imperial Highness. I argued to myself that I would bow to no one unless I felt that person to be a great human being, no matter what his rank or name. Since I never held this opinion about the Crown Prince and Princess, I never curtsied the whole time I knew them. I learned that they were not pleased with this independence of ours; my mother also refused to bow, even after watching Madame François-Ponçet, the wife of the representative of a great democracy, the social and official leader of the diplomatic corps, make her conventional curtsey.

I suppose it was an instinct which we felt unconsciously at first, and later justified to ourselves and held to, perhaps too tenaciously and stubbornly. Whenever I felt myself weakening, I remembered my father's wry comment when we were discussing it: "You know Thomas Carlyle had an interview with Queen Victoria, one of the greatest reigning monarchs. He did not bow, and when the interview was over, instead of

EG

walking out backwards, as was the unbroken rule, said good-bye, turned on his heel and walked out, his back to the Queen." My stubbornness also kept me from asking to be presented to the Queen of England, when all the other daughters of diplomats were flocking to London. Of course, in the society I lived in for four years, this was an almost un-heard-of heresy—but I was following the traditions and principles of my real life, not of the life I had adopted for a few years.

At the palace, on this evening, my brother and I sat quietly smoking and drinking beer, without knowing we were break-ing rules. After dinner, during which the Crown Prince and his wife flatteringly plied my brother with questions on Amer-ican history, of which they had heard he knew a great deal, and he answered with naturalness and oftentimes lack of tact, we went again into the main room. The conversation con-tinued, the hosts seemingly very interested in my brother's discussion and in the fact that there were very few real aristo-crats in American history who had left descendants. They affected great surprise when he told them many of the present outstanding families of America had no long lineage of name or fortune.

At about ten-thirty the Crown Princess rose—I supposed, to leave and go to bed, as is the custom of most parents when young people are around. We didn't know quite what to do, so we stood up and waited for her to tell us good night. After some time, all of us standing around, self-consciously doing nothing but gossiping, bantering and cautiously watching one another, I finally realized that she was signalling for us to go. We said good night and were soon on our way back to the city, much puzzled and quite pleased with the evening, in which no mention of politics had arisen. Later we were told that when the Crown Princess stood up, it was a sign for everyone in the party to leave, and you couldn't leave until she did!

Many times thereafter, when I was at their home, I longed for the moment when she would assemble a few devotees around her and start saying good night. It was a long ritual, lasting nearly an hour, because everyone had to come up, bow deeply, say a few words, bow again and leave. One time, at a very dull dance, it was almost two o'clock before I could go. Once or twice I broke all etiquette by slipping out before the Crown Princess had decided it was getting late.

I remember once, when we were all invited to a banquet at which they were to be present, my father and mother came in later, after another dinner. At ten-thirty I saw my father making his way to the host, obviously to take his leave. I rushed up to him and told him what was expected of the guests, and he simply answered: "I am very tired and exhausted. I am leaving, anyway." He went to the Crown Princess and told her he must go—probably one of the few times it had ever happened in her life—and she graciously acceded to his request (though he would have left, in any case). All of these *faux pas* on the part of our family led the Royal Family, as I have good reason to know, to think of us as rather callow and insolent Americans.

Several times I had lunch with the Crown Prince in his palace in Berlin, on Unter den Linden. He wanted me to try to curb some of Louis' obvious Americanisms. He felt his son could never be popular among Nazi Germans if he continued his natural blunt, frank, American ways. For some reason, I suppose because I was one of his son's best friends, he thought I could have some influence. I discovered, in these private lunches, that he didn't really approve of his son, in fact, felt some personal hostility to him. Louis, from the time he was a boy, never cared for military displays and training, and the fanfare of Royal pretentions. I soon saw that the Crown Prince was a rather pathetic spectacle of a man—frustrated, bitter, and jealous.

On the whole, the Crown Prince is and always was very unpopular in Germany, and now, except for a small group of Royalist supporters in the army and outside, is regarded with a sort of amused tolerance and contempt by the Nazis and most of the people. The Nazis remember with distaste the Hohenzollerns' personal friendship and royal patronage toward Jews, liberals, and artists.

The only active member of the S.A. among the Hohenzollerns is Prince August Wilhelm, the brother of the Crown
Prince. It was consistently rumoured in Berlin while I was
there that the Kaiser had not only advised "Auwie" to join
the Nazi ranks, but had given him large sums of money to
contribute to the campaign of Hitler. In the Kaiser's few
utterances and in his pregnant silences, it is quite evident that
he approves of Hitler, the only objection being that he himself
did not accomplish what the Leader has, and that the Leader
does not see fit to restore one member of his family. If he
finally reconciles himself to the fact that the farthest thing
from Hitler's mind is to share his glory with a Hohenzollern,
his only policy can be watchful waiting—in the hope that the
Nazis may make a blunder by which a military dictatorship
can be established, with a Hohenzollern as its figurehead; or
that, on the death of Hitler, the chaos and wrangling will be
so great that a restoration of his family will present the easiest
solution.

It is no secret that Nazis and Royalists alike are hoping for
the dissolution of the Soviet Union. Many members of the
Royalist groups, very close to the inner nucleus, would tell me
repeatedly: "Well, if Tukhachevsky can still be as powerful as
he seems to be in Russia, it is not impossible that the German
Reichswehr and the Red Army can in some way or other find
a means of realignment; a fine aristocrat like that cannot be a
wild Bolshevik and consequently would be inclined to favour
a more reasonable regime by which Germany and Russia could
unite once more." This was a bit naively expressed and not
without guile. What they really meant was something quite
different. The Royalists were hoping that Tukhachevsky
would either sell out to Nazi Germany or, that point being
finally settled by a shotgun, the chaos resulting from his
execution would make a step toward Russia's internal collapse
which would culminate—in their minds at least—in the
restoration of the Romanoffs. The Nazis, of course, had a
deeper laid scheme, though I am sure they would have accepted
temporarily the plan of the Royalists, realizing, of course, that
there is no such thing as an effective and functioning Royal

Family in Europe to-day and that the Kings would be but pawns in the hands of German dictators.

In any case, both gigantic fantasies have failed miserably. Nevertheless, the Kaiser still hopes and spins his futile and pathetic plots from his Doorn exile. And the Nazis notoriously organize plots and espionage groups in every country in the world, the Soviet Union not excepted.

As for the internal problem of the restoration of Royalty in Germany, I have never seen a sensible man, much less a Nazi, envisage this with any sense of reality. Even granting the will of the Nazis to have the Hohenzollerns back, which is beyond a sane man's imaginative powers, the Kaiser is still very unpopular, too old, and legally out of the question; the Crown Prince is disliked by the vast majority of Germans; and his sons are too young and erratic, or incompetent, for serious consideration.

General Beck, formerly Chief of Staff, and von Fritch of the Reichswehr, the former an ardent Royalist and the latter a Conservative of the old Hohenzollern school, have been deposed; not to mention Von Blomberg, an aristocratic traditionalist who, if he ever had courage of views and independence, apparently dropped them when he left the battlefield. It is true that these Generals and their clique were deposed not only because they formed a conservative Royalist bloc, but also because they were a check on Hitler's recklessness—for instance, they were opposed to the Spanish venture and to the Austrian putsch. Though they love war and are preparing steadily for it, they want no chances taken by the fanatic Adolph until they are absolutely sure of victory, lest one day some counter-action should be taken by the democratic powers against Hitler's aggression.

With little support from the Reichswehr, with no support from the Nazis, and being considered by most of the German people a dead issue, the Hohenzollerns still hang on, dreaming of former glory and empires, and future restoration. It is a tragi-comedy played in a sort of pathetic majestic triviality.

Their hope to take advantage of a situation that might be created by the death of Hitler, in case of an internal collapse

caused by a strong and effective opposition, or after an unsuccessful war, seems to be as unrealistic and far-fetched as their
original hope that Hitler would keep half-made promises and
restore them after his seizure of power, if they would in the
meantime lend support. It is hardly within possibility that the
mass of discontented and terribly oppressed German people
would on any of these occasions desire or permit a return of
a monarchy based on imperialism and exploitation—though
it, compared to Hitler's absolute rule, was fairly democratic.
The Imperial way of governing was a bitter experience, still
vivid and fresh in their memory.

Around the Hohenzollerns there was a curious group of
people who supported them, and yet would leave them at a
moment's notice. They were drawn and held, by some strange
German traditional instinct, to the monarchy. Though they
reviled the personal character and accomplishments of the
Crown Prince himself, they revered in some way, what he stood
for. These people comprised those who had been recognized
and given favours by the Kaiser, the intellectuals and artists
who had enjoyed patronage. For instance, there was an old
professor of archaeology or ancient history, who by a quirk
in the Kaiser's mentality had been honoured by his friendship
in the old days. He retained the most fanatic devotion to
the Royal Family—even though he knew of the life and futility
of the eldest son of the monarch—and his children were
hangers-on of the Crown Princess's ménage. One daughter,
a fairly intelligent woman of thirty or so, who acted quite
normally and humanly under different circumstances, was,
when in the presence of her mistress, the Princess, a nonentity,
a cringing sycophant. There were others like these, members
of old-time intellectual families, artists and painters and
musicians who, through habits of former patronage and
loyalty, still clung to the Hohenzollern group. Among the
younger artists and writers, occasionally one found a frequenter
of the Royal Palace functions, but they attended mainly for
reasons of opportunism. They thought they might meet other
people who would help them get along in their careers. Of
course, some of them had a personal fondness for one or

another member of the Royal Family, but on the whole there was little sense of loyalty among them, or confidence that they would be restored.

In Potsdam itself there is a nucleus of a pro-Royalist group —retired generals, former Ladies-in-Waiting and their daughters, relatives, and hangers-on—who are passionate and antiquated partisans of the Hohenzollern cause. Impoverished old women of noble birth, who brought out their moth-eaten ball dresses and valuable jewels once or twice a year for the Palace banquets; their uniformed husbands bedecked in orders bestowed years ago by the Kaiser, and their protected daughters, always make up a pathetic element at any Hohenzollern ball. The word "Potsdam" in Berlin society was a word of faint opprobrium and the expression "Don't be so Potsdam" was used to reprove people who suddenly became smug and hypocritical, or hopelessly dated in intellectual or social ideas. Many of these people, after a period of years, realized which side their bread was buttered on and swung over, half guiltily, to the Nazis.

There were, until a few years ago, many Royalist societies which held meetings on the Kaiser's birthday, or any other occasion obviously connected with Royal celebrations. They were attacked viciously in the Nazi press and eventually disbanded by Hitler. Also, as I have said, the defunct Stahlhelm, the society of war veterans, which was frankly anti-Nazi and pro-Hohenzollern, was liquidated less than a year after we arrived.

During the Purge of June, 1934, the Crown Prince was supposed to be in danger and "Auwie" arrested. The story went that Goering called in "Auwie" and questioned him as to his role and whereabouts in these troublous times. He answered at length. After Goering had finished with him, he is supposed to have remarked wryly to his adjutant: "Take 'Auwie' away —he is surely too stupid to have had anything to do with these things." However, I am sure they were temporarily suspected and watched, if not actually in danger. Hitler takes no chances. If there could be ambitious folk around anywhere, with even the slightest following, in such times of uncertainty, he would be sure automatically to keep them guarded and suppressed.

As for the supposed strong support in the Reichswehr itself,
I have always discounted it. There are many officers who traditionally respect and give allegiance to the former crowned
head, but few would do anything active to restore him. They
like to drink with members of the family, attend their social
gatherings, gossip and have fun with them, but I have known
very few who are in any way concerned or interested in
having them back on the throne.

5

When I arrived in Germany I thought I would have an
opportunity to meet some of the great German writers and
artists. To reveal how little the book-burning and persecution
of intellectuals meant to me, and how carelessly I had read the
American press, I still hoped to meet some of the outstanding
men of letters like Leonhard Frank, Döblin, Zweig, Remarque,
Mann, Feuchtwanger, Ludwig, Wassermann, and Hauptmann. Out of this group the only one who remained in Germany was Gerhardt Hauptmann, the author of the great play,
The Weavers, whom I never met and whom later I never
wanted to meet. He had become a good Nazi and had honours
heaped on him, far out of proportion to his fame. He was,
however, the only German writer of major distinction who
had accepted Nazi tenets and chosen to live by them. Of
course, he is a very old man.

It is interesting to realize that not one writer of merit,
except Hauptmann, capitulated to National Socialism. The
German writers were always in the vanguard of progressive
thought and had remarkable social and political development.
Feuchtwanger, whom I met some years later in Paris, told
me that the night before Hitler seized power there was a
dinner in the German Embassy at Washington, at which the
then German Ambassador, von Prittwitz, extolled Feuchtwanger as the finest example of the flowering of German
contemporary culture. The next day Hitler seized power,
and in a few weeks, Feuchtwanger was described as the
worst example of Jewish Marxist degeneracy, and his books

were burned in the public square. His property was seized, his house, capital, even his library confiscated, as well as the royalties his books brought into the German publishing house from abroad! This is, of course, only one instance of a regular procedure applied to all enemies of National Socialism, literary or otherwise.

I began to ask friends of mine, what had happened to the writers I admired. Even among the ardent Nazis I noticed a genuine sadness, no matter what rationalization they found for my benefit, when they discussed the fate of literature. They would attempt to justify the state of affairs by saying: "Of course, in a revolution one cannot expect art to flower immediately, and these men could not have remained in Germany because they were liberals, anarchists, Marxists, or Jews. It is too bad; but give us time, our literature will come again."

Many less famous writers and poets were imprisoned or put into concentration camps, sometimes killed. For instance, the poet Erich Muhsam died the most ghastly death, after infinite agony and humiliation. A friend of mine, in the camp at the same time, since escaped, described the scenes to me. The minor writers in many cases could not escape in time, had not the money with which to do so.

I knew about these facts shortly after I arrived in Germany because I met many people, Germans and foreigners, who were deeply concerned with the intellectual life of Germany. I was shocked, of course, but having been lulled into a critical paralysis through the steady stream of propaganda, I found myself for the first few months using the same arguments which were handed out to me, about the "revolution." Furthermore, I wanted to be as just and fair to the Nazis as was humanly possible.

However, I determined to see and talk to what writers there were left in Germany. I had several friends connected with magazines and publishing houses and I was well enough acquainted to make known my strange request. So I was introduced to one of the most picturesque and active publishers German literary life has ever had. Before Hitler, Ernst Rowohlt published most of the important and talented writers of Germany—many of them radicals, some Communists, others liberals and pacifists. He also published several of the best contemporary American writers, including Wolfe, Hemingway, and Faulkner.

He was a delightful man, of giant blond Aryan stature and complexion. He had a positively cherubic face, with innocent blue eyes, round, ruddy, plump cheeks and an irrepressible and spluttering humour. When I first arrived he was learning English and spoke very badly with a strong accent, but so amusingly and with such obvious delight in his mistakes and in his attempts to right them, that his bubbling, stumbling, lisping jargon was a positive joy to listen to. Rowohlt was a tremendous drinker and also a very serious and vital man. He loved life and freedom passionately, was tremendously proud of his past record, and spoke bluntly and honestly about any subject that arose. Since that time his firm has been taken over by the Nazi Party; he has been forced to submission in a more or less minor role in the publishing house and is a broken and tragic figure. He was the type of man who aroused and held the devotion and unswerving loyalty of his subordinates and who could attract anyone by his tremendous energy and intelligence. In his house in the early days, one could find the last remains of independent literary thought collectively gathered in Berlin. Now it is a different story.

At one party, a very drunken affair, but as always, extremely amusing and full of gaiety, I met Hans Heinz Ewers, formerly a writer of degenerate, cheap, lurid sex stories, the most famous of which was called "The Vampire." As soon as Hitler came to power, he smelled the way things were going and jumped hurriedly on the bandwaggon with a biography of Horst Wessel, now the official Nazi biography of the S.A. leader who was allegedly killed by Communists, and who was the composer of the Nazi national anthem which bears his name.

Ewers is wined and dined by official German circles, and even by diplomatic people, though I am proud to say he never came into our house. An old man with a monocle, trying desperately to appear younger than his years, he is to me one of the most disgusting types I have ever met. When he took my hand and kissed it, I shuddered at his touch. His hands were scaly, splotched with red dry sores, hard, repulsive. I wanted to wash my hands as quickly as possible after his handclasp. It seemed like contact with a toad's skin, or with a particularly repugnant reptile just losing its skin. His face, too, had the strange blotched and bloated complexion of a drunkard and a degenerate. His manners were soft, ingratiating, formally polite, but with salacious suggestiveness. I remember I was profoundly indignant when he told me he was married to an American. I went into the other room as soon as possible, to escape this loathsome creature and his eulogy of Nazism.

A few days later some friends of mine asked if I would like to meet Hans Fallada, the author of "Little Man, What Now?" which had created a stir in America shortly before I left. He was generally considered a minor but competent writer and I was anxious to meet him. He lived with his wife and family on a small farm near a village in Mecklenburg, a good two- or three-hour drive by car from Berlin.

It was a lovely spring day when we started, the young delicate green soft and blooming on the hills, in the trees and gardens. The chestnut trees all along the roads were glowing and luminous with their strange, upthrust flowers, the acacias' wine-sweet fragrance faint in the air.

When we had driven half-way, there was a violent spring storm. The rain fell heavily in long, strong strokes, the wind rushed through the trees. Little sharp lines of lightning lit up the sky, and the scene was wild and violent with colour, intense electric green and violet, lavender and grey.

We had an open roadster and were driving very fast, enjoying the rain in our faces, not wanting to put the top up. In a few minutes it was warm and moist again, the earth steaming and fragrant, the sun soft and bright on the flowing hills and beautiful lakes. Mecklenburg is one of the loveliest districts in North Germany, certainly the most beautiful I have ever been in. There is a gentleness to the landscape, in the rolling green hills and bright lakes, a lyricism and poetry in the softness and contour of the land and water.

We finally found the village and managed to struggle through the bad roads until we arrived at the modest cottage set by the lake and surrounded by a few acres of cultivated land.

Hans Fallada came out with his buxom, simple wife to meet us. We walked around a little and he described the farming he was doing, his wife proudly showing off her work in the garden. He was a stockily built man with blondish hair and charming, genial features; his wife plump, blonde, serene, with a pleasant face. They had two children, a young, bright-faced boy of four and an infant in arms. Their life seemed to be built around their family and their farm. He was isolated from life and happy in his isolation. There was some discussion and though I got the impression that he was not and could not be a Nazi—what artist is?—I felt a certain resignation in his attitude.

After a wholesome country dinner we took a long walk to the top of the highest hill. The panorama was splendid and there was a quiet haze of heat spread over the earth, the lakes and hills appeared to be resting softly, and life seemed peaceful. We took a lot of pictures, as is the German custom wherever one goes; went back to the house, followed by his dog; looked at his books, the foreign editions, he talking about his literary work to come, and we finally took our leave promising to come back soon.

But we never went back. This withdrawal from life was Hans Fallada's tragic solution to the problems that might have been troubling his peace. It was a temptation to which he had completely succumbed. And the impression of defeatism he gave us was saddening. Later I heard that he got into trouble on one of his rare visits to Berlin, that he was beaten up by some Storm Troopers and confined to the hospital for a week or two. But he seems to have settled his life in the simple, trivial pattern we saw on his farm, is still writing not very good books, and is for the moment lost to a deeper struggle with life. However, he is the one remaining author of recognized talent writing in Germany and one can watch as time goes on what this intellectual and emotional passivity will do to his talent.

In the course of four and a half years I made several feeble attempts to give literary parties. On one occasion, when a visiting American publisher was in Berlin for a few days, I asked a dear friend of mine, a highly sensitive and educated German married to an American in Berlin, who had known the earlier Berlin literary life and still had contacts with what remained, to arrange the party for me. She got together about forty people, writers, poets, publishers and magazine editors. It was a dull and, at the same time, tense afternoon. One poet, a year later, was put into a concentration camp. At the time I noticed he was sitting in the back of the library with a group of three or four people around him. They were talking quietly and cautiously, a sort of still living centre in the party. He was a man of about forty, with a strong, suffering face and deep soft voice. His wife had been arrested several months before, but I got no feeling of fear about him, rather a subdued strength turned inward, a tested courage of spirit and character, an endurance of heroic proportions.

The rest of the guests were standing around drinking heavily and devouring plates of food. Probably many of them were poor and actually ill-fed, and the others were nervous and anxious to conceal it. Many of them hovered around the American publisher in a pathetic eagerness to know what was happening in America. They revealed the avidity of the mentally starved. A few Jewish writers and critics looked uncomfortable and self-conscious. One of them has since emigrated to the United States, but his complex of persecution was so deeply rooted by that time that I am afraid his whole future has been warped.

In any case, this was the party at which I hoped to hear amusing conversation, some exchange of stimulating views, at least conversation on a higher plane than one is accustomed to in diplomatic society. But this party was so full of frustration and misery; of the strain laid upon the last scraps of minds and opinions of any freedom, by the ferreting-out conducted by the Secret Police; of tension, broken spirits, doomed courage or tragic and hated cowardice, that I vowed never to have such a group again in my house. Of course, later it would have been dangerous for any of these poor souls to be connected with a foreign Embassy, particularly the American one. I weakened, however, one other time, when the American writer Thomas Wolfe came to Berlin.

There was one other writer in Berlin whom I met on various occasions. He was a Russian émigré, his father having owned—so they said—most of the Siberian gold mines. He was patronized by a curious personality in Berlin society, a Baroness von Nostitz, who had been a model for Rodin years ago in Paris and whose father was then the German Ambassador. She was an enormous woman, of classic, ruined facial beauty and pale hair. Of an ancient and aristocratic lineage, she was the proud possessor of the only salon in Berlin. She cultivated and helped many writers, musicians and artists, all of mediocre talent, who thought the road to Fame was lined by such Baronesses and social entrees.

All the diplomats, many of the Royalty and their hangers-on, but very few National Socialists, attended her parties. She was a snob, social and intellectual, who wanted to attain distinction through her patronage of the non-existent arts of Nazi Germany. "Art for art's sake" was her motto, and the quality of her output, both in her parties and her sponsoring of talent, gave clear evidence of the superficiality of this dictum in these years of change. Outmoded, and outdated, her salon and the people who frequented it were shabby imitations of a former custom which had value and brilliance in dead ears. That the diplomats attended so religiously was another evidence to me of the bankruptcy of their life. From habit—because if a diplomat did not have on his calendar at least one or two parties a day in the season, he wouldn't feel *au courant*—from lassitude and snobbery, the diplomatic corps appeared regularly, and revealed as regularly a deadly boredom. I went once or twice and was amused to watch the immobile faces, the glittering eyes of women covered in furs and pretensions, anxious to see and be seen, peering from behind hands covering polite yawns or holding cigarettes and delicate cocktail glasses, chattering the same small eternal gossip between one another, sitting erect and paralyzed, their minds obviously on other things or simply not functioning, while the man or woman-of-the-hour sang a song or played the piano.

The Russian writer, for whom the Baroness held out high hopes, wrote several books in the few years I was there, all hailed enthusiastically by the Nazi press. They were inconsequential things which he attempted to colour with that morbid Russian quality so often and so badly imitated by second-rate writers. He visited the darkly beauteous daughter of the Greek Minister, Miss Rangabe, many times, and once or twice called on me, claiming that he received from us some unearthly quality of inspiration. He was very mystic and absorbed in himself, an exceedingly unattractive person both mentally and physically.

There may be some health somewhere in the creative field in Germany now. I do know there are a few left-wing writers, and writers of vitality and constructive ideology still at work. One man I know has completed a book which took him three years to write. It is, for the seeing eye, a complete and terrible denunciation of National Socialism, so carefully and brilliantly done that the Nazi press and Nazi critics to this day do not know that he is a revolutionary. But those who are aware of it preserve the secret closely and hold precious in their hearts the daring and genius of the author.

Once or twice there is some subtle writing of this nature in magazines as well. At one time in a popular magazine in Germany there appeared an article about conditions in the Ukraine. Within a few days everyone of intelligence saw clearly that the article was really describing the conditions in Germany, and rumours began to fly. This was a bit too obviously done and, as I remember, the editor of the magazine is now in prison on a trumped-up charge of homosexuality. Other articles get by, however, and it is not always the most difficult thing in the world to pass the often stupid Nazi censorship. The fact that occasionally such things happen in books and magazines, heartens tremendously the creative artists and gives them a feeling of some solidarity with the others of their craft.

6

Thomas Wolfe came to Germany two years after we arrived. National Socialism had already settled down into its pattern of oppression and exploitation. There were no more illusions about the revolution to come, or about Hitler's promises both to the outside world and to his followers. It was, after two years, a cynical, cruel, ruthless rape of the German people, made fact by regular procedure.

But Wolfe came, strangely enough with high enthusiasm about Germany—many American writers are naive politically until they have some personal experience with Fascism and oppression. He had studied and loved the great German writers and artists and felt more closely akin to the Germanic spirit than to any other. It took him some time to learn what was happening, as it does most people who have not been passionately interested in the political and economic developments in Europe. What really finished his illusions about Germany were his observation and experience with men and women whose lives and spirit had been crushed by the terror. He came back again the following year, attended the Olympics, and learned his final lesson.

I had a party for Tom almost the day he arrived. Again, we tried to get together some interesting writers and critics. But this time it was hopeless. His German publisher, Rowohlt, came, of course, and a few others; but I filled in with American friends and the Embassy staff, who had heard vaguely that Tom was a distinguished writer and flocked to take a look at a freak. Part of the trouble was that the American Embassy was known to be extremely critical of Nazi Germany and we dreaded to ask intellectuals or free-thinking people, for fear the German officials would take this opportunity to observe them, follow them, or in other ways intimidate them. In fact, in the last year and a half, not more than half a dozen antagonists of the National Socialist regime came to our house. If I wanted to see these friends, I would arrange for it in a way to ensure their safety.

The Germans, even the Nazis, loved Thomas Wolfe. He

had long articles written about him, comparing him to a much-loved Bavarian poet of the people. His book "Look Homeward Angel" had been acclaimed by pre-Hitler Germany, and his personality and later works by post-Hitler critics. He wrote several articles about Germany and his impressions, some of which appeared in newspapers and others in magazines. The fanatic Hitler-followers accepted and praised him, the enemies of Hitler were devoted to his personality, respected the power and lyricism of his prose. In fact, there actually seemed to be something Germanic about him which they all could claim. If he were alive now, I doubt if he could return to the country; certainly the official Nazi attitude is one of hostility. He had written things since then on Germany, after the impact of study and observation had touched his mind and heart, which could never be published there. It would not surprise me if his books, past and future, were confiscated.

In his short month or two there the first time, he became a legend around Berlin. For the first time since Hitler's coming to power, the famous Romanisches Café, formerly the centre of literary lights, artists and intellectuals, took on life. He seemed to give a sort of animation to the streets and café. People began shyly to enter the almost deserted café. Tom, a huge man of six feet six, with the face of a great poet, strode the streets, oblivious of the sensation he created, with his long powerful strides, his head high, his posture free and full of a lumbering rhythm.

To the desolateness of the intellectual life of Germany, Thomas Wolfe was like a symbol of the past when great writers were great men. Something of the angel and the demon in him, as his best friend once told me, he gave back to the intellectual and creative people of Berlin a sense of their past, of the dignity and power and freedom of a mind not under stress. Certainly he was the most vital experience literary Berlin had had in the Hitler years, and, for months after, people would gather to talk of him. But when he had left, the famous café, no longer animated by his booming voice and reckless gestures, with his circle of friends and

FG

admirers around him, again was deserted and silent. I have heard that he attracted men to the café who had not been in such public places since Hitler; and that the Secret Police, aware of this, planted spies for weeks after in the café, to try to ferret out some free opinion that might have been less cautiously expressed after the sense of security and oblivion of terror that Wolfe's presence had given them.

Part of Tom's uncritical attitude toward Nazism can be explained by his own state of delirium. He had just published his book, "Of Time and the River," after five years of writing, during which time most of the critics said he was through, that he had written himself out in his first book and would never be able to repeat his success. He had escaped from America before publication-time and fled to Paris. His book had been an overwhelming success immediately and was on the best-seller list in a few days, with the critics proclaiming him one of the greatest writers of his time. He was in a state of high nervous tension, wherein everything took on the proportions of a gigantic and infinitely beautiful dream. He loved everything and everyone, his high spirits flooded everything he did, thought, saw, or felt. And his moods of despair were equally terrifying in their intensity. He was mad with the music of his own personality and power, almost beside himself, and no one could come near him without feeling the charged atmosphere of his tremendous excitement.

Several of us took a trip with Tom to Weimar, the home of Goethe in his adult and later years, and to the Wartburg. We tried futilely to show him that all was not unconditionally superb in Germany. He was to learn for himself; in the meantime, he was in a ferment, taking all of it in and waiting for the passion of the moment to become quieter.

He was fascinated by the little garden house of Goethe and measured his height against that of the great poet, to find that he, Tom, was taller; and stood almost hypnotized by the famous saddle chair upon which Goethe composed. The little house somehow pleased us all more than the pretentious city house, which we saw later. We walked around the grounds, enjoyed the smooth green lawns and magnificent trees. A storm was rising and we stopped for a moment to listen to the wind in the trees, wild and full, like music from an organ, like a great poem. The sky was darkening and the trees twisting and raging in the weird and beautiful symphony of sound. We thought of Walpurgis Nacht.

We visited the town house where Goethe lived pompously after he had become a citizen of great stature and a public servant. The atmosphere here was stuffy; one felt within the walls of this place that Goethe's soul had atrophied. There was no longer the sympathy for the youthful Goethe, the dreamer, the seeker, the troubled genius, passionate and baffled in his attempt to find meaning in the destiny of the human race. He had become the burgher, self-satisfied, smug, quite conscious of his role in the world and in literature, shutting himself off from people, including the faithful Christiana who could not trespass into his section of the house, and the struggle of the human heart. In the garden were one or two "blut büchen," red beech trees, flaming against the blue sky.

We went finally to his tomb and that of Schiller. There were very few flowers on Goethe's, but Schiller's tomb was heavy and almost concealed with floral tributes from admirers, among whom were National Socialist societies. Outside was another blood beech, with magnificent rich crimson foliage, as if it had sprung, burning, from the heart of the poet.

We drove on through the soft early-summer air and scenery, through luxuriant fields, some covered with the German mustard plant, like a huge golden wave falling and undulating over the earth. At Eisenach we found the spirit of Luther, if not around us at least in ourselves. We took pleasure in refreshing our memory of one of the greatest and simplest of Germans. In an hotel on the top of the mountain, *Die Wartburg*, about which many legends have arisen and which is the scene of the Venusberg drama, we drank cold Moselle wine and then walked around the castle. It was dark outside, but one could distinguish, among the churning, stormy clouds the rugged outline of the mountain. Below were the small, yellow lights of Eisenach. Here the scene was morbid and romantic, with some of the strange barbarism of Wagner, peopled with the dark heroes and legends of the new Nazi religion. Though the scene appealed to me in some ways, I could not help a feeling of revulsion, remembering what a revival of Wagner's grandiose magic and a perversion of heroic Germanic legend had become, in Nazi symbolism and ideology.

Next morning, misty and cold, we visited the castle where Luther had stayed in retirement to write his Bible. The ink-spot on the wall is amusingly preserved, to remind visitors that Luther had a very human reaction to the devil.

On the way back to Berlin we passed again through the Harz mountains, covered with black forests, which inspired the Brothers Grimm and many an ancient German to pass along a lore of beauty and imagination to succeeding generations.

The trip was a joy and a revelation. We were made conscious again of the Germany of the past; great, deep, courageous chapters in the history of literature and progress were unfolded. I think I learned at this time, once and for all, not to confuse the real German character and people with their present oppressors. Hitler will undoubtedly have a role in history, but it will be an unsavoury one, one which the inheritors of the great literary, artistic, philosophic traditions of giant men will detest remembering.

Tom left soon after, with many of his illusions intact, though some were wavering. The following year he returned, a much soberer person, this time eager to learn what lay beneath the surface of Nazi success and effectiveness. He met even more Germans than in the first year, learned what made the wheels go around, in the partisans as well as the non-partisans of the regime. He still drank convivially with Rowohlt during long evenings of violence—since both men were very emotional—and discussion. What he concluded about the effects of National Socialism on human society and freedom, he had already written, and though he carried with him always—as most of us do who know anything about Germany and its people, past and present—the warm affection and reverence they have so marvellously deserved, his feeling for their tragic frustration left him no alternative but to stay away from present-day Germany.

Tom has died of a brain infection in a Baltimore hospital. His death is one of the great losses in American literature. Despite the uneven work, the occasional careless and unimportant writing, here was a talent whose magnitude and promise were and are to my mind unmatched by any other contemporary American writer. His lyricism bears the stamp of true and living poetry, his characterizations will remain in human memory long after his bones are dust. Tom, at his death, was already a major writer and was unmistakably American. His sense of the American scene, his intuitions, brilliance, and poetry produced some of the finest interpretations of America in literature. His lust for life, the stature and grandeur of his soul, the roaring fury and joy of the demonic angel he was, the conflict of good and bad within him are all now irrevocably lost in body. But his writing still lives not only for those who loved and revered him, but also for future generations. He was a legend, a hope, a glowing promise and his generation seems curiously paralyzed, sterile and trivial without him. There will be many people who will cavil and carp at him now that he is dead—many who have already said that madness produced his greatness. Tom was not mad, unless madness means one man's almost unbearably sensitive reaction to life's struggles and dreams, conflicts and terrors, meanness and splendour. Perhaps his understanding and vision were too intense for him to endure, but he has captured in beautiful prose, for all the petty depreciators to read and learn from the feeling of America—its glistening cities and plains and people—of the secret, deep, dark heart of life, of the mortality of man's body, the immortality driving his dreams and the restless, confused and hopeful world in which they wander and flower.

V

THE PRESS CORPS

THE NEWSPAPERMEN, AMERICAN and English, living in Berlin these years were on a pretty high level and certainly, as far as I was concerned, were a steady source of amusement, enlightenment, and cynical realism. They were the most articulately intelligent group in Berlin and the group I saw the most of. Furthermore, they were people whom we could in no way endanger, so they could be constant friends and companions without causing strain to any of us.

When we first arrived in Berlin, the Counsellor was the rather silly Protocol man who had very strict rules about the conduct of the Embassy. He attempted to bully my father into a social and official ostracism of all newspapermen. He was very angry that they had the audacity even to ask for interviews and statements. We thought it very strange indeed, particularly remembering the way President Roosevelt had handled the American press. We concluded later that the Counsellor had an almost psychopathic loathing of newspapermen, perhaps because he considered them socially inferior or because they may have been unkind and contemptuous of him. We listened for a few days to his advice which we thought must be fairly well-founded and just. We learned later that the same man had in the identical pompous way attempted to make the preceding Ambassador agree to this procedure. The former Ambassador had so resented the Counsellor's intrusion that he had not only disregarded all of his advice but had actually tried many times to get him transferred from the Berlin post.

The Counsellor applied his theory to the Consulate people also—in fact, they were outcasts as far as the American Embassy was concerned—they and the journalists. This also struck us as an extraordinary procedure since the Consulate people were also servants of the United States Government, and in many cases more efficient and conscientious than the diplomats. The Counsellor succeeded in his plan only so long as we remained ignorant of customary procedure and of his past record. There was one embarrassing episode, in which my father yielded to the demands of his Counsellor (who said it was the accepted Protocol at our and other Embassies) and didn't invite the Consul General, or his staff to our first diplomatic reception. We thought the separation of two branches of American Government service in social functions was both ridiculous and snobbish. The Consul General left town on that day, perhaps to save himself from such an artificial situation.

However, later, in fact almost the next time we entertained, we invited both newspapermen and the consular staff. And my father was the first Ambassador to establish the new precedent of co-operation, both professional and social, of these two formerly rival groups. All this seems trivial in the recounting but one can hardly imagine the tempest in the teapot the whole matter caused at the time we dared to defy rule and tradition. So after a few months, in which time we got out orientation, we chose our friends from among whatever groups were open to us, and newspaper people as well as the consulate staff had free access to our home both at official and more personal functions.

When we first arrived there were many interesting newspapermen among whom were Knickerbocker, Edgar Ansel Mowrer, Junius Wood, Victor Bodker (a representative of the English Reuter service), Norman Ebbutt, and Sigrid Schultz. All except the last have been transferred or deported from Germany but a new batch of younger men came in their places. Ralph Barnes came from Russia a couple of years after we arrived, and the New York *Times* continued its universal policy of keeping men of foreign extraction at the head of its staff—two venerables with strange and difficult names: Otto Tolischus and Guido Enderis. Hearst was represented by Karl von Wiegand, as head of the European office—an old, charming, naïve, and loyal soul who was a devoted partisan to the royalty—and a young man named Shirer and his assistant

Huss. The Associated Press kept Louis Lochner, a middle-aged and extremely able man, a Social Democrat of pre-Hitler vintage and also an ardent monarchist, rather disliked by the rest of the press corps, maybe because of his "scoops," maybe because of his slight pomposity. The United Press found in Fred Oeschsner an intelligent, sound, conservative reporter who had pretensions to complete objectivity and developed quite a theory about it. However, he was a friendly, loyal and warmhearted person.

These, and a scattering of others, a Lithuanian, French, and Russian, particularly some loyal British newspapermen who were thrown out of Germany and whom I didn't know too well, constituted this group of people whom I saw most of, and liked the best, in Germany. They, for the most part, had the most realistic and honest approach to foreign affairs I knew—diplomats being too frozen-mouthed or too conservative, too scared or too conventional to express openly more than a half dozen opinions a year. They had sources of information almost as valuable and reliable as those of the diplomats—in fact, quite a few diplomats, in our and other staffs, respected and used their information constantly. They employed informers, or voluntary informers came to them without reward, who were in almost every ministry and activity in Germany. And they protected these people so carefully that I heard of only a few contacts being broken by detection while I was over there.

Sometimes the journalists went off on wild-goose chases, got stories that were clearly implausible, but on the whole the stories that came from Germany, from most of the people I have mentioned, presented a pretty accurate picture of what was happening there. When I hear in America of the gross exaggeration of the newspaper accounts of Nazi Germany, I am amazed at the naïveté or the pro-Fascist leanings of the speaker. Because the newspapermen I knew were amazingly conscientious, had excellent sources, both German, foreign and diplomatic, and knew Germany and the developments better than most people. Ebbutt, of the London *Times*, for instance, had lived in Germany for twelve years—Sigrid Schultz for ten, and the New York *Times* correspondents for about the same length of time. Karl von Wiegand has studied the European scene for almost twenty years. So these men knew both the Hitler and the pre-Hitler days in many cases; if not, they got to work immediately with the language, inherited the contacts of their predecessors, read source books, travelled the country, and met the German people.

It was well known to everyone that every newspaper office had its spies. Germans were planted on one excuse or another, in the outer or inner office, as translators, secretaries, information agents, or what-not. Their role was so obvious that there was a good deal of joking about it, though naturally at the same time extreme resentment and disgust. One journalist told me: "It's the goddamnedest nuisance. Hans appears at my elbow all the time as guileless as a new-born babe, and I have to spend most of my time thinking out ways and means to give him the slip." Not only was this espionage in the office a common and discussed occurrence—so was the presence of spies and followers after hours. Both Mowrer and Ebbutt were followed religiously, and their apartments watched and reported on. The secret contacts were impossible to arrange in their private homes; they had to use somewhat the same conspiratorial method practised among all opposition groups.

Of course, these tactics described above were employed by the Nazis mainly with newspapermen who had the most knowledge and effective contacts. Often the journalists were summoned before the Secret Police to explain a certain hostile dispatch, and by this summons given an implied threat and warning.

The Taverne, an interesting Italian restaurant, was the centre of the journalists' social gatherings. Every night from ten until two—sometimes later—they would gather there for beer, or scotch and sodas, and discuss the stories of the day, the stories that most of them had already sent to their papers. Friends of mine in foreign Embassies, some of the best informed men in Berlin, made it a point to go there every few nights to listen to the discussions. There was a sort of friendly exchange of news between the journalists themselves, and

often between them and the diplomats. At the Stamm Tisch,
or Reserved Table for eight to ten people, I would often see
eighteen to twenty people crowded together in ardent discussion. Only those very much in the know, or very close to
newspaper circles, could occupy a seat there. At first a lot of
Nazis and S.A. people frequented the place out of curiosity
and interest in real news. Later we began to feel that they
were carefully selected and placed there to get what information they could. Even Dietrich, Nazi press chief, Hanfstaengl,
and Diels, were seen about and appeared to be on intimate
terms with the journalists. Finally, the Nazis received an order
not to go to the Taverne. We figured out that, even though
at first they had wanted to come, and later been planted on
us, they were finally forbidden permission to go there because
the news and information of the journalists were too dangerous
and demoralizing for Nazis to listen to!

2

Norman Ebbutt, a dour, dark little Englishman and his
friend, Mrs. Holmes, reigned at this table. Almost any time
you could see him silent, with a pipe jammed in between his
teeth, his right arm supported high on his chest by his left, silent,
glowering, keen eyes examining the people around him. He
was certainly one of the most brilliant newspapermen in
Berlin, if not in Europe. Known to be violently anti-Hitler
he was a sharp and effective thorn in the side of the Nazis. He
never spoke when it was unnecessary, had a profound contempt for anyone who could not show intellectual integrity
and training. Therefore the glumness, against which many
people complained, was a conservation of his own energy and
a barrier to idle talk. He had a dry sense of humour and a deep
sense of loyalty and definitely possessed more knowledge,
understanding, and information about Nazi Germany than
anyone there, in or out of his position.

In fact, it was rumoured constantly that he was the mainstay
not only of the London *Times* foreign service but also of the
British Foreign Office. His reports were supposed to go to the

Prime Minister as well as to his paper, and he was trusted and relied upon implicitly by the British Ambassador Phipps. It is said that when von Ribbentrop was sent as Ambassador to England he had two things in his portfolio to accomplish immediately: remove Phipps and expel Ebbutt from Germany. Otherwise, in the minds of the Nazis and the conservative Fascist set-up represented by Chamberlain, England could never come to terms with Germany. It is a coincidence and maybe more that both men were manœuvred out of Germany, Ebbutt in a scandalous and heartless way, Phipps less openly and more honourably, and incidentally, to his wife's and his own intense pleasure.

Ebbutt was far from a socialist though this, among other things, was said by his enemies in an attempt to discredit him. He was a militant and progressive democrat who had known Germany in better days and who knew and understood the Germanic temperament and background as thoroughly as any scholar of the subject. He was horrified and infinitely grieved, personally, by the results and plans of National Socialism. Furthermore, his knowledge of economics and politics led him to discard completely the Nazi ideology.

Since the London *Times* has always played a very shrewd game of pro-Fascist ball, Norman had to be especially careful in his dispatches. Often they were kept out of the paper, or put in an inconspicuous place, or garbled in such a way as to sound almost innocuous. To combat this he developed a highly elaborate and delicately implicative style in which he said what he wanted to, and implied more, without being detected. This came to be known in Berlin as the "Ebbutt style," which was the envy of every other newspaperman. By this caution and brilliance, no matter what happened to his reports, garbled or cut or misplaced, they "carried a wallop" that no one could miss, if he had a grain of intelligence. I am sure he was retained on the *Times* as long as he was because he could so cleverly conceal and yet reveal his hostility, and also because as long as Eden and Vansittart were in the Foreign Office, they valued his work highly and used his reports very advantageously.

To be admired and respected, considered the dean (in no stuffy sense) of the journalists' corps, is no easy position to hold among cynical newspapermen. But no matter what personal likes or dislikes entered into the judgment of Ebbutt and his ménage, I have never heard a newspaperman, or for that matter any informed person, German or diplomatic, say anything derogatory about Norman's intelligence. He rendered a service for many years to what was left of progressive England. When the forces against progress took over the reins, Ebbutt was sacrificed. Another indication of his position in Berlin was revealed in the profound and bitter indignation everyone felt when he was practically "booted out" of Germany by the Nazis and the pro-Fascist bloc in the British Government.

The Ebbutts' parties were always among the most interesting in Berlin—certainly not comparable to the pretentious and dull diplomatic affairs, where one could endure an evening only if a small group of friends could spot a corner and have a quiet talk for a little while. In the simple but roomy apartment of Norman and his wife, there were held small dinners, buffet suppers, *bier abends*, and cocktail parties, at which one could find most of the people worth talking to in Berlin. Up until the last six months, even later, of their stay, there was a scattering of Germans, some of them Nazis, asked purposely by the Ebbutts, and, when these weren't present, there were former German officials, titled, German-Jewish, intellectual, artistic, and other people who had been known and respected in pre-Hitler days, and who still had something to say and refreshing attitudes to reveal.

Sometimes these parties became hilarious brawls, as most newspaper parties did before they were over, and the intimate friends stayed on to drink, say what they really thought about foreign affairs in general, Nazi policies in particular. These groups would cluster around the fireplace in another and cosier room, interrupted only occasionally by a sharp jangle from the telephone—a message from the office or another story about to break—and we would then really begin to hear the fascinating inside stories of all present. Mrs. Holmes, a handsome, voluble and infinitely courageous woman, murmur-ing on in her soft voice in one corner of the room, Norman, standing listening or analyzing in his brilliant and long-viewed interpretation some new move of the Nazis or Great Britain. He and Mrs. Holmes seemed to work admirably together, she supplying the intuition and keenness of a remarkably agile mind and Norman fitting and piecing together, co-ordinating all he heard through his own mental processes, into their conclusions. In my last two years in Germany these parties were among the high spots in my life.

When the story broke in England that several Nazi journalists had been found guilty of espionage, that there were about three times more German journalists in London than papers they represented, and that they were to be deported, everyone immediately thought that the Nazis, as a reprisal, would manage somehow to get Norman Ebbutt out of Germany, especially since they knew his capacities and uncompromising critical attitudes. And in a few days, as we all feared, the Nazis asked for his recall.

What actually transpired between von Ribbentrop and the British Foreign Office, or between the German Foreign Office and the British, perhaps only they could reveal. It is clear that the *Times* was either threatened by the British Foreign Office, or was glad to be rid of bad business in the person of Norman Ebbutt. In any case, Norman Ebbutt, one memorable after-noon, spent several hours with my mother, Mrs. Holmes, and me, indicating confidentially some of the manœuvring that had been resorted to. The *Times* refused to support Norman in his protest—the Nazis, among other ridiculous and venomous charges, had accused him of possessing military information, and he was ordered out of the country, the order to take effect in something like two or three days. Norman felt very bitterly about the *Times*' conduct during the whole affair and was convinced that higher officials were at work, both in Germany and in Britain to remove him.

The crowd at the station when he left, bringing their little gifts and flower bouquets and words of sadness and good luck for his future, all the journalists in Berlin, even Birchell of the New York *Times*, a few brave Germans and some foreigners, indicated pathetically and touchingly what loyalty can be like in Nazi Germany, how people can stick by friends who tell the truth, even when their own personal safety might be jeopardized. Ebbutt stood around, almost with tears in his eyes, profoundly touched, talking with friends until the train left—bitter, and sad to leave twelve years of living and study and friends. All of his idiosyncrasies, his brilliance, humour, and integrity became doubly endeared to all of us—even those who had not been too close or too friendly over the years— when the test came of our devotion to his sincerity and ideals. Certainly, Berlin life was emptier without him and his wife.

Ebbutt was sent back to England and into a comparatively unimportant position on the *Times*. He was preparing a book on Germany and had begun to write it when he was seized with a paralytic stroke. If he does not recover sufficiently to carry through his work, the outside world will certainly have lost one of its best estimates and analyses of the Nazi and pre-Nazi backgrounds. And without question, he stands another victim, both intellectually, professionally, and physically, of Nazi persecution.

The only other journalist in Berlin, whose parties really rivalled the Ebbutts' in solidity of interest and unusual guests was Sigrid Schultz of the Chicago *Tribune*. For many years she had an attractive apartment on Dornberger Strasse with a small garden and a tremendous studio room with a fireplace. She and her mother, with the aid of one cook, would manage large affairs, serve, talk, entertain, and even do some of the cooking. Though she had written many critical dispatches, and was known to be in general unsympathetic to the regime, many Nazis came to her gatherings, and in some cases quite high officials. She also, like the Ebbutts, had her coterie of intellectuals, artists, singers, actors, musicians, and writers. There was, of course, no rivalry between the two families and Sigrid was a devoted friend of Mrs. Holmes.

Sigrid Schultz was oftentimes a bit patronized by her male colleagues, mainly because of her sex, though their excuse for occasionally laughing her off was that her stories were hysterical.

As a matter of fact, Sigrid had just as many and just as few wild stories as the rest—and much of her confidential information, some of which she used in her papers and some of which she kept to herself or for trusted friends—was proved to be on an exact and high plane of accuracy. I think some of her male colleagues were a little jealous that a woman could scurry around and track down so much good stuff. In any case, though I didn't especially like her at first, as I got to know her I recognized a woman of real warmth, sincerity, and talent. She was certainly one of the kindest and most loyal people I met over there. She supported, as far as her scant means would allow, several people who were derelicts for one reason or another, and once she had made a friend there was nothing that could sway her fierce loyalty. Sometimes she was a little over-ardent, too passionate in her judgments of people and events, but her personality with its charm and warmth, eagerness and courage, made her much loved in Berlin.

She had at her home regularly—she specialized in *bier abends* and informal lunches—diplomats, Germans, foreigners in general, enemies and friends of the regime, and enthusiastic Nazis themselves. At one dinner, she had one of the highest aides of Hitler, a youngish man, who had some human qualities to which no doubt she appealed, along with diplomats known to be hostile to the regime. These dinners were almost always interesting though if unofficial Germans were present there was an atmosphere of caution and fear. My mother and father often went to her home, and enjoyed the simplicity and intelligent atmosphere. Mother was especially fond of Sigrid and, as I remember, they exchanged gifts like pork and beans, and cigarettes, which could only be had in Germany at a fabulous price, and jellies and canned things Sigrid and her mother put up themselves.

Another journalist family to which I became very attached personally was that of Bill and Tess Shirer, representatives of Hearst in Berlin. Though they were both too young and too poor to give elaborate parties, I went often to their home in a group of five or six and never failed to have them to every party I gave. Bill was by far, in my mind, the best and clearest thinker as to the economic implications of Fascism, among the group in Berlin. He was a cultured person as well, having followed and participated in new writing and publishing ventures (as, for instance, Whit Burnett and Martha Foley's *Story*) in Vienna and read voluminously in almost every field. This interest and training was what first drew me to him. When later I learned that his knowledge and reporting of Berlin events was not from the pure journalistic and objective angle, but from a careful and formulated analysis and study of Fascism, our friendship was firmly cemented. His wife, Tess, was a beautiful, shy, and glowing Viennese girl with great intellectual integrity, firmness, and discrimination. The two of them in my last year and a half in Berlin became my closest and dearest friends.

On the whole, they were the most anti-social of the newspaper crowd. They were happy in themselves, read and worked together, arrived at conclusions about life and social progress that did not fit well into the picture they found themselves involved in. They didn't like artificial or stupid people —they definitely felt no kinship with German Nazis, and were shy in making friends among their own group. However, they had a small circle around them with whom they were content and productive. Bill is now European chief of Columbia Broadcasting with headquarters in Switzerland.

Dorothy and Fred Oeschener of the United Press bureau belonged also to this younger and livelier set of newspaper people. Dorothy was a loquacious blonde, sometimes beautiful, always striking, who, though she had a sense of humour, took herself very seriously. She had a quaintness and naïveté and also sincerity about her that attracted me immediately and I, furthermore, was intrigued by her obvious and passionately expressed (especially when she had a few drinks) love of her husband who took it all rather magnificently in his stride. She introduced the first artificial fingernails to Berlin society (nervous as a cat, she bit her nails to the quick), possessed a lovely wire-haired terrier which was a constant source of delight to my brother, a game of darts, and a swell set of Jensen silver.

Her husband was a little unimaginative but extremely nice, conscientious, accurate, and unsensational. Fred rarely got excited about anything—if he ever did, you could be sure it was an important bit of news. Most other correspondents, as I may have indicated, were almost always in a state of jitters about one thing or another and usually with full justification. Fred was as loyal and accommodating and kindhearted as was his wife, and during the years I knew them, they never for an instant hesitated to lend help, or assist in any emergency. They gave their home and their time almost too freely and lavishly to visiting foreigners and newspapermen. Many people in Berlin considered Fred to be rather pro-Nazi in his thinking, but I knew that, even though they enjoyed and took advantage of the comparatively easy and interesting life they led, their attitudes towards Fascism were critical, though Dorothy was not especially aware of the issues involved, except as they affected her personally and her management of her home. Many of Fred's colleagues criticized indirectly what they called a certain pompousness, but I always believed that this stiffness of character came rather from habits of life than from affectation.

I always enjoyed going to their parties and invariably found interesting people there. Especially do I remember their entertaining Robert La Follette and his wife, who were in Germany in the summer of 1937. La Follette was getting fullest information on Fascism, and had not the slightest illusion at the time about it and its destructive and militant nature. But he was very careful, in mixed gatherings, to avoid the subject. One afternoon at Dorothy's he sounded off, in best senatorial manner, with resonant voice and oratorical twists and verbal pyrotechnics, gesticulating and addressing a throng of from three to six people, on the Supreme Court issue. One could easily imagine oneself in the gallery of the Senate, and Dorothy's small apartment and few guests were soon magnified by Bob's vastness of gesture and tone into that very august building and assembly. Bob's little-boy pudgy face and his wife's serious, and at the same time irreverent, attention did not diminish the effect.

Gg

Another young and animated couple, who were in Berlin the last two years of my stay, were the Ralph Barneses who had spent five years in Moscow as *Herald Tribune* correspondent. Ralph was the most painstaking, nervous, and maddening newspaper hound I have ever met. He had a naïveté about news-gathering that was extraordinary in one of his years and experience. Every bit of information, no matter how trivial or unconnected it was, he would track down to its last source, sacrificing no one and no thing in his attempt to lay its ghost. Sometimes he would have something when he finally got there but as often as not he would find himself holding the bag. He was extremely excitable and definitely didn't like the Nazis. But he had neither the cynicism nor the incisive keenness, the "nose for news," that many of his colleagues had. He went about the whole business of news-hunting in an earnest, passionate, stammering way. Sometimes he got scoops through this procedure, sometimes he was left out on a limb. He was erratic and had most endearing traits of character and wore a continual expression of intense worry on his face. He was extremely argumentative and tenacious and many a night Bill Shirer, my brother, the two wives, Ralph, and I stayed up late at night heatedly discussing various theoretical approaches to Fascism. He was sensitive and had a child-like innocence of personality, cherishing a hurt or a grudge a long time. But I was devoted to him and his strangely beautiful, passive, and understanding wife, Esther.

Once or twice my father and mother were amused and slightly annoyed at his midnight appearance at the Embassy. He is supposed to have gotten William Bullitt out of bed on various occasions in Moscow. My father simply invited him, and on one occasion Bill Shirer who accompanied him, upstairs to his bedroom, to discuss the matter they were so eagerly pursuing. My mother, always intensely interested in everything that went on, threw on her dressing robe and went to my father's room, anxious not to miss the latest development, no matter what it was or on what subject.

The Duells of the Chicago *Daily News* came from Rome with well-developed attitudes, and information and experience on Fascism and Nazism. Duell was young, intelligent, and attractive. They were considered a little standoffish and were so absorbed in family life and childbearing that only very intimate friends saw much of them. As one of the most promising young journalists in Berlin, Wallie Duell's reliability and acumen stand without question.

Louis Lochner and his Austrian wife belonged to a somewhat older set. He represented the Associated Press. Louis was a short, bald-headed, bulbous looking man, a little resembling a gnome, somewhat officious and patronizing toward some people. Among his most intimate and devoted friends were the widow of Stresemann and her son, and the Fritz Kreislers. Louis Lochner entertained many of the Nazi bigwigs, even those closest to Hitler, and his parties on the whole were more official and serious than others of his professional clan.

He and his lovely wife were ardent Royalists and one of their dearest friends was the young Prince Louis Ferdinand, who, by the way, was very popular among the correspondents in general and felt himself completely at home and enlivened in their company. Lochner more than any other correspondent had more regular, and at the time completely accurate, stories about the restoration of the Monarchy. These stories came in almost with every season, and always seemed to be perfectly authentic. However, nothing happened and we began to have a joke among ourselves about it. We never knew whether wishful thinking was the source and origin of these rumours, or whether more conscious design went into their circulation. Some people thought that the Hohenzollerns themselves spread the stories of their imminent restoration; others thought that Hitler and his group encouraged the dissemination of such gossip to discredit the Hohenzollerns, or to indicate to the population that the Nazi policy of Royalist suppression was justified.

Louis Lochner, at the time of the purge in 1934, was perhaps the most distrait man in Berlin among the foreign groups. Many of his personal friends and acquaintances were victims and he was consequently very bitter. He greatly feared that the Hohenzollerns would be arrested. In fact, several correspondents told us at the time that a police cordon had been thrown around the Potsdam palace. He was white-faced and nervous these few weeks and made regular visits to my father. He had always an air of great conspiracy and secrecy about him. He would take father aside, and the two of them, joined occasionally by another diplomat, would stay in a huddle, heads together, talking over newest events.

Louis was also a good friend of Hanfstaengl and was one of the first to get the news of his disgrace. At a tea party I gave, Lochner was present, telling his story of Putzi having been packed off in an airplane with sealed directions to the pilots to take him to Spain. One of the pilots told Putzi what was planned and in store for him and told him that, if he would get off at Leipzig, he could run for safety. So, according to Lochner, he had disappeared and never been seen again, his aged mother in a state of desperation as to his fate. Our Naval Attaché at this moment said quietly, "Why, I saw him only a few days ago at Hotel V.—in Zurich." Lochner almost knocked over the guests in his dash for the telephone!

Louis was a very capable newspaperman, warmly liked and admired by most people who knew him. Greatly respected by diplomats as well as other people in Berlin, there was hardly an official or unofficial function or party at which Louis was not present, circulating among his friends, listening to bits of news and giving his own, talking seriously with diplomats and Germans. He is a man of somewhat old-fashioned ideas, a seasoned and unshakable liberal, sadly out of place in Nazi Germany.

The New York *Times* has chosen a very strange man as their European jack of all trades. Frederick Birchell, one-time Pulitzer Prize winner, dashes about Europe chasing every new crisis and sometimes anticipating them. He is about sixty, I should judge, was formerly on the home staff of the paper he represents, and is an Englishman. Short, slight, with a little pointed white goatee, without a knowledge of the German language, despite long residence there, he can turn out as rosy a picture of Nazi Germany as anyone, anywhere! He was critical of Nazism until he fell a victim to the mass hysteria at a Nazi Party Congress. From that time on, despite the heckling of his colleagues, he managed to maintain a consistently favourable interpretation of Nazi policy. Lately, after winning the prize for his earlier reporting of Nazi activity and "seeing the light," Europe rather than Germany has been his assignment. When he made his miraculous appearance at the station to say good-bye to the Ebbutts, everyone whispered with surprise and some contempt, wondering what pressure or snobbishness had led him to participate in such an unfriendly demonstration—unfriendly, that is, as far as the Nazis were concerned. I didn't see much of Birchell, and when I did it was from social necessity. I must say that, despite my personal opinion of him as an opportunistic journalist, he was always extremely cordial and particularly decent in his appraisals of my father's role in the Nazi scene.

The other two *Times* correspondents, Guido Enderis and Otto Tolischus, were on the whole able and interesting men. They were journalists seasoned in their trade, without a scrap of idealism, as far as I could determine, and without an illusion as to men's personalities, actions, or motives. They seemed to regard journalism as their business and to have perfected it as such. They chased down stories, estimated present and future events carefully and cynically, and formed a sort of *Times* club of their own. Something about them indicated their attitude of being the aristocracy of their trade. Hardboiled, tough, seemingly without passion, they did their job and did it well. Enderis, a short, stoutish man, of a gargoyle ugliness which was strangely attractive, seemed to have tremendous mental stamina, a sinewy, unconventional, and assured personality. His character had salt and punch—he was more of the Junius Wood school and tradition than anyone else in Berlin and one felt always a certain challenge when listening to his pungent, sharp, and wiry speech.

Ross, their assistant, a much younger man, was a quiet, wordless, almost dour fellow, whom I liked rather well, after the first year of misunderstanding when he thought I was a Nazi and I thought he was impertinent. He did a lot of the work in the *Times* outfit and was sincere, wry, and passionate.

Victor Bodker was the English Reuter correspondent when we arrived. He had an excellent sense of humour, didn't give a damn about Fascism, at this time, one way or another. Singing hilariously and telling tall stories of all colours and varieties, he was a blustering, lovable person with great generosity of character. The first year he was a very good friend of my brother's and mine and he made me a confidante to whom he came with all his troubles, which were world-shaking when he was drunk, and trivial (even in his own eyes) when he was sober. His main concern as a newspaperman was to get a story, the more sensational the better, and he didn't care how he got it. He became, towards the end of his stay, quite sympathetic to the Nazis, and he fell in love with a girl who was a strong Nazi partisan. Later, he learned better, and his real change of heart came when he saw at first hand the rape of Spain by the Fascist powers, including his own country.

I will never forget a party at his house—and he gave very amusing ones—when I was invited with a young secretary from the Soviet Embassy. Present at the same dinner was Diels, the Secret Police Chief who didn't know the Russian was going to be there (the Russian was also in the dark as to the guest list—as was I). Two other guests were a crazy young attaché of the English Embassy, sharp-witted, heavy-drinking, and extremely amusing; and his girl friend, a white Russian. The Russian held his own, returning all the subtle, barbed, and dangerous conversation of the Secret Police head, with even better wit and surer mastery of the situation. In fact he seemed to have the time of his life in this rather extraordinary situation. The white Russian girl, in the presence of a Red Russian, refused to speak and pretended not to understand her own language when spoken by him, and kept a frigid and offended reserve during the entire evening. Victor looked like a pleased bad boy. I am sure he and the Russian enjoyed this party, its tense situation and rivalry of wits, more than all the others. It was completely unexpected and therefore more exciting. The party came to be quite a legend in Berlin and, of course, quotations from the conversation spread very fast.

Bodker, who, by the time he left, had become almost a legend himself in Berlin, was succeeded by a young Englishman whom I thought for several years somewhat inconsequential. Gordon Young was shy, but a really good sort underneath and an intelligent newspaperman with real critical ability and a set of constructive ideas. I was sorry to see him go and most of his colleagues considered that he had done an excellent newspaper job, in fact, much acuter and much more progressive in effect than Victor's. He was sincere, intelligent, conscientious.

The *Manchester Guardian* correspondent was a rather vague and unassuming man whom I don't remember very clearly one way or another. His personality had not much colour and certainly his reports were not equal to those of the *Times* or the English agencies. I understand that the Foreign Editor of the *Guardian,* who lived for a while in Berlin before and after the Nazis came to power, was the real brains behind the *Guardian's* German reports. As everyone knows, there was no comparison between the two papers in the editorial policy toward Germany, the *Guardian* being critical, intelligent and far-sightedly anti-Fascist.

There was an English newspaperman in Berlin who succeeded the colourful and extraordinarily able Tom Delmar, who was correspondent of the *Daily Express.* I remember one conversation on Spain at a small tea I gave at which Bill and Tess Shirer and the Pantons were present. They were discussing the Spanish Government and the Rebels. It seemed unaccountable to me that Panton and Bill should be agreeing on every point in this highly controversial issue. Finally, when a remark something like this came out, "but the Rebels are being supported by Russia," it dawned on all of us that we had been talking about opposite groups—to Panton, the Government was the Franco group and considering the Rebels were the Loyalists who in his mind had brought on the revolution and war. We thought we had been using acceptable terms to one another.

I have spent so much time and space on the newspapermen I came to know and understand and see so much of, because they were the group that was helping to mould and form world opinion on Nazism and its methods and ends. To indicate their merit and reliability, their personal quirks and connections, their training, ideals and background and experience, may help the reader to judge with what degree of accuracy and disinterestedness they view the Nazi scene and may give him a clue to their future reports and biases. With the attitudes and perspective I got from regular contact with the diplomats, combined with the inside news I learned from my newspaper acquaintances, I could understand better both the methods of effecting the dictatorship of Fascism internally and the points of view developed toward Fascism among people in other countries.

3

In my first two and a half years in Berlin, the newspaper crowd mixed pretty regularly and intimately with the German Nazi official friends and sympathisers. For instance, when I first arrived Knickerbocker described to me a luncheon engagement he had with Dr. Goebbels at the famous Horcher restaurant. Goebbels apparently was not then so vicious and arrogant toward the foreign press as he was later and entertained them and was entertained by them fairly informally. Hanfstaengl and Diels, of course, appeared regularly, almost up to their last minute in Berlin, at newspaper functions. Putzi was at that time and until his disgrace, chief of the Verbindungs Stab and necessarily had to connect himself with the foreign press but he was, even so, very close to Hitler and had many inside stories, true and false, about various happenings in Nazi Germany, which he delighted to tell, sometimes quite indiscreetly.

Diels, until he was "kicked upstairs" as Governor of the Province of Cologne, and then later Hanover, enjoyed these newspaper circles and their parties, notwithstanding his professional capacity and assignment to be there. Besides that he was bored by the stuffy formalities of Berlin life and the fanatic discussions of his own party members, for Diels was essentially an anarchist in his personal and intellectual life, an opportunist and cynic politically. Among newspapermen and their free conversations, these and other high party officials found a certain release, a liberty of action and speech which they had not forgotten from the days before the imposition of the rigid dictatorship.

Often one could meet Nazis on the level of the human, rather than the divinely appointed. Very often the parties, after a certain stage in the evening—when both the newspapermen and the Nazis felt that they had fulfilled their duties of extracting information from one another—became hilarious and boisterous. There was a free interchange of humour, fun, mutual intimacy. Stories, anecdotes, barbed jibes, inside gossip would fly back and forth. And everyone really enjoyed himself, without feeling any sinister atmosphere.

After the purge of June, 1934, a good part of this atmosphere was dispelled almost overnight. Nazis were forbidden to have too much contact with diplomats and foreigners in general. There was soon to be a black-list of restaurants, private homes, and diplomatic houses and functions. Nazis were told they must counteract the vicious effects of the corruption of the S.A. ranks and chiefs. They could not spend much money, they could not entertain extravagantly or freely, they must not get drunk or behave unseemingly; they must, in other words, behave like soldiers of the new religion, pure and above reproach. Above all, they must not be contaminated by the attitudes and gossip of foreigners and foreign press groups.

These instructions were not rigidly observed at first—in fact, it took over a year to effect the boycott of informal contact with foreigners and diplomats. But it definitely put a damper on the former natural and easy association with the press. Though for the next year there was still intimate, rather surreptitious, contact with the press, most people felt and resented the restraint imposed on them, and the press people, on the whole, were furious at the wholesale and unbridled attacks that appeared in the German press after their news and interpretation of the Purge, despite the fact that the German press attempted rather lamely, in garbled quotations, to prove that the world powers gave their blessings and sanction on all the killings of that bloody week.

During the last two years of our stay in Berlin there was as severe a brand upon the foreign press as there was upon the diplomats. We felt as if we had a sign on our door, SCARLET FEVER—DANGEROUS AND CONTAGIOUS—KEEP OUT. Of course the Italian Embassy and the Japanese, with their press correspondents, were as thick as thieves with the Nazis, though when we came and for some time after (until as a matter of fact the Berlin-Rome axis had become the mutual policy), the Italians were even more hostile to the Nazis—and unconcealedly—than the French.

The German officials and ministries saw the press representatives when there was a story they wanted foreign publicity on, and occasionally when interviews were demanded, and once in a while attended official functions given by newspapermen and in turn invited them to a few of theirs. However, even these were cut down to the minimum. And, in the winter of 1937, when the Press gave its annual ball, heretofore attended by hundreds of Germans and high officials like Goebbels and Goering, not a single German of any consequence appeared. This was clearly a slap in the face of the international press which was not taken warmly.

There were a few German press people who were, if not liked, at least tolerated and entertained by the foreign correspondents. Karl Silex, editor of the *Deutsche Allgemeine Zeitung*, had lived in London for many years as representative of his paper. He was less than competent as a journalist, certainly not equal to an editor's position. But, since every German newspaperman received orders as to what he could write, it didn't much matter if he were able or not.

Another German newspaperman, much more respected and much shrewder than Karl Silex, was Paul Scheffer, editor of the *Berliner Tageblatt*. I personally had a stronger distaste for him than for Silex, for I considered him much subtler, with a sharp, analytic mind. He was formerly a liberal nationalist, who, people told me, had social-democratic leanings, connections, and friends before Hitler. He was once correspondent in Moscow for eight years, and was quite a good friend of Louis Fischer, nicknamed the "Red Pope," with whom he made a long trip to the Caucasus—just the two of them—and consequently became intimate. I remember an incident that occurred at our Embassy which clearly revealed to me the character of Scheffer. We were having a New Year's reception in 1935 when Louis Fischer happened to be passing through Berlin from Russia. We invited him. Louis was talking to a man, near my father, almost next to the receiving line. Paul Scheffer came in, shook hands with my father and mother, looked once at Louis very distantly and coldly, and passed on without speaking.

He was a short fat man who looked something like a big grey toad. He had a heavy, pontifical manner, each sentence weighted with significance, and a look on his face which demanded and anticipated silence and attention while he was speaking. However, his logic was always exact, his words cautious, his meanings devious and evasive.

Scheffer was a passionate nationalist—this, from the German point of view, must be stated to his credit. That he could, for whatever reason, find a solution to his political and emotional uncertainties in Nazism remains to his lasting discredit, both mentally and morally.

Scheffer was reported constantly to be at odds with the Nazis. He was certainly more independent in his paper than was Silex in his. But if he did not observe the letter of the law, he was, on the surface, in agreement with the general policy. In 1937 he was sent as correspondent to the East, Near and Far, and since the fall of that year has been living in America, until recently a correspondent of his paper there.

4

There were a few correspondents who came regularly through Berlin, and among these was Vernon Bartlett.

Bartlett, at first with strong pro-Nazi tendencies, soon turned against the regime in Germany. He now edits an anti-Fascist magazine in England and is on the regular staff of the *News Chronicle*.[1] One time in the Taverne, after a trip

[1] In the fall of 1938, Vernon Bartlett was elected to Parliament on an anti-Chamberlain programme.

to Spain, he met the brother of Dietrich, chief press man of the Nazis, and a thoroughly disagreeable man. The conversation turned on events in Spain, wherein Vernon passionately defended the Government. Dietrich, of course, argued that Spain was controlled by the Communists. Vernon denied this vehemently. Dietrich fixed a stony eye on him and asked the question, "Would you choose socialism in preference to National Socialism if you were faced with the choice?" Vernon replied, "Why, naturally, how can anyone ask such a question?" The conversation continued, Dietrich knowing that the former Nazi pride was irrevocably an enemy, while he pretended it made no difference in the attitude of the Nazis towards a visitor. Vernon then asked, "All right, if what you say is true, will you please get me a visitor's ticket to Hitler's birthday celebration" (or some such affair that was going on at the time). Dietrich winced, but said he would, since the Nazis were afraid of no press interpretation, inimical or otherwise, of their politics or celebrations. Of course, the ticket, due the next day, never arrived, and the Nazis and Vernon Bartlett, their former apologist, had drawn swords.

Vernon never felt quite safe thereafter in Germany. His magazine and his work on the paper were so consistently, intelligently, and influentially anti-Nazi, he feared there would be reprisals of one sort or another. A nice person, between forty and fifty, a little bald and snub-nosed, somewhat resembling Walter Duranty, he was one of the most interesting and least affected Englishmen I had met in my years abroad. The last time I saw him, in Geneva in 1937, he had not altered his position in the slightest. He is a firm and militant liberal, a left Social Democrat and no more, but his experiences in Germany and Spain had so aroused his indignation and sense of justice that he could, honourably and intellectually, take no other course. He said, the last time I saw him, that his relations with Anthony Eden, whom he had seen a great deal while he dealt with foreign affairs, and who seemed also to be his close friend, were losing their old cordiality. Perhaps Eden's demotion has opened his eyes to the courageous, intelligent and honest Vernon Bartlett.

A man of an entirely different calibre is Jules Sauerwein, foreign editor of *Paris Soir*. He is known in Europe as "pengo Jules" because of some transaction he made with the Hungarian Government. A big, enormously paunched, white-haired man, with long sharp nose, and bright ruthless calculating eyes, on the surface he is more of a gourmet and connoisseur of women than he is a journalist. But Jules Sauerwein cannot be dismissed with such light gossip. He is one of the most dangerous journalists in France and the fact that he is foreign editor of a newspaper with a huge circulation gives one pause.

I met Jules first when he was in Chicago lecturing for the Harris Foundation series. I thought then he was a rather impressive looking old man who took abnormal delight in the Sally Rand fan dance at the Fair. Later I saw him in Berlin when he was covering one of the first Nazi Congresses. Again I had long chats with him in Geneva, and the last time I saw him he was covering the Nazi Congress in September, 1937. Both in Geneva and in Berlin he was always travelling in the company of high officials and, especially in Berlin, he was treated so royally one expected him any minute to take out the keys of the city. There is no question that he is let in on many official sessions of the Nazis; that he has a tremendous amount of and continual access to, confidential information; and that he is allowed into the highest circles, almost on an equality basis, even into the innermost sanctum.

He is deathly afraid of Socialism and fully believes in the magnificent destiny of Nazi Germany. He told me in Geneva that he was in favour of Anschluss and that he was convinced Germany would dominate Central Europe, if not all of it—and would be right in so doing. Holding this opinion, it is certainly true that he is closer than almost any other journalist in Europe to the Nazi officials, in whatever subtle, devious, or even militant fashion at his disposal. It is a depressing and frightening commentary on the conservative elements in France, including the press, that he has a position of such influence with a leading newspaper.

There was a continual stream of foreign journalists, most of whom did not stay long enough for me to remember them. When Duranty came to town, which was two or three times a year, sometimes less, there was general rejoicing. Duranty can be one of the wittiest men in the world. He drinks too heavily, granted, but drink rarely impairs his humour or his logic. His collection of amusing and instructive anecdotes, about almost every subject and experience you can imagine, seems endless. Stuffy people dislike him because he says what he thinks in a very unconventional and picturesque manner, though, when necessary, he can be as diplomatic as the rest— perhaps more so because he has been often the trusted confidant of many of them.

One time he came to pick me up at a frightfully boring dinner party given by our Military Attaché. He stayed for a moment and of course questions were asked about his travels and his experiences. He talked boldly, wittily and objectively. The wife of the host was so horrified at his language, his slightly intoxicated state, and his ideas, that she visibly, after a few not too delicate insults, breathed a sigh of relief when I started to go. Duranty, for some people, is hard medicine to take—for the rest, no matter how much they might disapprove of his private life, he is a delightful specimen of sophisticated mentality and an irresistible raconteur.

Short, slight in build, baldish, with a wide mobile but ugly-friendly mouth, an amusing snub nose, sharp, small, quick-moving bright blue-grey eyes, Duranty shows on his face his Irish ancestry, his pugnacity, and shrewd mind. He has a wooden leg, as a result of a railroad accident in France, which he has learned to manipulate very well and which in no way embarrasses him. He is an Englishman by birth but has been the New York *Times* correspondent for many years in Moscow. His two main passions in life seem to be America and Russia—whose people he calls "my Russians."

He declares to his friends and foes alike that he is an "opportunist." He asserts that he has no real sympathy or passion for Russia or Russians. He has lived through the worst period of the Russian Revolution, really voluntarily— for he could have had other positions—and only a persistent belief in their general objectives and a fondness for the people themselves could have been his inner rewards and furnished his real satisfaction. He has said often that he bet on Stalin when there was uncertainty as to who was to follow Lenin, and that the reason he stayed on was his purely objective desire to see the working out and effectiveness of a going-concern. There is no doubt that Walter Duranty is the most eminent of journalists reporting the Russian scene, and that his attitudes and interpretations are objective. He is a colour-ful writer and thinker; his mind does not work only along the dry statistical line; his instincts are dramatic and he found perfect material for this dramatic instinct in the Revolution. He fully recognizes, mentally and emotionally, that the Russian Revolution was one of the turning points in modern history. It is of everlasting credit to the *Times* that their editors saw the value and brilliance and understanding of his dispatches.

He is supposed to have an uncanny "nose for news." He claims he can smell an event long before other correspondents, that his senses are so attuned to Russian psychology he can pick up through his sensory antennæ events and news that other men find only when the change is on them, in process of accomplishment. Walter is a great prophet, and as with most prophets makes many mistakes, but I would on the other hand trust for the most part his prognostication of future developments more than I would that of anyone else. He is experienced, cynical in a constructive realistic fashion, and tremendously sensitive.

He is, of course, more trusted by the Russians than are his colleagues. When Litvinov came to the United States at the time arrangements were being made for American recogni-tion, Walter went with him and no doubt was consulted on various problems. He has the confidence of many high officials and diplomats all over the world, and it is said that his contacts with the British Foreign Office were even more reliable and interesting than those of Norman Ebbutt.

In Germany he was often at our house and my father depended on his information of developments in the Soviet

Union and the East in general. Mother, of course, was keenly alive to his personality and fascinated by his stories and news.

In Moscow he holds a rather sanctified position among his colleagues. There are some reactionary correspondents who pretend to discredit him, but all of them, when they are in a tough spot, trust his interpretation, though they rather resent the position he holds with Soviet and foreign officialdom and as leader of the foreign press. When the Moscow trials were beginning, one rather venomous journalist said that Walter never appeared at the sessions, that he sat at home and wrote his news from what he knew would happen and from the information he might have gotten from other sources while the others sweated every day and even far into the night to report the courtroom drama.

I faced Walter with these charges and he admitted them to some degree. He said that he had attended sessions regularly but that he did not spend every minute of the day when they were going on, in the courtroom. He knew all the people involved, most of them personally and over a long period of time, he knew their past records, and he knew the charges against them. It was ridiculous for him to be as attentive as the rest of the correspondents. Certainly, his dispatches were more accurate and colourful than those of his critics and the *Times* found out later, in the last trials, that Harold Denny, not so competent or dramatic, came to the same conclusions about the events.

This little ugly-fascinating Englishman, with his beautiful and precise language, his wit and lightness, his sharp and sometimes prim incisiveness, found in Russia and its people a kinship that transcended race, nationality, and boundaries. Because of his strange sympathy and understanding of the Slavic race, his mental and emotional identification with their problems and struggles, his sense of at-homeness in a land that sprawls over one-sixth of the earth's surface, he has done one of the most superb and consistently brilliant jobs of reporting in modern-day journalism, and is listened to and respected by bankers and intellectuals, workers and employers, college students and retired arm officers, diplomats, and officials.

There were few other such interesting men who came through Berlin in line of duty or travel. John Whitaker author of "Fear Came on Europe," was there for a while. He looked a little like a movie actor, lovely big eyes with curling eyelashes, nice mouth and teeth, and slightly weak chin and smeared with charm. Despite his rather social self-consciously fascinating manner, I think he was both sincere and able. He had been in Italy—I had heard his reporting was somewhat pro-Fascist but I doubt it very much. He seemed to be an honest progressive and pretty clear-thinking individual. He went to Franco's lines for a time and came out completely disillusioned, if he ever had any illusions, and disgusted. He said he had never seen such a motley crew of degenerates, aristocrats, generals, and supporters—weaklings sustained internally mainly by their arrogance and corruption. He made one naive remark to me—he thought the Loyalists should not have been trained by an International Brigade—yet he was horrified at the rawness of the Spanish recruits and the fact that they were sent as tenderfoots to the front line. He didn't seem to realize that they were in a desperate situation where man-power of whatever calibre was absolutely imperative, and furthermore that the International Brigade not only served as a training school but as a tremendous and almost incalculably important moral support. However, he was genuinely in sympathy with the Loyalists, and a likeable, if flashy, young man.

Of course, there was a continual stream of visiting newspapermen, heads of agencies like Webb Miller, editors like Roy Howard and Colonel Knox (who, by the way, whatever one can say about him on other scores, became a militant anti-Fascist and anti-Nazi, due to some extent to efforts of the excellent representatives his paper had in Rome and in Berlin), correspondents like John Gunther, who came from other parts of Europe on temporary duty or for some special story, but either didn't stay long enough, or were there when I was absent, so that I had no real impression of them. My parents told me they had entertained Colonel Knox and asked him if he didn't want to meet some of the "key" Nazis—which

HG

was the usual demand of eminent visitors. He snorted vigorously in the negative, adding that he wouldn't want to meet them anywhere or under any circumstances.

Hearst, of course, made regular visits for a time and was the honoured guest of the Nazis on several occasions. Naturally we had no contact with him. I remember the family was taking a tour through Germany one Fall—mainly to escape attending a Party Congress—and we stopped for lunch at Rothenburg, one of the perfect gems of European medieval towns. At the historic restaurant, my father was asked to sign the register, which he did rather reluctantly, and without examining it. After he had signed, he looked at the other names on the register and was shocked to see that he had signed his name almost directly under that of William Randolph Hearst. Hearst had been there several days before, most likely after attending the Congress. Of course, my father couldn't rub out the ink signature, but I recall his repugnance and the day that was spoiled because of his inadvertence. These were the days when rumours were thick and fast that Hearst was a devoted admirer of Hitler and that there had even been a financial deal between them.

VI

PURGE OF 1934

THE SPRING OF my first year in Germany approached as I became more and more critical and reserved about the Nazi regime. I had been reading steadily, not only the foreign and German press but articles and books and even Nazi propaganda material. I had met, increasingly, men and women who with their friends were victimised by the dictatorship. I began to learn of the deals that made the Nazi seizure of power possible, the contacts between Hitler, "the pure idealist" who was working for the benefit of his people, and Thyssen, Krupp, and other industrialists and the Junkers. I had witnessed the Reichstag trials and knew of the terrible and tragic deception of the German people Hitler had perpetrated through the Fire. Nazis, I knew, either held their silence on this subject or clearly indicated that they didn't believe that the Communists were responsible for the outrage. I saw the defendants with my own eyes, heard and later read the testimony, and realized that even the Nazis and their stooges, the judges, could not continue the fraud and were forced to release the defendants.

My friend in the French Embassy, who had lived and studied many years in Germany before the Nazis came to power, who knew and understood their mentality and their historic and economic background, was with me constantly, and explained and analyzed many moves and policies for me. I began to know newspapermen and diplomats who had access to information that was sound and accurate. Furthermore, the Nazis themselves began to talk to me more openly about certain measures that were being taken by the government in contradiction to their original promises or as evasions of their original programme. Some complained of this thing, some of that, but almost everyone was dissatisfied, some even going so far as to predict the fall of Hitler.

The growingly vicious attacks against the Soviet Union and all Communists, radicals, democrats, and liberals were too fantastic for anyone to believe. Russia as a nation of "baby-eaters" and untold tortures began to assume proportions of ridiculousness even a confirmed anti-Communist could not stomach. A curiosity began to grow in me as to the nature of this government, so loathed in Germany, and its people, described as so utterly ruthless. No human being at any time in any age could possibly have been responsible for the horrors accredited to Soviet citizens. Of course along with this reaction, grew the desire to see and know a nation and people so profoundly effective, so powerful that a good Nazi must shiver in his boots when the name was mentioned. I couldn't believe that Communists, democrats, and liberals could be responsible for as many things as the Nazis described again and again. If so, there was definite reason for everyone to go and see these monsters of intrigue, power, murder and rape, and to find out just what their capacities were. I began to meet and know many German Jews who didn't look or act as if they were ready to kill babies, rape innocent women, plot the downfall of civilization, destroy the decencies and morality of Western society. They didn't have huge bulbous noses, protruding eyes, jagged wolf's teeth, and inch-high foreheads; their hands weren't dripping with blood; they weren't branded with the hammer and sickle. The "Jewish-Marxist" International was clearly a ghastly nightmare in the diseased brain of National Socialism. When all democrats and liberals were included in this dreadful apocalypse of a destructive devouring storm raging over the world, I turned from laughter and cynicism to anger and a profound contempt for the Nazi government in their attempt to permeate the population they pretended to love with such flagrant untruths. To this day I believe that, if anyone wants a true picture of Hitler and his cohorts, an evaluation of their mental and emotional hysteria, he should take out a week's subscription to Julius Streicher's *Der Stürmer*. If he can endure any more issues he no longer belongs to

civilized humanity. This is the paper officially recognized and
blessed by the Fuehrer himself—the editor, a short, stout, bald,
bullet-headed man with a mean and surly look, is one of his
closest friends, an "old fighter" who is definitely a psychopathic case. There is not an intelligent Nazi who has not
blushed with shame over this scurrilous sheet, and who does
not consistently do everything in his power to discredit it and
influence the Nazis, in whatever way he can, to withdraw it.
They apologize quite openly and abjectly to diplomats and
foreign visitors for its appearance and have no answer when
the foreigner pointedly says, "But Streicher is one of Hitler's
dearest and most trusted friends."

So, by the spring of 1934, through the combination of stupid
propaganda, information, study, and contact with friends,
Nazis, diplomats, and enemies of the regime, I was as opposed
to the system of National Socialism as I could be, though I
still attempted to keep my hostility guarded and unexpressed.
I was determined to go to the bottom of the reasons for such
propaganda and to study and observe and listen very carefully
to everything that happened and was said. For this reason I
planned a month's trip to the Soviet Union, to arm myself
with first-hand information on the subject about which they
had the deepest obsession. Furthermore, all sorts of people
began to tell me, including enemies of the regime, that Russia
and Germany and their systems of government were exactly
alike. They couldn't answer my queries as to why, then, was
there such a deadly hatred between them.

I was not in the least anti-German, only anti-Nazi, by now
fairly clear in my conception of Fascism. I loved the German
people and still do. Their qualities of simplicity and honesty,
a sort of childlike warmth and friendliness, their discipline,
adaptability, and curiosity (if only these qualities could be
used and directed properly) would endear them to anyone.
The rigidity and disagreeable arrogance so often associated
with the Prussian type, and the brutality that often goes with
it, are not characteristic of the large mass of people. By the
spring of 1934 what I had heard, seen, and felt, revealed to
me that conditions of living were worse than in pre-Hitler

days, that the most complicated and heartbreaking system of terror ruled the country and repressed the freedom and happiness of the people, and that German leaders were inevitably leading these docile and kindly masses into another war against their will and their knowledge and for which they would have to pay not only with their homes, property, and civilization, but also with their very lives.

Though there was still much talk of Hitler's imminent collapse, and though all of us believed that the economic storm ahead would perhaps lead to his downfall, a counter-revolution or an organized opposition did not seem to be in the offing and was the farthest thing from our minds. There were many rumours concerning a Hohenzollern restoration, the discontent of the German population, the dissent and disorganization within Party ranks and a possible purge of Hitler's personnel. Before June 30th, the atmosphere had become tense and electric. Everyone felt there was something in the air but didn't know what it was.

2

At this time I was seeing a great deal of Rolf Diels. He was extremely nervous and sometimes sick of acute stomach and heart disorders. He was in constant fear of his life. One time, when he, my brother, and I went to a restaurant in the country, near Wannsee, he told us dramatically that he anticipated being shot at any moment. We didn't take too seriously what he said, thinking that he was a melodramatic sort of fellow anyway, and that his job was one in which anyone might become hysterical or paranoiac. But it seemed a little strange to us that he didn't want to be seen in the city or among crowds. Of course, he had told me before that the S.A. were more friendly to him than the S.S., of which he was a member. I took for granted that inter-party intrigues and jealousies, which he had indicated long before, were responsible for his feeling of fear and imminent assassination.

One time he told me he was going to Switzerland to a sanatorium, that he had been very ill and needed a cure and a rest. This was in the spring. When he came back I called him up and he asked my brother and me to come around to his apartment to see him. His wife was there—a pathetic passive-looking creature who must have gone through hell living with Diels. He dismissed her brusquely and greeted both of us. He was lying on a couch in his living-room with loaded pistols on the table beside him, and had a large map stretched out in front of him, elaborately marked with circles and signs and different coloured inks. It was a map of Germany and marked on it were the nuclei of the Secret Police agents and organization. It was a terrifying spectacle to me— all the lines and designs spelled brutality, torture, sacrifice of innumerable human lives—it was a vast spider-web of intrigue, carefully and effectively spun, woven with the blood, sinew, brain and nerves of thousands of Germans. He said proudly, "You know most of this is my work. I have really organized the most effective system of espionage Germany has ever known." This was the Social Democrat who had once worked as chief of police under Severing, the Minister of Prussia—the man who had once given his mind and work to a supposedly humanitarian and democratic system.

I asked him why he was so fearful when he obviously had so much power in his hands. He replied this time, and many times before and after, "Because I know too much." Many of the prominent people who were murdered during the Purge "knew too much"—about Hitler's seizure of power and, among other things, the Reichstag fire. Diels was one of the few I knew, whom I and many others thought was in full possession of such information, who escaped death. Hanfstaengl was another.

Many times in these weeks when Diels seemed to cling to me, my brother, and the Embassy in a sort of desperation when his mind and imagination were harassed with fears and fantasies of having been poisoned by his enemies, I recalled the picture of Diels and Goering facing the wiry vital dark-haired Dimitroff—Diels, sinister and self-confident behind the enormous red-faced General, supposedly his friend. He knew about the Fire, it was sure, and he knew a lot about other things, even less savoury, in the lives of those with whom he associated most and saw daily.

And now in these weeks he was like a frightened rabbit, with, however, a certain fatalism in his temperament. In some ways the danger he thought he was in was a challenge to his slyness and shrewdness. Could he outwit them or not, could he escape them or not? He told me several times it would help him if I were seen in public with him. At that time, still, the Germans were very respectful of the United States, her attitudes toward Germany, and her representatives. To be in close contact with the American Embassy was of some definite advantage. I remember a very nice friend of mine, a Jewish boy, told me at several cocktail parties where we met, "Martha, you are very silly, and you are playing with fire. In the first place, you are being used by Diels, perhaps because he actually needs some protection, perhaps only because he pretends to—but in any case it is very dangerous to take sides in such a matter or to identify yourself with any particular man in the Nazi group. There is some sort of trouble ahead and you may get yourself unwittingly involved."

However, I saw no reason whatsoever not to see a lot of Diels if I could. I was extremely interested in his type and his conversation. He gave me, consciously and unconsciously, a picture of the backstage workings of espionage that I could not have got anywhere else. Furthermore, I was young and reckless enough to want to be as closely in on every situation as I possibly could, even though my friends might think it dangerous. I knew also that Diels could learn nothing from me since I knew nothing and that, furthermore, if I had known anything he would have known it directly from my father (who never concealed his attitudes on Nazi blunders, even in the beginning), or indirectly from his highly efficient Secret Police system. Finally, I was convinced that I could be of no help to Diels because Nazis are not the kind to let anyone stand in the way if they want to "get their man," and under no circumstances would a foreigner, especially the daughter of a diplomat, become involved in any embarrassing or troublesome row.

So I went out with Diels for drives in the country and to night clubs where we knew we would be seen. One Rolf Reiner, an adjutant of Roehm, spoke to us often and one time, when Diels had left the table for a moment, came to me and said that Diels was in trouble and that I should not antagonize the Nazis by being seen with him. This same Reiner was later imprisoned for some time, came out with a shaved head, and was rumoured to have given away all the secrets he knew in connection with Roehm and others as a price for his freedom. Reiner was nevertheless out of the S.A. and is now in some business in Berlin, distrusted by most people who know him.

One memorable afternoon Diels told me that he had not only gone to Switzerland for his health. When I asked him if as I had heard he had taken his private papers out of Germany and placed them in the hands of a reliable friend in Zurich to be published immediately in case he was shot, he looked at me closely and said that would be the only threat he could hold over the Nazis. I doubt, in the first place, that he took them out and, in the second, that the Nazis would have done other than shoot him if they had wanted to, even with such a threat.

I believe the reason Diels was demoted to his position in Cologne was that he had outlived his usefulness. He had constructed an effectively functioning secret police and he knew too much to be retained. Furthermore, Diels is a man that the Nazis never did trust and would have been stupid in so doing. With his record they could draw but one conclusion, one that everyone else drew—Diels was an opportunist, with a thirst for power, ready for activity in no matter what regime. To give him too high a position would be dangerous. Added to this was, no doubt, the fact that Diels hated Goebbels and was probably envied by Goering. Here was a young man, directly under Goering, rising steadily in power and influence which, if allowed free rein, could damage Goering's own prestige. Goering was surely jealous of Diels and ready to get rid of him at an appropriate moment. Diels no doubt made many criticisms of the men around Hitler, spoke of them perhaps openly in Nazi meetings as he did in private conversation, and was slated to pay the price.

One time he told me that he had gained the resentment of the Nazis because of a strong protest he made against the murder of several prisoners in a concentration camp, I think near Stettin. He demanded, so he said, the execution of the S.S. guards responsible for the murder. Very likely he told Hitler, or those close to him, that the Nazi movement would be discredited, not only abroad but also dangerously so within the country, if such brutality were allowed to continue in this flagrant fashion. Not that he pitied the prisoners or had any moral or humanitarian indignation. Simply, the regime would be undermined and consequently his position would be less secure and important. He had much more concern, as I have indicated before, for foreign opinion than his colleagues and he worked always very fairly with the American Embassy and Consulate.

In fact, when he was in such desperate fear of his position and life, he asked us if we could not in some way bolster his position. He suggested that his friend, Messersmith, the then Consul General, should write to the Nazi Government indicating how valuable it was to have a reasonable and sane man in such a position. Messersmith, when I spoke of Diels once in conversation, was very sympathetic toward him and would have liked to assist him since he believed Diels was one of the most rational of Nazis in high position. Of course, it was impossible to do anything for Diels, and many people believed, as the Purge broke suddenly on us, that he would be shot.

As I said before, no one knew exactly in what form the tension would break. Most of us knew something was brewing. There was a lot of grumbling in the S.A.; there were many complaints not against Hitler but against the men around him, and Roehm was conspicuously absent from Berlin and the inner circle.

We knew also that Roehm, leader of the S.A., was taking altogether too many vacations. In the papers one would read of Roehm's visit to this and that place far from Berlin, or that he was on extended leave. Less and less did this "old fighter"

—one of the dearest and closest friends of the Leader, over a
period of ten years and more, who was called tenderly "du"
(thou) by his comrade Adolf—appear in the closed corpora-
tion of Hitler men. He was rarely seen with him, as rarely
consulted—in fact, it looked as if he were being given the
slip by his old friend. He was immensely popular among the
ranks of his semi-military people's army, the S.A., without
whose aid Hitler could never have seized power and for whom,
with their class, he had made the so-called "revolution."
Hitler seemed, to most people, to be taking a chance—an-
tagonizing and cold-shouldering a man who had wielded such
power and who had formed the earliest organized supporters.
Beyond that, supposition or theory did not venture.

I remember my father had invited Roehm, whom he had
met several times and whose invitations to *bier abends* he had
both accepted and declined over this period of time, to a stag
dinner to be given in the first week of July, 1934. His other
guests included Goering, von Bülow of the Foreign Office,
the Crown Prince, and various other Germans and diplomats.
He received a very polite and friendly note from Roehm saying he could not come because he would be out of town.
Goering also declined on a similar pretext. After that time my
father never again invited Goering to his house. From his
point of view, Goering had been responsible for the murder
of several hundred people in Berlin—and he declared that he
never had and never would knowingly entertain murderers.

Two weeks before the Purge, von Papen had made an
extraordinarily courageous speech at Marburg. It had been
suppressed, and then later, I believe, was privately circulated
in large numbers. In this speech von Papen had attacked the
radical members of the party, high and low, who were consciously and unconsciously destroying its prestige both inside
and out. It sounded rather reckless, even democratic-conserva-
tive in tone, and the whole of Berlin was agog at his daring.
They couldn't imagine what he meant. What radical elements?
I do not know to this day whether von Papen had in mind
the Roehm elements in the party and in the leadership, or
whether he was cutting closer to the bone by implying that

the men around Hitler and in high favour with him were the uncontrollable and dangerous ones. I should venture, since the article was suppressed and since von Papen missed being executed by the skin of his teeth, that he meant the latter.

He came to a lunch we gave a few days before the 30th of June. He seemed self-confident and as suave as usual. My father said later, however, that he had spoken very nervously and in apprehension. I noticed the two men, deep in conversation, standing by the fireplace in the library after lunch and wondered what von Papen was saying. His speech had been delivered and the official attitude of the Nazis towards it pretty clearly revealed. He must, of course, have been scared within an inch of his life, if he really knew what was going on within his party and if he had really intended to strike against the men close to and in favour with Hitler.

Also at the same lunch was Madame Cerrutti, wife of the Italian Ambassador who was a bitter enemy of Hitler at the time. Madame Cerrutti was a Hungarian Jewess whose sympathies naturally were far from the ideology and plans of the Hitler regime. She sat by my father in a state of near-collapse, hardly speaking, pale, preoccupied, and jumpy. Father said later that she had murmured to him several times during the lunch, in varying forms of expression, "Mr. Ambassador, something terrible is going to happen in Germany I feel it in the air." How she got her information or prescience no one ever knew!

3

Saturday, June 30th, was as beautiful and warm a day as we had yet had in Germany. I determined to spend the day on the beach, imitating the German habit of acquiring a sunburn as early as possible in the season. I had a date with a friend of mine, a young secretary in a foreign Embassy. In less than a week, I planned to go to Russia and, since I had heard the heat was unbearable, I was getting in training as well.

We took down the top of the Ford roadster and drove to Gross Glienicke, a lovely and fairly private lake near Wannsee.

I baked in the sun the whole day, retiring to the shade only
for cooling drinks and sandwiches. It was a beautiful serene
blue day, the lake shimmering and glittering in front of us,
and the sun spreading its fire over us. It was a silent and soft
day—we didn't even have the energy or desire to talk politics
or discuss the new tension in the atmosphere. At six o'clock
we decided we had had enough sun and we drove slowly and
quietly back to Berlin, our heads giddy and our bodies burning
from the sun.

We passed through lanes of acacia trees, their beautiful
white clustered blossoms, like bunches of rich ivory-tinted
grapes, falling heavily forward and down, their scent like ripe
grapes in the sun-laden air. Then there would be lanes of
green coolness as we sped by luxuriant dark trees, then a
stretch of sun-warmed sharp pine odour, almost like dry
pungent dust in the nostrils.

We were not thinking of yesterday or to-morrow, of the
Nazis or of politics. Men and women were speeding by us both
ways on bicycles, with small children in little wagons on the
side, or in baskets on the front; a swift throb of a motorcycle
mounted with strange goggled figures from another world,
women carrying flowers, sturdy men walking with knapsacks
by their sides. It was a homely, hot, and friendly day—I had
my skirts pulled up to the edge of my bathing suit underneath, to get the last touch of the sun and the sudden cooling breezes which came when we had a long road of swiftness
before us. I was happy, pleased with my day and my companion, full of sympathy for the earnest, simple kindly German people, so obviously taking a hard-earned walk or rest,
enjoying themselves and their countryside so intensely.

It was six o'clock when we drove into Berlin. I pulled down
my skirt and sat up straight and proper as befits a diplomat's
daughter. The atmosphere had changed, fewer people were
on the streets, many of them in curious static groups. Soon we
noticed there was an unusual number of police standing
around. As we drove nearer and nearer to the heart of the
city, we saw heavy army trucks, machine guns, many soldiers,
S.S. men, and especially large numbers of the green uniformed

Goering police—and no S.A. men. The familiar Brown Shirt
was significantly absent. As we came closer to home, we
realized something very serious was happening. More truck-
loads of arms and soldiers on the edges of the streets and in the
parks, some streets blocked off, guards and police everywhere.
Hardly a person dressed in civilian clothes could be seen as
we neared Tiergarten Strasse, and traffic seemed to have
stopped. We had a diplomatic number so were allowed free
passage. Across from our house entrance was another sinister
lining of trucks, soldiers, and the paraphernalia of war. Stan-
darten Strasse, only a few blocks from our entrance, was roped
off, and a cordon of police thrown around it. This was the
street whose name had been changed to honour the distinguished Roehm, favourite of Hitler.

My companion was alarmed by this time. He let me off at
the head of the lane that led to our Embassy and sped away
to his own. I flew towards the house in the broiling sun. Breaking suddenly into our darkened house, the cool air striking me
in the face, I turned a little dizzy, my eyes blinded for a
moment from the lack of light. I stumbled up the first flight of
stairs. When I got halfway up I saw the shadowy figure of
my brother at the head of the steps. He called out nervously,

"Martha, is that you? Where have you been? We were worried about you. Von Schleicher has been shot. We don't know
what is happening. There is martial law in Berlin."

For a second my mind didn't register the name Schleicher.
Then slowly I remembered. He was an army officer of the old
school, a man whose name recalled the old saying, "soldier
and gentleman"; he had been Prime Minister for a short
period and had been betrayed, so they said, by his former
friend von Papen. He was one of the shrewdest politicians of
the old school—and, of course, much shrewder than the Nazis.
He had a great deal of influence in the Reichswehr and was a
deadly enemy of the Nazis who feared that his brilliant
manœuvring and more liberal policies would some day tempt
him into political ambitions to outwit Hitler.

I sat down, still confused and terribly distressed. Why had
they shot him? What had he done? Hitler surely couldn't

shoot all people who opposed him, or who had opposed him
before 1933. I heard my brother's voice running on excitedly,

"They not only killed him but they killed his wife as well.
It is rumoured that several of Goering's police entered his house
and asked for him. The servant said he was out in the garden
with his wife. The men went straight through the house,
through his study, and into the garden. Their backs were
turned to the house and to the men who came for them. They
fired several times in their backs."

The courtly, attractive, and clever Schleicher had known
too much about Hitler, had watched his rise to power and had
remained too important and influential a person for Hitler
to leave around among the living. But what about his wife?

We heard many varying stories during the next few days as
to when and how they met their death, this old soldier and his
wife—but the stories never varied as to one detail: they had
been shot in the back. It was so shocking a murder, even to
many of the Nazis, that Goering denied his police had had
anything to do with it. The Nazis covered up the murderers
—no one knew their names or their positions. It was said that
Goering later ordered them to be executed because they had
carried out their commands with such drastic and indiscreet
effectiveness. Some people deny that Goering knew anything
about it, that he definitely had not ordered the killing of
Schleicher and certainly not of his wife. But it is certain that
no such terrible retribution would have been meted out to these
people, had they not been clearly indicated on the black list
for arrest, if not worse. Perhaps the murderers became panicky
when they saw Frau von Schleicher, and realized that only a
dead person can't tell stories—or perhaps they coldbloodedly
knew they would shoot her, too, if she were there to witness
the death of her husband. The indignation and wrath of the
foreign press broke upon an outraged world—and the Nazis
had only one excuse, one escape from responsibility, which they
used repeatedly—and that was ignorance of the murder, though
they charged Schleicher with treason. I think the facts of the
case and of Nazi conduct and history in the last five years
speak for themselves only too obviously.

My mother came downstairs, and we all sat in the green reception room talking apprehensively, trying to piece out the picture. My brother continued with his story of the events of the day and the night before, which he had heard from newspapermen and some of our young diplomatic friends who had been phoning us frantically all day. My father was in the office preparing telegrams for the State Department. We closed all the doors as we noticed the servants loitering around the hall, softly entering the room on every pretext. They looked white and scared. Of course, we couldn't, and didn't, trust them for an instant.

Roehm had been caught in the night or early Saturday morning, after Hitler and Goebbels had flown from Bonn, Hitler having been with the Krupps a day or two before. Supposedly there was to be an uprising Saturday morning—to be led by Roehm—and Hitler found Roehm soddenly asleep, in bed with one of his young S.A. friends, after a riotous evening! He awakened and arrested him, made him dress and tore the insignia from his uniform and dragged him to prison along with his friends. Some people say he was shot that night in bed, others that he was shot early Saturday morning in prison. But the accepted story is, strangely enough, the one the Nazis themselves have told. Roehm was held in prison for two days and a night and offered but one alternative—suicide—which he resolutely refused. He denied to his last moment that he had been engaged in any treasonable act against his leader and proclaimed his loyalty to Hitler until they shot him.

One of Hitler's charges against him, in fact one of the first charges, was homosexuality. It seemed strange, even to the gullible German people, that Hitler would suddenly, for this reason, murder an old friend, a comrade of "du" intimacy, whom he had known to be a homosexual ever since they joined forces some ten years before this event. Roehm was accused of corrupting the moral of his army, of living extravagantly and licentiously on the people's money. But Hitler had been aware of this for many years, and furthermore Roehm lived no more extravagantly than his cohorts, Goering and others, and not much more licentiously.

In fact, it was such an open secret that Hitler and Roehm had been the dearest of friends through long years of trials and tribulations, that the rumours, when I first arrived, did not exclude slurs on Hitler's personal morality, though no proof could be presented against him.

By the middle afternoon of the 30th June Roehm was arrested and von Schleicher shot. Berlin was being governed by Goering, while Hitler and his little dark clubfooted friend were cleaning up Bavaria in their inimitable way. It was continually repeated during these days that Goering had planned to liquidate Goebbels as well as less important figures —and that the only reason Goebbels escaped being murdered was his anticipation of Goering's intentions and his consequent absence from Berlin and shadowing of Hitler himself. Goering's police were in charge. A heavy hand, dark with vengeance, was striking here and there, everywhere, sometimes according to plan, sometimes by whim, even carelessly, because a little more blood could not deepen or change the stain already there. Hundreds were killed that week in Berlin, over a thousand in Germany. Would there be disorder, would there be rioting, would there be a revolution, would the German people take this occasion to rise up and overthrow the masters of their misery? Those were the questions foremost in our minds and in the minds of most people.

We sat around whispering over the possibilities. I decided to postpone—perhaps even cancel—my trip to Russia. Telephone calls came in regularly, and Fritz, the short, blond, obsequious, efficient, Slavic-faced butler, was at our heels every time we moved. I think he was afraid to learn what his Fuehrer had done. I am sure he was afraid of the consequences; and the dread of going home alone that night through the Berlin streets was clear on his face.

During the next two days newspapermen called to give us further reports; two friends, each from a foreign democratic Embassy, asked if they could come over Monday night. A Nazi leader was going to speak, was to put the people's minds at rest and explain the lightning-like fury of their dictator.

By the time dinner was served we had quite a party of
I G

people preparing, for various reasons—personal and otherwise —to listen to the speech at the American Embassy. Victor Bodker, Walter Duranty (who happened to be passing through town), the two Embassy secretaries, a friend of my brother's, a young aristocrat in the S.S., and strangely enough, Elmina Rangabe—the curious, sensational dark Greek girl—with her escort, shrewd Herr Thomsen, who was in the Chancellery of the Leader himself.

Our family had a silent meal, interrupted occasionally by indignant outbursts from one or another member of the family—my mother, for instance, unable to recover from the horror of the von Schleichers' ignominious murder. None of us anticipated with any calm the outbreak of a revolution. Yet this was to be considered—and seriously. The situation was foreboding. Our only consolation during this day and the uneasy days that preceded and followed—until it became clear that Hitler had liquidated all chances of protest or revolt—was that we were together.

My father was pale and excited, with the usual reserve he showed when under strain. He was the least talkative and the most profoundly distressed of our family, having spent a harassing day listening to stories and rumours that came to him from all sources, and working on reports and telegrams. He seemed to feel, as most people did, that revolution was not improbable.

Elmina arrived, looking tense and highly emotional, with an unusual splotch of colour in her olive cheeks, her black hair knotted low in a coil on her neck. For the first time, she expressed real fear and disgust at what was happening—and it was the last time. Thomsen, by her side, was as suave and cool as usual, though later, after the radio speech, when he talked alone with my father, he seemed a little agitated.

Bodker was alive and stimulated, eagerly on the scent of news such as he hadn't reported before in his life. My brother's friend, in the S.S., was more nervous and alarmed than anyone present. He looked as if he had seen a ghost. Walter Duranty, used to revolutions and sensations, was witty but outraged—dry, sharp, and contemptuous in his conversation. There was no repression in the general talk that night, and it must have made good hearing and reading later for the Nazis, as it was no doubt reported duly by two people there.

Armand was cold with apprehension, unable to sit in one place longer than a few moments. He no doubt already knew the charge that would be made, not too closely veiled, against his chief, François-Ponçet.

We all moved from the green room into the ballroom where we formed a circle waiting to hear Goebbels. The voice finally broke from the radio onto our listening ears. As I remember, it was not a long speech but was delivered with all the mastery of oratory and demagogy Goebbels is noted for. An incomparable speaker, he manipulates his voice and tones, crescendos and diminuendos, rhythm and timing, as if he were handling a musical instrument. His voice can be honeyed with softness and persuasion, brittle with sarcasm, deep with wrath—he hisses like a snake and coos like a dove.

I have heard the Doctor speak on many occasions, and each time the words are clear and formed, controlled and inhuman. He doesn't get the fuzzy, furry tones of Hitler and Goering, he never allows his voice to go into a screaming hysteria or break into the sharp and hideous staccatos of his Leader. On the other hand, one senses there is not a sincere note in anything he utters. He is conscious of the mastery of his art; he uses his brain, his twists his logic, but there is never a sign of a heartbeat, real or affectedly real, in a syllable he emits so cautiously from his thin, cruel, subtle mind and mouth. To me, Goebbels as a personality is symbolized by his voice. Inhuman and opportunistic, he is the type of supremely malevolent hypocrite that National Socialism can produce. He is the most hated man in Germany. Among his own party groups and among the people, there is always the fear of his power with Hitler, his mental savagery, his instability, and of that product of his cunning brain, the Bureau of Propaganda and Enlightenment.

There were many sarcastic smiles that passed between our family and our friends that night as we listened to Goebbels trying to explain the swift and devastating wrath of his master in striking death to the heart of all opposition. He admitted a small number of dead, viciously attacked habits of vice and sexual aberration and extravagance, and pretended that Roehm had planned an insurrection against Hitler, in collaboration with a foreign power, by implication with Schleicher and others.

I saw Armand wince and blanch with rage when he heard the charge against a foreign power. We learned later that François-Ponçet was, according to the Nazis, supposed to be in the conspiracy along with Roehm and Schleicher to overthrow Hitler, and that parties had been held at various homes with these three men, among others, plotting the downfall of the Third Reich. It was too absurd for even a child to believe. But the accusation was made public, and Ponçet told my father that he was so indignant and insulted that he would never again shake hands with Hitler. In a few weeks, however, all was forgotten. At one time all the newspaper correspondents said that Ponçet was one of Hitler's closest friends and that he consulted often with him—Ponçet being a man who had access to the Leader's presence at all times.

We went to the library and continued our discussion. We were told that von Papen was under arrest in his apartment and that several of his secretaries had been arrested and one shot. Jung, who wrote the Marburg speech, and von Bose, the closest men to Papen, had been shot in Papen's office two days before—Saturday. Von Tschirsky, who later was released and fled to Vienna, was arrested, his head shaved. He was kept in prison for a month or more, being told every day that he was to be shot. Kaggeneck had disappeared and was not found for many weeks later—it was said that he had spent his time running from house to house, hotel to hotel, never staying in the same place long enough to be identified or found. He probably thus escaped death at a time when killing was the mode and personal vengeance was allowed free play in every part of Germany.

Reiner, the adjutant of Roehm, was arrested and held prisoner for many months. I had been at a party at Roehm's house only a week before the Purge. Roehm did not appear but Reiner was the host. It was a very lavish affair in an elaborate home. A bar downstairs supplied all that could be desired by the jaded palates. Beautiful decorations, a fine dance orchestra, lovely and magnificently gowned women, men from all classes of society—coarse and refined, rich and poor, degenerates and innocents alike. It was one of the strangest parties I had been to in Berlin and one of the motliest. I didn't like, for the most part, the type of women there, and I didn't like the loose, drunken atmosphere. It seemed strained and ugly to me. So I left at about ten-thirty. I heard later that it turned out to be a rather disgusting affair.

This same Reiner, after months in prison, came out pale, with his hair shorn, having missed execution by the skin of his teeth, permanently disgraced in the S.A. And as I have said, unsavoury rumours circulated as to how he bought his freedom.

The slogan of these days, when you met a friend on the street, was, as we learned, by Saturday night, "*Lebst du noch*" —which means, translated freely, "Are you still among the living?" I told Thomsen that this was the rumour going around and he frowned angrily. A true story was of a certain Schmitt who was a marked man, an S.A. fellow, in Munich. The Hitler fanatics went after him and shot him. Later they discovered that they had got the wrong Schmitt, so they summarily returned the ashes to his wife, with an apology presented in person by a Nazi. Many wives and families were notified of the decease of their husbands and fathers in this manner.

The evening wore on, father and mother going to bed rather early. Stories were flying thick and fast. Heines and Ernst were shot, both leaders of the S.A., Ernst supposed to be a rather able man, Heines one of the most dissolute and disgusting men in the entire Nazi ranks. Klausner of the Catholic Party (centre) and Gregor Strasser, an early Nazi fighter, had been brutally murdered. My father recalled that Ernst had been sent to him almost a year before when the indignities against American citizens were occurring every day. He came to the office very officially dressed, clicked his heels, gave the Nazi salute and proceeded to read out a page of apology, most sincere in sound and encouraging in promise, for the conduct of his S.A. men. He clicked his heels again, saluted formally and bowed himself out. Father's humorous account of this Nazi apology delighted many people, and his own informality as Ambassador quite dismayed the handsome and apparently effective S.A. leader. In any case, this same young man, Ernst, was about to leave on a boat from Bremen with his wife, for a trip, when the "fury" of the Leader broke upon him. He was seized on the ship, carried back to Berlin, and thrown in prison. Saturday night, I believe, he was executed in Lichterfelde.

My brother's friend had positively hair-raising stories to tell about what was happening at Lichterfelde, a prison in a suburb outside Berlin which had been transformed into a shooting gallery, with human bodies as targets. The S.S. guards were on twenty-four hour duty, indicating that the Nazis thought there would be revolution and that their picked troops had better be on the job.

This one young man was reporting regularly to Lichterfelde. He told us that a court-martial was set up in which a few Nazis, including Goering, were the judges. The charges were made and the sentence passed—without the defendant having a chance to say a word—and the victim led before a firing squad, the whole procedure taking place in a few minutes. Different groups of S.S. men did the shooting—they were told that there was a blank cartridge somewhere among the ten or twelve guns used, and each man could think that his shot was not the one that hit the human target. There was a huge hole dug outside the camp where supposedly the bodies were thrown in. They were to be burned later and returned to their families in packages through the mails, or kept in small boxes to be called for at post offices.

At this time, and also later, we learned that several young foreign office attachés, with S.S. or other affiliations, were forced to be present at the execution, to witness the entire scene—no doubt, the Nazis' conception of self-discipline; the steeling of character put into practice. I know, however, that they were young, sensitive boys whose souls were shocked and sickened by this enforced and unwilled participation in the horrible drama.

An eyewitness of Ernst's murder said that Ernst had died very bravely, without a shadow of fear on his face, proclaiming loudly to the last that he was completely innocent of the charges made against him and that he had always remained loyal to the Leader—his dying words "Long live the Leader. Heil Hitler."

Some of the stories we heard that night were so ghastly and cruel—and incidentally made such good news—that Bodker rushed to his office and sent a special story—which, if anyone cares to look it up (Reuter News Service, June 30, and days following, 1934), I can guarantee will make informative and reliable background.

That night was a nerve-racking one for all of us. Walter Duranty was engaged in rapid fire dialogue with Thomsen and my two friends in the foreign embassies. The latter, of course, had to maintain a certain discretion and caution in what they said, but Duranty felt no such restriction. With his stick striking the floor in emphasis, sitting precariously on the edge of the sofa whenever he was excited, he answered Thomsen's pointed and sarcastic questions about Russia and asked equally pointed and sarcastic questions of Thomsen on Germany, and especially on events of the past two days. Elmina, watching the trend of the conversation, heatedly defended Germany and the action of the Nazis. She really hero-worshipped Hitler and told me often that she thought he was one of the greatest men who ever lived.

After the other guests had left, my brother went out with the newspapermen to dig up some more news, and I went to bed.

It was a sleepless night I spent—I suppose, all of us spent. I heard, as I had also on Saturday and Sunday, the faint sound of shooting as a sort of counterpoint to fitful and disturbed dreams. My personal experience of that night did not vary from that of my friends. Many people told me that the shots from Lichterfelde could be heard most of the night, and a friend of mine who lived near this suburb reported that intermittently throughout the night and during that awful week he was awakened by the deadly staccato metal sound.

4

On the 1st of July my father said he wanted to drive by von Papen's house and see what was happening. We drove slowly by the house, and I saw the young son of von Papen —who was a dear friend of mine—standing behind the curtains. Our car bore, of course, a diplomatic number, and as we passed we noticed the black-uniformed guard staring at us. The young son told us later that the family was deeply appreciative of our gesture, as no other diplomatic car had come near their house on that Sunday.

In the afternoon my father announced that he was going to stop by and leave cards at von Papen's house. He sent in his card with a handwritten message, "I hope we may call on you soon." My father knew quite well what he was doing. He had no sympathy whatsoever for von Papen or his record —black with cowardice, devious with espionage and betrayal. He liked him personally, as did most people. But he left his card as a protest against the brutality of the Nazis. That men who had not been proved guilty should be murdered outright, without trial, was a shock my parents never got over. And it was said that von Papen might be executed any moment.

On Monday I had a telephone call from the young son of von Papen. He was to be allowed to leave his apartment to take his final examination at the University of Berlin. He made a date with me on Wednesday, July 4th. I knew we were going to have a tea for all the Americans in Berlin on that day, but I thought I would have time to see him for a moment and I felt he was much more important at this moment than twenty such teas. On Monday and Tuesday more rumours came in of deaths, suicides, arrests. The well-known Treviranus, a political figure of some importance before Hitler, was supposed to be on the black list. The S.S. men came for him in his house. He was notified by either a servant or someone staying in his house of what was happening. He was playing tennis behind the house, but he threw down the racket, scaled the garden wall, took a taxi, and escaped before the men had time to get beyond the person at the door. Treviranus, so the story went later, hid himself in the house of a friend for a few days and then somehow managed to get passage to England where, as far as I know, he is still living.

Louis Lochner and others reported that the Hohenzollerns were in serious danger. My father got word to the Crown Prince that he thought it best to call off the dinner that was planned for that week—and the Crown Prince was only too happy to accede to his discretion. My father felt that any contact with a foreigner or a foreign Embassy at this time would be dangerous for a German in high position—or, for that matter, in any position. These were the days of insinuations about foreigners and diplomats, warnings to Germans not to appear in diplomatic or foreign houses.

I recalled during these days what Diels had told me before the Purge broke. He was now secure in Cologne, seemingly safe at least, with the unpleasant job of organizing espionage in this district and of bringing the Catholics and Catholic opposition around to the Nazis—at which, by the way, he failed miserably. He told me, in the late spring, that soon there was to be disclosed a vast network of espionage, involving high personages among foreign groups in Berlin who were working in direct co-operation with Germans in official positions. This was his way, I suppose, of indicating to us what the charges would be at the time of the Bloody June 30th.

Many people told us how the adjutants of von Papen had been arrested and shot. These stories were corroborated later by various men close to von Papen. One young secretary was in the office at the time the Nazis came for von Bose, von Papen's most trusted secretary. Von Bose's associate knew something was brewing so, as he led them into the office, he ran back to the waiting-room pretending to forget something he had left there. He took this opportunity to escape. The S.S. men asked von Bose to announce them to someone else in the office. As he turned his back they shot him.

On Wednesday, several hundred Americans, the Embassy and Consulate staff, newspapermen, Germans, and a few diplomats, came to celebrate our Day of Independence. The house was beautifully decorated with red, white, and blue flower sprays tastefully arranged on all the tables, little American flags, and favours. Our dining room table, stretched out to its full length, was creaking with heavy plates of food and drink. The orchestra played American songs softly, and my mother and father stood at the entrance to the ballroom to greet the guests. The July day was hot though not clear and many guests went out on the terrace, lingered on the stone steps, and wandered through the garden, sitting at small tables or walking on the grass or gravel paths. Externally it looked like any other Fourth of July celebration observed by every American Embassy in Europe. People chattered and gossiped, devoured the food, and made 'way with the punch, sought cool shadowy places and laughed freely.

My mother looked lovely in a long flowing blue and white dress, the subdued light flooding around her, her hair pure silver, and her voice soft and southern and gracious. Only the unusual bright flush on her fair skin and the quick keen look in her almost black eyes indicated that her mind and emotions were on other things than her duty of being a good hostess to the throngs of people around her. But she stood there by the side of my father, smiling softly and making the necessary light conversation.

My father looked as humorous as always—he was usually dreadfully bored by these affairs but his sense of humour saved him from showing it too much—whimsical and ironic expressions playing over his face, and implicative meanings in his conversation. (My brother and I, feeling still a sense of indignation and anger, were very undiplomatic when we greeted some young Germans with the now common phrase, "*Lebst du noch?*" We thought we were being sarcastic, revealing to the Germans some of the fury we felt. No doubt many of them thought the remark bad taste. Some Nazis showed extreme irritation.) When the newspapermen arrived, they, one by one, pulled father out of the receiving line, and were seen

leaning their heads together rather noticeably while my mother
and I greeted the guests. The same thing happened when our
staff members arrived—so it seemed that there were still things
happening on Wednesday after the Bloody Saturday. I stood
in between my father and mother part of the time, and he
managed to whisper, between arrivals, that everything was
now in control of the Nazis, and that all danger of revolution
had vanished.

The butler came to me and said quietly, "*Der junge Herr
von Papen* is downstairs waiting for you." I touched my mother's
arm—she knew that he was coming—and slowly made my
way out of the mob of people around us.

The tall, thin, sharp-featured blond young fellow took my
arm and we walked quickly out into the park. He apologized
for having interrupted our celebration. But I assured him that
I was glad, and anxious to see him as soon as possible. We
looked around to see if we were followed, and after some
precautions, went into an open air café for a drink and talk.

His face, with the long sharp nose, narrow bone structure,
thin, rather cynical mouth, had a certain fine beauty—like
that of a blond fox. He had a swift sense of humour, a keen
but non-intellectual mind, and a great deal of sportsmanship
and charm. He was one of the most beautiful and graceful
dancers in Berlin. To dance a waltz with him at a ball—as I
loved to do—was like living in music itself.

He was nervous, clearly, and showed the strain he had been
under. On Monday when I spoke to him over the telephone
I had told him that my father had left his visiting card on
Sunday. Today he said that his father hadn't received the card
until a few hours before. He believed that the S.S. men on
guard over their house those two days had taken the card
immediately to the Secret Police where it had remained these
two or three days, being examined, checked, and reported
on by all and sundry—perhaps even carried to much higher
personages in the government. Of course the old and young
von Papen believed that what really saved von Papen from
death during these days was Hindenburg's protection—it was
well known that Hindenburg loved von Papen almost like a

son. It is not known just how conscious the old warrior was of the events going on around him in the latter years of his life. There are many conflicting reports—some people say he was as alive and interested in German and foreign affairs as ever before and that his mind functioned as well as it ever had—others say in the last year or two he was too feeble and old to know what was happening, his mind almost like a baby's. My father, however, saw him at a formal reception a few months before the Purge and told us he seemed to be the same as when they first met in 1933.

In any case, no matter what his condition, the Nazis were afraid to touch von Papen while Hindenburg was living, no matter how good an accusation they could trump up against the Vice Chancellor.

The von Papens on Saturday were held virtually in prison in their apartment, neither father nor son allowed to leave the house. There were S.S. guards posted in their apartment and also downstairs at the entrance. Von Papen was allowed to see no one, and was led to believe from hour to hour that he might be taken out and shot. It was a harrowing day for both of them. Von Papen in all his checkered and curious and questionable career which had involved some danger and demanded some daring, never had experienced such a period of anxiety. Certainty of death sometimes makes more endurable the period of life left to one. Von Papen did not know until Sunday or Monday evening whether Hitler would decide to execute him or not. Both he and his son knew that von Bose, Jung and others whom von Papen trusted and liked personally very much, had been murdered, and that several other of his friends had either been arrested or had disappeared. The charges against von Papen were that he had conspired against Hitler and that he had been in contact with Roehm and Schleicher in plotting the overthrow of the Leader.

The young son, Franz, agreed that these were the most ridiculous statements that the Nazis had yet made against people they wanted to get rid of. He said his father and Schleicher had become deadly enemies; that Schleicher had always hated and been jealous of his father. He categorically denied that his father had even seen Schleicher on terms of any intimacy whatsoever in the last year or two. He concluded that the charge associating his father's name with Roehm's was even more ridiculous and impossible. The elder von Papen apparently held Roehm in great contempt both socially and otherwise. That the head of a fine aristocratic Catholic family of wealth and position should be conspiring with a riffraff gangster of questionable morals and violent political past and present, to overthrow a man he had helped manœuvre into power, was too patently fantastic a story for a child to believe. The elder von Papen thought Schleicher was terribly ambitious and unprincipled, and even might want to put himself into a position of importance again—which, by the way, would be a fairly accurate picture of von Papen himself—but more than that his mind did not accept.

Franz told of his father's resignation handed to Hitler on Tuesday. He said both of them were bitter and furious that, his father being charged with such humiliating things, Hitler refused to allow von Papen to resign!

At the time I was talking to the young man and pitying his nervous and distraught manner, I thought what a shame it was that he remained in ignorance of his father's political corruption and what a burden it must have been to have a father of such stamp.

When I left the son, I felt that at least two lives had been spared for the moment, and one hoped-for career ruined. Shortly after, von Papen was demoted from his position in the Foreign Office, though I believe he was never allowed the honour of resigning, and given the unsavoury job of annexing Austria which was accomplished in 1938. Whether or not it was partially the accomplishment of von Papen no one knows definitely. In any case, a close worker and collaborator of his was once more found dead in the river—no doubt a victim of Nazi violence. Von Papen's role before and during Hitler's seizure of power has been so devious and fantastic, one scarcely can formulate a clear picture of his numberless betrayals or find a clear design behind them. Certainly he is not a great statesman or a disinterested man. His career and politics lead to only one conclusion: von Papen is a man never to be trusted by any group in power. His own thirst for position and control has led him into strange and contradictory attitudes and activities. An opportunist of unmistakable ambitions, he might have been a lesser Tallyrand, had he had greater love for Germany than for himself, or had he had any real talent whatsoever. It will be interesting to follow the next stage in his career.

Franzie, dear friend of careless, nonchalant days and ways of life, spirit of all lighthearted parties, of humorous, gay, critical, and tolerant attitudes, realized suddenly and brutally that he was a victim, and not through his own fault, of a group which held power in his country. However, young von Papen was one of the least tragic of the cases I knew about, and I don't want to over emphasize the disruption caused in his life. I fear that he is the type of young man, brought up in conventional indulgence and accustomed to privilege, whose easy-going attitude toward life is only sharpened and increased by the cynicism and fatalism he now feels.

Towards the end of the week, when von Papen was clearly out of danger, he drove his low-numbered car over in front of our Embassy. He and his young son got out conspicuously and entered my father's office. The older man had a long conversation of about an hour, while the son waited.

Newspapermen were frantic with excitement as the news was passed about. They all knew the long black car—with licence number IA 99—and could not mistake von Papen's intention of announcing boldly that he had support in the American Embassy, if not in Germany. I must repeat again that the Germans were still respectful, and a bit awed by American public opinion at this time. To prevent misunderstanding of my father's position it must be emphasized that he had no respect or affection for von Papen at any time, and that he only wanted to register in no unmistakable terms his disgust with Nazi methods.

The journalists, as soon as von Papen left, besieged my father in his office and by telephone to find out what this gesture meant and what von Papen had told him. No doubt von Papen received many queries of the same kind. Both men kept a profound silence to the press. My father said later he was astounded by what von Papen had told him, and questioned him as to the advisability of publicly flaunting his visit. However, no further trouble came to von Papen, and the incident was closed.

5

We received, either on Saturday or Sunday, through very indirect and reliable sources, a telegram from a German in London asking if something couldn't be done to aid his family living in Berlin. We happened to know the wife, though very casually, and liked her very much. We did not like to interfere in internal affairs, but, against the advice of von Bülow —one of the secretaries of State in the Foreign Office—my mother and I went to call on the woman in question, feeling that a personal and private visit between women had nothing to do with Nazi affairs.

We entered the suburban villa, and were announced by a red-eyed servant girl. A dark, slender woman came in the room after a moment. She, of course, remembered our faces and knew who we were. She apparently didn't know what was the occasion of our visit so we sat quietly talking for a moment before we told her of the telegram. The woman broke into tears and sobbed softly with her hands before her face. She looked like a completely broken human being. Dark and attractive, the thinness of her face, the deep circles under her swollen eyes and the persistent nervousness of her speech and gestures indicated to us what a terrible strain she had been under.

She told us that a month or so before, she, as a member of a wealthy, well-known, and respected family, had entertained several of the men accused of plotting the overthrow of Hitler. She said that a foreign diplomat had been there, but the dinner was simply in the line of her social duties and position, and no political discussion had taken place. The Nazis accused her husband of being in on the conspiracy because he had entertained these men at the same dinner. She said that if her husband returned from London—where he had gone on a business visit—he would certainly be charged with treason or perhaps shot first. She was deeply touched by her husband's telegram, carefully sent to reliable and high-placed people, in her interest—and also by our "courageous concern."

Her son had been summarily arrested—without a charge and without explanation—and her house searched, her own passport taken from her. She knew that, unless she escaped, something might happen to her and that her house and belongings would surely be confiscated.

When she spoke of her son her self-control collapsed and she became hysterical with fear. He might already be dead, he might be tortured, he might be in a concentration camp. She asked if we could do anything for him. She said perhaps if I would show some concern about him, visit him, or take cigarettes to him, the Nazis would realize he was being observed by a foreign diplomat's family. We promised to do what we could and left her in a pathetic state.

We spoke to various people we knew who had some influence in Government circles, and also with some other diplomats. In a few weeks the boy was released, safe but pretty scared. The mother slowly got some of her finest household treasures out of Germany or in houses of friends. She asked us to buy or take some of her priceless bits, but we decided not to. Her son, using his own passport, took a night train out of Germany, across a border where the customs' inspection occurs in the middle of the night. He got through safely and let his mother know immediately.

She came around to see my mother using an assumed name —Carrie—that was agreed on between them. The servants didn't recognize her—and she spoke excellent English which helped her disguise. We feared that if she were reported to be visiting our Embassy, it would get her in trouble and make us suspect.

She was, by this time, receiving the help of several other people interested in an innocent woman's safety. She told us of mysterious telephone calls, visits, and letters she had been receiving, and of her daily terror. A way had been found, she said, to get her out of Germany, using another passport and travelling by airplane. She was leaving the next day. She bade my mother a sad and affectionate farewell and promised to send a card as soon as she arrived. In a few days we had a simple postcard from London. "Arrived safe and sound. Deepest gratitude and love. Carrie." Though we ourselves had done nothing personally to get her out of Germany, she was everlastingly grateful that we had told others in positions of influence, Germans and diplomats, of her plight.

Of course, many of the Embassies at this time took a personal interest in the victims of the Purge and, when the cases were obviously unfair and cruel, or involved personal friends whom they knew to be beyond reproach, intervened to the extent of calling the attention of high-placed and more humane Nazis to them. In a few cases I heard of later, two foreign Embassies actually effected, as the story went, the escape of several accused persons, in immediate danger, without notifying the German officials.

This period of June 30th and the week following is, even to this day, one of the least known and most speculated upon in Nazi German history. Of course, there were many more vicious and devastating rumours than I have repeated, but so unverified that I don't like to recall them. The atmosphere of Berlin—and I am sure it was the same all over Germany—was as tense as I have ever felt before or since. Later there were more war-scares, and international uneasiness, but the internal situation was never so measurably acute.

People very well informed outside Germany, and in contact with various opposition within, tell me that during this first week they had their suitcases packed, expecting and hoping that the regime would so alter either by revolution or modification that they could return to their native land.

Hitler a few weeks later called together the Reichstag, invited the diplomatic corps, and gave a speech in which he tried to explain the whole series of events. My father was no less cynical than the rest of the diplomats who listened to the hysterical oratory.

KG

The general theory among diplomats, trained observers, more moderate Nazis, and newspapermen was that Hitler and Goering and Goebbels did not descend in God-like wrath on Roehm and Schleicher and the rest because they were attempting a counter-revolution. On the contrary, no evidence has been offered in any way acceptable to an intelligent person that convicts Roehm of such a plot with such strange and different-minded cohorts. It is hard to believe that the potential leader of a counter-revolution to take place on Saturday would be in bed drunk the night before!

However, there is not much doubt that a large number of S.A. men were discontented with the discrepancy between Hitler's programme and his practice. The "revolution" supposedly made for them was getting out of their hands and into the hands of people they detested and distrusted. There is no doubt that Roehm was jealous of the men who were superseding him around Hitler. It is generally believed by those who know what facts there are at hand, that, at most, Roehm wanted to dispose of those men, or at least destroy their influence, and remind his beloved Leader of his own trustworthiness—his and his loyal army's. The men of whom he was jealous and whose policies and hold on Hitler he disapproved of, anticipated his antagonism, warned Hitler or perhaps even deceived him into believing that the old fighter was betraying him. They thought the best way to be rid of Roehm's criticism and past affectionate friendship with the Leader was to eliminate him. There is not much question also that, had Goering been able to get hold of the Doctor, whom he loathes, he would have disposed of him as well. But Hitler is very shrewd in his handling of these two men, infinitely valuable, each in his way, to the Nazi movement. He plays one off against another—when Goebbels seems to be too much in favour and there is gossip about it, Hitler shifts his attention and honours to Goering.

As for Schleicher, as I have already stated, the men around Hitler, and very likely Hitler himself, feared the old army officer's potential political influence, and decided that, as killing was the accepted technique of the moment, they might as

well cook up a plot whereby they could involve Schleicher and
accuse him of treason, thus making his "liquidation" necessary. The other murders of these days were committed along
these same lines of opportunistic action. Everyone could be
accused of plotting either with the S.A., or with the Reich-
wehr (tied up the Schleicher), or with a foreign power,
represented by François-Ponçet. But the men murdered in
Germany these days were the men who either didn't approve
of Hitler's advisers or those who were possible future rivals
of these advisers. Naturally, a lot of people who were either
actively or silently opposed to Hitler could, under the screen
of counter-revolution the Nazis set up, be quietly taken
care of.

VII

TO RUSSIA

I HAD HAD ENOUGH of blood and terror to last me for the rest of my life, though I still saw and learned of plenty as the years went on. The terrible fear that reigned in Germany demoralized the people almost under our eyes. My parents and my diplomatic friends still thought there was a possibility of an uprising of the suffering German people. But it seemed to me that Hitler, with the use of terror and espionage and his self-appointed control of legal and illegal methods, had the country pretty well in hand. There was no revolution in sight, so I decided to go to Russia as soon as possible. Within a week after the outbreak of the Purge I was on my way. I was certainly glad to be out of it. I figured that I could fly back in a day if there were trouble.

Both my parents, and my brother as well, were reluctant to see me go to Russia for a month. But I was determined to see the workings of another system so often compared with the German.

Though I was travelling alone, I tried to ease their minds with a white lie: I was going to meet several people on the plane and we were going to travel through the country in a group. I think my father suspected this was not true; and my mother was disturbed because Russia seemed to her a wild, distant, and strange country where anything could happen.

I said good-bye to my father early in the morning in his bedroom and he said wryly but affectionately, "Well, dear daughter, I hope you take care of yourself and have an interesting trip. It seems like a wild goose chase to me." I kissed him fondly and attempted to reassure him.

Mother and my brother took me to the airplane, Mother with tears in her eyes. She feared that something would happen in Germany while I was away, that I would get sick or have trouble in Russia, and the family would be separated. I promised to write her and gave her an elaborate plan of my itinerary, swore I had been inoculated against all diseases. In her mind, she saw Russia as a country full of reckless Bolsheviks, abounding with typhus, Black Plague, smallpox, and typhoid, as well as mysterious diseases unknown to the western world.

I mounted the beautiful tri-motor Junker 'plane. Some photographers rushed up and got a snapshot. I didn't realize or have any conception at the time of news value, and near diplomatic scandal, this trip would cause. The daughter of the Ambassador to Nazi Germany CHOOSES to visit the Soviet Union. I suppose my father had this definitely in mind when he advised against my going, but with his usual tolerance of, and sympathy with, his children's curiosity and development, he didn't say a word to me on this score.

This was my first airplane flight and it was to be one of ten hours. I waved energetically and a little sadly at my mother and brother, but the excitement and newness of the adventure that stretched before me soon overcame any qualms I felt about disobeying and leaving my family behind.

We ran into a bank of clouds that looked as if the sky was full of cotton; then, a little later, rain, and slight wind-storm. But, on the whole, it was a beautiful flight, and I kept my nose glued to the window, watching the cloud and sun shadows on the earth below, the complicated, rich, and varied texture of the soil and topography, like different designs in soft and brilliant coloured and woven cloths. I constantly marvelled at the power and the lightness of the airplane that seemed so heavy yet quivered all over with every wind-stir and air-current. We made several stops for the everlastingly boring customs inspection, and, in Talinn, Esthonia, changed into a small four-passenger 'plane for the hop to Leningrad.

2

Leningrad's airport was swarming with people—it was a holiday and everyone came out to see the 'planes, the landings and take-offs. The people were poorly clad, according to

American standards, and had strange faces, high cheekbones, rather Oriental in cast—Finnish or Eskimo types—the women with white cloths bound around their heads, the men in dark blouses. Occasionally there was a careless casual brown uniform among the masses of people.

I was met by a pretty rosy-faced girl guide and, as we drove through the streets in the Intourist car, I noticed the grey uniform drabness brightened by innumerable flaming red flags flown from buildings. The people shuffled along, it seemed to me, neither happily nor unhappily, talking and loitering, some standing in breadlines, some listening to the loudspeakers placed at intervals throughout the city.

It was still very light outside though it was eight o'clock. After a late dinner, which was served by very independent, self-respecting waiters—not like the cringing obsequious service of German servants—I went to bed behind blue velvet curtains in a luxurious room in the Astoria hotel. I heard voices and steps outside my window far into the night, and when I closed my eyes at twelve or one it was still like early twilight in the streets. These are known as the "white nights" of Leningrad and are famous all over the world—lasting only a few weeks in June and July.

In the morning we looked around Leningrad a little before going to the country. It is one of the most potentially beautiful cities in Europe, with its wide and gracious streets and squares, the vistas, and the parks. Though much of the old Leningrad was in a terrible state of disrepair—paint peeling off the buildings and plaster loose—there was a great deal of bustle and activity, old buildings being attended to, streets being relaid, new structures rising everywhere.

The men were attractive with their light or dark blouses worn over their trousers and bound at the waist; the women looked dowdier; but in both sexes one observed quite often a striking beauty of face—brown, strong-boned, with wide set eyes, and friendly large mouths.

Leningrad is a great industrial centre and is, consequently, drab and smoky, though many people consider it much more magnificent and exciting than Moscow. Most of the old buildings and churches have been preserved; the main cathedral is now an anti-religious museum, serving as a visual education to the workers who were so long exploited by the immensely rich and corrupt Russian church.

The Winter Palace of the Czars, scene of riot, protest, and revolution, is a museum open for a small fee to everyone. Again, through education and propaganda, the worker is instructed as to the activities of his former capitalistic masters. For instance, in one of the palaces outside the city there is a placard describing and showing the food and table decoration of one banquet of a Czar or Czarina. It is suggestively pointed out that one banquet alone cost as much as a worker got in several years.

Other buildings are turned into schools, scientific and educational institutions, for the workers. Smolny Institute, formerly an exclusive girls' school for daughters of aristocrats, is now occupied by the Leningrad Soviet. In this structure are the two or three starkly simple rooms Lenin lived in.

I went to several factories near Leningrad and was impressed with the hospitals, nurseries, kitchens, and recreation centres provided for the workers. They work seven hours a day, have an hour for lunch and recreation, and two weeks' to a month's paid vacation every year, and enjoy every sixth day as a holiday. Former palaces and mansions, and their parks, are turned into homes of culture and rest, playgrounds, medical centres, children's schools or vacation places. All of this is done for workers by other workers who are the head of the state, as a beginning toward giving them the privileges and opportunities they deserve as the creators of the nation's wealth—and not as a means to pacify and keep them in hand, not as a sop to prevent other demands, rising self-respect, or a feeling of power.

We spent a day in the country looking at the palaces of the Czars, those of Peter and Catherine the Great, Elizabeth, Alexander, and the last Czar, "Nickey." Catherine's palace, once painted gold and blue on the outside (now a dazzling white) had the most magnificent rooms that I have ever seen—of lapis lazuli, amber, other precious and semi-precious stones, gold and silver as the materials for pillars, floors, furniture, walls and with every conceivable decoration and bric-a-brac. Contingents of workers were being constantly shown through these palaces, or were on little excursions of their own, their faces showing disgust as they saw the cost, graphically explained everywhere, and the ways the money was raised to cover it. The other palaces were equally lavish, and the fountains—outside Peter the Great's—more beautifully designed than those of Versailles.

The last Czar's palace was pathetic. All rooms of faded and very bourgeois grandeur, they were covered with family pictures, with innumerable icons (cheap and priceless mixed together), a hodge-podge of bad taste and tawdriness, of simple-mindedness and superstition. The rule of Rasputin could be seen everywhere, and I was repelled to see a bit of food, left on his plate, that had been saved by the last Czarina to reverence and worship in her private rooms.

I left Leningrad with mixed sentiments. I was beginning to get a sense of the country, of its past, present, and future. I was shocked by the poverty that still existed; I was amazed at the efforts everywhere to put all the good things of life at the disposal of the workers; and I was beginning to understand what Czarism must have meant to the millions of people ground down under its heel.

I remember best the beautiful vista across the Neva, with the fortress of Peter and Paul in the background, the long, broad avenue following this strange river, the openness and breadth of the streets and squares, the architectural gems of the past so carefully and meticulously preserved and used for a common good, I had always been told that the barbaric Russians had destroyed everything of beauty, all of the palaces and magnificent dwellings, the ancient and the modern churches. Therefore, I was astounded to see that all of these buildings were intact, were being used for educational purposes or for medical or recreational centres.

I came away with a picture of a vast and sprawling city, excellently planned, full of bustle and constructive activity, street-cars crowded, women participating in all sorts of work (as traffic cops, for instance, and street-car conductors); luminous nights, when the whole urban population came out to walk in the streets or in the parks, to talk and entertain themselves; streets dirty, drab, littered, slowly beginning to take on the aspect of cleanliness and newness; a city full of memories of the past and gigantic dreams of the future, the first city I had seen in my whole life which was completely in the hands of the proletariat, struggling, striving, learning bitterly by experience, sacrificing and dreaming.

At first I didn't like to recognize the fact that the class I was used to seeing and living with all my life was nowhere in evidence. I resented the fact that beautiful private mansions with exquisite marble statuary, gold brocade furniture, mirrors, and small and large luxuries, had been given over to the simple, toiling people to enjoy and rest in. Later I was touched by the care they took of these valuables, the tenderness with which they handled and preserved them—as if they, clumsy, hard-working, newly arisen to life and power, were proclaiming their appreciation of and sensitiveness to the fine things of life.

There were few private cars, no sign of the wealth and luxury of a privileged class, no elegance of dress; I saw no night clubs and found no expensive shops. However, there were movies, parks, lectures, entertainment, theatres, and ballets in abundance for the simplest and poorest person to enjoy, many of them entirely free.

I don't quite know why I was so disappointed. I came to Russia with practically no preparation for what was there. That there was no exploitation, no sign of the vast differences between the rich and poor (because a classless society was slowly being effected); that the working people were really in control of their own life and future, should and did please me, of course, but it came, nevertheless, as a great shock. I didn't feel quite at home with these masses of people—and I felt a little conspicuous—yet I was challenged by them and aghast at the enormity of the programme of education, reconstruction, and organization ahead of them.

What pleased me most, even in this early stage of my Russian trip, and something that lay at the back of my mind

for a long time before I realized its meaning, was the absolute
lack of military display. I saw few Red Army soldiers, and
even one small parade, but they were all so simple, so incon-
spicuously dressed, so modest and even careless in appearance,
I could hardly believe they were part of the formidable Soviet
Red Army. There was no provocative or insolent behaviour,
no militaristic propaganda and fanfare; there was a complete
lack of arrogance and exhibitionism which I had come to
believe, after my German residence, necessary adjuncts to a
military machine. Where was this terrible regimentation I
had heard so much about? How could it be so prevalent if
even the highest expression of regimentation—the army—
was conspicuously without it?

3

I arrived in Moscow after a curious night on the International Sleeper. Completely unaware of the Russian custom
of putting men and women together in Pullman cars, I was
shocked to see a young Italian make his way into my compartment after I had gone to bed, and start undressing in his
berth across from mine. He saw my chagrin apparently
because he started an apologetic flow of conversation which
I didn't understand. Finally, we found a common language
—French—and he explained the situation to me. He assured
me that I need not feel afraid, that it was a common experience
for all tourists in Russia, and that if I had a brother I would
understand how he regarded me. After many more elaborate
and friendly fraternal protestations, I felt safe and went
soundly to sleep, disturbed only by a bedbug who concentrated
his friendly feelings on my left shoulder.

From the moment I arrived at Moscow until the day I left
I was entranced by the city. People looked gayer and better-
dressed, there was more traffic in the streets—though, of course,
always the ubiquitous street car loaded beyond capacity—
everything looked cleaner and more prosperous, shops were
nicer and more numerous, there seemed to be a sort of
ebullient vitality and love of life everywhere. In fact, I liked

Moscow so much that I often said later I couldn't understand why Intourist would ever route its tourists through Leningrad first. One felt in Moscow that the struggle was over, that the fruits of victory were being cherished and enjoyed by everyone.

I felt much more energetic and cheerful here than I did in Leningrad and so rushed into a week of hectic and fascinating sightseeing. I visited factories and nurseries and law courts, museums of art (though nothing, in my mind, compares to the superb collection of paintings in the Hermitage in Leningrad, unless it is the museum of modern art in Moscow where there is a fine collection of the best French moderns) and museums of revolution, government buildings, theatres, ballets, hospitals and movies, churches, workers' apartment buildings, parks and homes of "culture and rest."

By this time I was getting used to the simplicity of dress and manners of people on the streets. I dressed accordingly in a simple blouse and skirt and began to feel more in my element.

One day we went to a Prophylactorium, or a home for reformed prostitutes. Formerly, there were thousands upon thousands of prostitutes in Russia plying their pitiable trade, mainly from economic necessity. During a Nishni-Novgorod Fair, famous the world over for the meeting of merchants from east and west, 60,000 of them came there for the duration of the Fair. Now, there were only 200 prostitutes in Moscow itself. Those who came voluntarily to the hospital were taken care of for a year, absolutely without charge, given careful medical treatment, and taught a trade. The decline in prostitution was explained to me by these facts: economic change entitled everyone, including women, to hold jobs; easy marriage and divorce laws; the lack of a rich and corrupt class who could afford and support prostitutes. Most men who themselves had jobs were married, not "chained," to women they wanted, women who could also have jobs or careers if they wanted them.

As in Leningrad, there were practically no soldiers in the streets, no military displays or parades. In fact, on the surface there was not the slightest indication that the population of Moscow was being regimented. There were seemingly no laws involving social behaviour, no *"verboten"* signs—there seemed to be a natural, easy-going, informal social intercourse among all people. They bore no rubber stamp of caste, class, or profession, and seemed to have a self-respect, an individuality and dignity that had nothing to do with their plain living or dressing, their jobs or salaries.

Ambassador Bullitt called one day and asked me to lunch at his home. He was very lively and attractive superficially—a bald-headed, glistening face, with intense light eyes, a curious nervous vitality in his vivacious speech and glances, a strong egotism under the brittleness and instability. To me a man who inspires the immediate question—What is he really like underneath, what would be his character and personality at home, every day, when the mask was dropped?—is a man to be suspicious of and one not to be trusted.

He told me, and a few other tourists at his lunch, that Russia was definitely better off than she was before the Revolution, but that it would take at least forty to fifty years to effect any real or measurable progress. He said Russia didn't depress him because he had had no illusions about what could be accomplished, though he became very irritated at the slow way things got done or didn't get done at all. The reason he gave for the latter was fear and inefficiency in minor officials. Bullitt felt that they were either too untrained in their jobs or too frightened of their immediate chief to take any initiative. He concluded that this government was simply one autocracy that had been substituted for another, the Czarist. In a final "pat" on the back for the Soviet System, he added that at least children weren't starving in the streets as they had been when he was in Russia in the early days, though 5,000,000 he stated had starved to death in 1932–33.

Bullitt, at that time, was still the avowed friend of the Soviet Union, was teaching the Red Army to play polo, was giving sensational "zoo" parties for the diplomatic corps and Soviet officials, and being very much the "big brother" of the U.S.S.R. The Russians, intensely satisfied by the recognition of their country by America, were anxious to be friendly with any representative our country might choose to send.

All the Russians I have talked to in recent years say that they were very glad that Bullitt left and Davies came. With Davies they knew exactly what to expect. He was a capitalist proclaiming no love for their country or their ideals. By background, training, marriage, and position he was an inevitable enemy of socialism. But they knew where they stood with him and could act accordingly. In view of Bullitt's present anti-Soviet, pro-French-German rapprochement attitude, it is not surprising to find the Russians sincerely embittered about "romantic revolutionaries" for Ambassadors.

I met a few members of Bullitt's staff and decided that my time would be better spent in my study of Russian conditions if I gave the American Embassy a wide berth. I saw Walter Duranty a few times, talking, gossiping, and complaining freely, tapping his stick in impatience, loving the Russians and being exasperated by them, his manner relaxed, natural and happy. Needless to say, Walter was not always so gay and charming in Moscow, because the Russian climate and inconveniences began to wear on him as it did on most foreigners. These facts of discomfort never prevented him, however, from keeping his perspective on what they were planning and accomplishing.

I spent an afternoon in the Kremlin, on a hill overlooking the town and directly above the Red Square. Here the Soviet government has many of its departments and offices and carries on much of its administrative and other work. Within the ancient and beautiful Kremlin walls, the head of the Soviet State, Joseph Stalin, lives very modestly in a few small rooms most of the time when he is not occupying his unpretentious villa in the country. We saw the churches in which all the Czars were crowned and buried. We went into the Treasury which contains all the priceless relics of ancient and modern times which the Soviet Government has preserved and guarded well. Robes of priests and high dignitaries in the church sewed thick with pearls and priceless jewels; jewellery of former monarchs that rivals anything I have ever seen or that my imagination could have conceived; dresses and ornaments and furniture and crowns and carriages, all so thickly set with invaluable stones that one gasps to think of the price. Certainly it was a most magnificent display of fabulous wealth, almost like an Arabian Nights story. I wanted to leave after seeing the first floor of it. It called to my mind a picture of blood, misery, gaunt starvation of millions of people whose very lives had been sucked away by church and state. One can well imagine what it meant to the worker who viewed it.

Of course, I had been told that the Russians had either destroyed, sold, or confiscated all the priceless gems of the past, so the irony of seeing this museum of horrors was even more intense and amusing. Naturally, besides its historical value and interest, it has a tremendous educational value for foreigners as well as Russians. No one seeing this building, heavy with riches, can draw other than one conclusion: the Revolution, in simple human terms, becomes more visually and graphically understandable.

Though Moscow still suffers severely from insufficient housing, there are workers' apartment buildings growing up everywhere, inadequate in number it is true, and hastily put together. However, they are modern, light and simple in design. The worker pays, or did at that time, for his apartment by the space he uses, averaging from ten to thirty roubles a month. We saw a lot of these and also a very impressive hospital, with all the newest medical instruments and research equipment. I was interested in an educational device in the waiting room. On an electric billboard were a series of medical questions and answers. The worker had to plug in the question then guess which was the answer and plug that in on the other side. If he had guessed correctly, there was flashed a red Correct, if not, he could try and try again.

One night before I left, two or three of us went to dinner at a hotel across the river in Moscow. The dining-room was on a top floor and overlooked the river, the city itself, the Kremlin, and the Red Square. In the setting sun the spires and domes and cupolas and minarets of the city looked fairy-like. Some of the churches had gold domes with innumerable stars on them and then a gold cross on the top From this cross were suspended gold necklaces that floated delicately down to be caught in the stars on the dome below. With the sun shimmering on them they looked like lacy, delicate, gilded cobwebs. Across from us rose the hill of the Kremlin with the stern and ancient walls around a small city of almost oriental aspect, the soft dark gold sky cut by the glittering outlines of domes and crosses, sharp spires, and one church crowned with ten golden balls that seemed almost to be jingling. One could see the shape of St. Basil's Cathedral at one end of the Red Square, fantastic in the tawny light, like a sudden vision out of the Wizard of Oz. Below us was the soft dark rim of the river, quietly flowing and encircling this part of the incredible and fascinating city.

We left the hotel, as twilight was falling, to walk back through the Red Square and to my hotel. This tremendous open paved square is one of the most beautiful in Europe. On one end is St. Basil's Cathedral whose myriad domes and spires and cupolas, coloured like an ancient and softened rainbow, was now mellow and old, hardly discernible, as if seen through a mist, twilight subduing the colours and casting a dim light on the strange structure, making the church tantalizing and rich like an old and beautiful painting under a film of dust. On another side and end were buildings used as government offices and a museum. Under the Kremlin walls is the tomb of Lenin, a tremendous structure of black stone and dark red porphyry, of stark, commanding, and unforgettable simplicity. On each side of it are long parallel lines of white stone representing the graves of the Revolutionary dead. Through the square now was silence and a soft, translucent green-grey light, like the green luminosity of fresh bright forests in early dawn. It was so thrilling that we stood still for a few minutes, without a word passing between us.

I had one more day before continuing my trip through Russia. I was reluctant and sad to leave Moscow. I felt I had only touched on the things I should have done and seen. Lenin's tomb was to be visited, but for the present his body was being treated again. When I finally did see it a few years later, it was under quite different circumstances. On a cold, bright winter day, I waited in an endless line of patient workers, a line that stretched almost the full length of the Red Square. I walked in the mausoleum and down some darkish corridors before I entered the room in which his body is placed. Under a coffin of glass, Lenin lies at full length for the view of everyone, his body marvellously preserved for many years to come. The visitor is not allowed to stop moving, but he may scrutinize closely and take very slow steps. One hand resolutely clenched by his side, a vast dome of a forehead, a scraggly reddish beard, and the most delicately modelled nose and mouth vividly recall what the Revolution's hero must have been like in life. The eyes are small, with a sharp, slanting Mongolian line, and set far apart, the face pure, beautiful. I expected to see a much fiercer and coarser face, a stronger and larger body. His build was slight, his body perhaps even smaller now than in real life (though he was a short man) because of the unavoidable shrinking that takes place in the embalming process. Though the face and skin were almost wax-like in appearance, one could sense the tense and living vitality that must have been Lenin's. The workers around me were oblivious of everything, each drinking in every smallest detail of the still figure who helped effect their freedom. There was no expression of fear, awe or superstition; only one of respect, curiosity, and warm love. A few old women sniffed. In a few moments the time was up and I was out again in the crystal-clear, cold, ringing air of a Moscow winter.

4

I had planned a trip down the Volga, so I packed my few things, said good-bye to my friends, and left on the night train for Gorki, armed with insect-powder, smelling salts, and some toilet paper I stole from my hotel. By this time I had gotten into my stride again. I felt I knew a little more about Russia and the Russians—I felt no sadness, depression, or foreignness as I did in Leningrad. I felt freer and lighter—more eased of tension than I had in over a year of European living. Adventure seemed to be calling to me for the first time in my life and my mind was open and fresh for it. I was eager to take in the discomforts, dreams, and disillusions so abundant in a country still strange and distant to me, though it had disconcerting familiarities that touched deep chords in my experience and hopes. Maybe the conscience and idealism that lie latent in most of mankind were being stimulated and awakened in me; maybe it was only the curiosity of an eager but callow girl, challenging all new experiences in sight.

On the train to Gorki that night there were only two of us who were English-speaking, in addition to my guide, of course, who spoke English fluently but with a strong accent. My travelling companion was an old man of German descent, American by citizenship, around seventy I judged, white-haired, sharp blue eyes in a sharp, puckish face, an ardent Communist who had been taking his vacation in Russia every two or three years since the Revolution. He was in some American business and seemed to be quite well off. Russia and Russians were his hobby, his weakness, his passion. He was to accompany me on my long tour down the Volga and into the Caucasus. He bored me at times with his long-winded and wildly expressed partisanship—nothing the Russians had ever done or could do was wrong!—but he was such an agreeable, gentle, and kindly old soul that I became quite fond of him.

We arrived at Gorki the next morning, safe and sound, without any bedbug bites!—and were taken for a drive over the town, which was swarming with people and crowded with markets for the collective farms surrounding the city. There was an enormous Ford factory near by but too far for us to visit. The Russians had a contract with Ford whereby they promised for a certain number of years not to put out their own models. I think the time is up now and the Russians are free to turn out their own product. When I went back for the second time I saw the most beautiful limousines that looked as comfortable and speedy as our Lincolns—the small cars as well were flooding the streets of Moscow several years later. They learned quickly—apparently with the help of the Ford factories in furnishing technicians, materials, and designs.

I remember very little about Gorki except that it was an

Lg

ancient and hot town, the birthplace of the famous Soviet
writer, Maxim Gorki, son of a simple carpenter, after whom
it was named. Formerly, it was Nishni Novgorod, the busiest
and most bustling of merchant towns in this part of the world,
where the famous Fair had been regularly held.

We spent only a few hours there but long enough to discover
that there was a Park of Culture and Rest, new factories, a
maternity hospital, modern, clean, and light workers' quarters.

My guide and I were discussing, on the way to the boat,
whether our steamer would be a new or old one. I was dismayed to see that it definitely looked as if it had been long
in service. However, I had the best accommodation possible
and a cabin to myself. It contained one bed, had a sort of
washbasin-sink, a small cracked mirror and shelf under it.
Under my bed and on the walls were long grey bugs, a bit
messy when killed, many cockroaches, whom by now I considered loyal friends, and innumerable stains all over the cabin
where other occupants had smashed various insects. Along the
wall by the side of my bed was a long dark red streak which
mystified me completely. I never did figure out what it was,
though my lurid imagination conjured up scenes of freshly
committed murder. I took the bed apart to look for bedbugs,
and, finding none, sprinkled the bed and room profusely with
my insect-powder. I felt much better, until I went to the
"ladies' room" which was primitive in that it didn't seem to
work at all. Fortunately, I had my own toilet paper. I consoled
myself with the thought that at least one doesn't have to live
in toilets—and I knew they were doing everything to make a
backward population clean and sanitary. But it took time!

We went out on deck and wandered over the whole ship.
Everything was clean, freshly painted, and attractive—so I
vowed I would reserve myself a spot outside and sleep there.
I made friends with the genial chubby Captain, a Volga
German, his mate, and an entrancing young son of six. No
one spoke anything but Russian. We had delicious food, in
fact, about the best food I had had in Russia. Caviar three
times a day, or more often if you wanted it, cucumbers in
sour cream, fresh and cooked fruits, marvellous nourishing

Russian soups, excellent meats, butter, ice-cream, fish. . . .
The hot tea drunk in glasses, ubiquitous in Russia, was served
constantly.

I took a lot of sun baths on the upper deck, tried to learn
the Russian alphabet, a few phrases, read books and wrote
letters. It was broiling hot, over 100 degrees every day, and
I suppose it was foolish of me to stay so long in the sun. In
a few days I was the colour of a freshly boiled lobster and
profusely adorned with sun-blisters. The waitress, the woman
who cleaned up my room, the Captain, and his mate all
were very worried about my sun-habits and urged me, with
many sympathetic and commanding gesticulations, to stay
in the shade.

The wide, pale, dreamy, blue river, curving softly ahead and
behind us, was heavy with traffic—all sorts of transport cargoes
including huge rafts, loaded heavily with timber. On each
side were signs of great activity, and it seemed well balanced
between the industrial and the agricultural—new collective
farms, new industrial factories, workers' apartment buildings,
parks, playgrounds, and schools.

We made a few stops for the loading or unloading of goods,
and at Kazan, the capital of the Tartar Republic, we halted for
several hours. It was a thriving industrial town, and workers
poured out from the hold with huge sacks, twice their size,
full, perhaps, of vegetables or potatoes for the market. Others
came on, equally heavily loaded. A tragic scene ensued at
one of these stops. I saw a middle-aged woman of heavy calm
features, black bobbed hair, pale, quiet, contained, approach
the gangway. She had two tremendous burdens on her back.
She paused for a moment, laid one down, laboriously found her
money tied up in a little rag hid between her breasts, opened
the sack and put it in. She then tied the sack up again, left
the other one protected by a friend of hers on the dock, and
took her burden with the money into the boat. She came back
to get the other one, obviously too heavy to be carried except
by itself. At this moment the whistle blew, the gangplank was
raised, and the scurrying peasants—I could see them running
blocks away, late for the boat—were held back by the guard

with a rope. The woman went up to the road and carried on an animated conversation with the guard but it was too late. She saw the boat begin to pull out. Then I saw a human face go insane with fear; the calm lines were ravaged and convulsed, she screamed with rage and grief, she wept, she pleaded and finally attempted to throw herself into the river.

I was horrified and shaken with pity as I saw her writhing in the hands of two guards, her precious cargo moving away from her. Very likely the little rag contained a few kopeks or roubles for which she was ready to give her life. It is unbelievable to western eyes and conceptions that such poverty can exist. For the elimination of this forever from national life, the Russian state is bending its every effort. Here along the Volga, one of the poorest sections of the vast land, one sees indications everywhere of the progress being made.

That night, while discussing this and other things, I learned that, in the years 1919–21, the Volga region experienced the most ghastly famine in Russia. In fact, until very recently, the Volga has been the worst area for periodical famines; for hundreds and hundreds of years people have died of starvation and disease. In the early years of the Revolution, crop failures resulted in ever-spreading misery throughout this area. For miles and miles around each town there was not a living thing to be seen. Dogs, cats, horses, rats, every animate thing, had been devoured by the famishing population. As things got no better, mothers would throw their children in the Volga, some would kill them and eat them, a man would kill another for a potato peeling. Then epidemic and disease set in, the remaining population became easy and tragic prey to the wave of death sweeping over the region.

One luckier family had potato peeling and occasionally black bread, as a luxury, for months and months on end. When finally relief came and they saw white bread again, they were so awed and afraid that they stood around looking at it on the table for a whole day without touching it.

At night, on deck, men and women sat up very late, the men singing in sad, pure liquid notes, the dark dreamlike river flowing slowly on, gently swishing against the boat's steady passage through the quiet water. In the daytime it is one of the broadest and most beautiful rivers I have ever seen, a colour of blue almost unmatched, and a soft blue-pearl mist floating languidly over it always. One sees it in a sort of pale blue luminous haze, moving gracefully and steadily like a sail in a slow wind, curving and straightening and curving again in a curious blue stillness; rolling, luxuriant, jewel-green hills on each side that look as if they would be soft, deep velvet to the touch. Then, nearing a town suddenly, a space cleared and a high bone-white modern building arises, rest-homes or apartments for the workers, new factories with billowing plumes of smoke, playgrounds, clubs, and hospitals like clean, strong growths on the festering body of former poverty and drabness.

We passed the town where Lenin was born and stopped at Samara, the capital of the middle Volga region. In this section the early revolutionary leader Razin started his roaring march of protest that was to reach Moscow itself. Saratov, the capital of the autonomous German Republic, the location of one of the largest combine factories in the Union, is modern and industrialized.

The scenery of the lower Volga was less and less interesting, green hills giving way to sand and clay banks. There were many cement factories and sawmills, the transport on the river became increasingly one of timber. We saw a lot of gay nude-bathing on the shores as we moved slowly on. A man with a dark, strong Caucasian face got on board at Saratov wearing a brilliant coat, like the coat of many colours in the Bible—a military aviator.

At Stalingrad, where we got off, a bustling new city with an amazing development on the outskirts—a modern workers' village—is located the second largest tractor factory in Russia. In 1932, the town had 200,000 people, now has a population of at least 400,000. I felt here the growth and importance of the newly industrialized cities of the Soviet Union, and imagine that it is only in the infancy of its development.

In terrific heat we took the train from here to Rostov, passing the monotonous flat Don Basin region, the richest mining section in the country. The architecture of the houses began to change—they were small adobe dwellings of white or mud colour with straw roofs, which had open-air ovens for cooking.

There were so many impressive things to see at Rostov that, despite the heat, I was hardly still for a moment. Milk factories, a workers' city growing up at the edge of the old city, hospitals, theatres, parks where people promenade, flirt, sing, and drink until late at night—I inspected everything, remembered the cleanliness of the workers, the medical and educational care taken of them, and couldn't help marvelling over the fact that everything good in life was being supplied for the vast majority of the population. There was no race hatred, no class antagonism, no grinding down of individuality under brutal economic laws that kept, in other countries, the poor always poorer, the rich always richer.

In the park there were joyful laughing couples dressed nicely, the men dark and handsome, white shirts with bright embroidery falling over their trousers and gracefully belted. Occasionally an army officer in simple khaki shirt and blue pants walked modestly alone or arm in arm with a comrade, singing and flirting with chattering passing girls. When I went to sleep after one o'clock, the city was still humming with activity, music was playing near by, people were talking and walking under my window, the sky was sparkling with clear fresh stars and cut cleanly with a brilliant crescent moon. As I kept travelling farther south I felt gayer and lighter, surer of myself and more at home with the people, appreciative of the striving and struggling of the masses for education and a free and prosperous life, tensely making comparisons with the smug, arrogant, militaristic automaton of Nazi Germany. I knew the progress I was witnessing had been bought at a terrific price and it was still being effected in grief and growing pains, in disillusion and sharp iron discipline—but the people themselves didn't seem to be paying the penalty. They seemed happy and free in gesture and speech, mingling with each other on a plane where human pride and dignity of work were dominant, and completely without the insane prejudice, the ever-present brutal heavy hand of the military machine.

We took the night train for Ordjonikidze, a rather large town on the edge of the Caucasus mountains. My fat, good-natured girl guide and I moved into a compartment with two army officers, but it was so untidy and dirty that I walked up and down the train until I found a cleaner one. In the meantime, my companion had told the officers my opinion of their habits. They were a little hurt but got to work immediately. They bustled about, got a broom from the conductress, swept, brushed, and tidied up the compartment, combed their hair and straightened their clothes. Then they came to the cleaner compartment we had found (the train being full to capacity and only a few women in our car), apologized humbly in Russian, asked our pardon for being such dirty, careless pigs, and then pleaded with us to join them. I was greatly touched, and of course we accepted their invitation.

Both men were charming—one a young Red Army officer, short, thin, almost completely bald, with a lively little face, who was so full of spirit and fun that he jumped and scrambled about like a monkey. They began to sing Russian army songs and folk songs to us and soon our compartment was crowded with others who came to join in the gaiety. The Russians are such communal people, both in their present and past, that they never enjoy being alone when there is any sort of community life going on. All of us sang and the train rumbled on, our voices loud and strong. The conductress, when she was not busy, stood by the door of the jammed compartment, laughing and cheering us on. Finally, they got tired of singing and started an animated conversation which was duly translated to me—about Russian women, and how they should now become softer and more feminine, the time being past for them to be and act like men.

Time came for dinner and we brought out some fresh fruit and biscuits from our package. The men offered us their wine and meat and we had a delightful picnic supper. The little monkey-man had to get off—he was going to a sanatorium in this district for a month's vacation—and we all stood by the window and waved him farewell kisses. We watched the moon for a while, streaming over the fragrant land, and finally went to bed, after I had sprayed all the berths with my insect-powder, much to the general amusement of the passengers.

There was nothing much to see in Ordjonikidze. It was blazingly hot and we rode around the city over rough roads. The men and women were darker and darker as we went south, with huge liquid black eyes and an Asiatic cast to their faces. The men wore the usual picturesque embroidered blouses and some had tall fur hats on their heads, even in this heat. It is a city of thirty-two different nationalities, and, of course, far from communized as yet. In fact, near the city, in the high mountains, one of which is among the highest in Europe, there lives an undisturbed savage mountain tribe. Their dwelling place is called the *city of the dead*. Tourists must go escorted by reliable Russian guides and by horseback. They live the primitive isolated life they led five hundred years ago. Men will kill one another for looking at each other's wives, and their wives are killed if they expose their faces. During childbirth women are thrown into cellars dug in the ground and forced to stay there two days after the child is born. Un-aided, they must bear their children, attend to themselves and the infants. They are then allowed to return to tribal life.

The night we arrived in Ordjonikidze we went to the home of the Party leader of the town—who had joined in the sing-ing on the train. It was a simple two- or three-room flat, very bare and clean. They brought out everything they had in store for visitors and friends—bread, jam, vodka, wine, tea, candy, caviar—and pressed us to eat heartily. I knew they would be disappointed if I didn't, so I ate as much as I could of their food. Other people came in, there was talk and singing and jokes. I learned a few Russian phrases and I taught them a few English ones. I was moved by their open friendliness and I finally had experienced, among complete strangers, the world-famous Russian hospitality—whereby all Russians open their homes and firesides to the utter stranger, eager to have him share all the food in the house, happy in new-found com-panionship and gaiety.

The next day we took an automobile for Tiflis, deep in Georgia, of which it is the capital. We passed through some of the wildest and most terrifying scenery I have known—not unlike parts of our Rockies. Huge, golden-coloured mountains, without foliage, sharp and fantastic in outline; fierce roaring mud-grey glacial streams in between; dark romantic-looking men riding furiously over the mountain paths on horseback, their high fur hats stiff in the wind. Many of the mountain tops were covered with snow, others shrouded with clouds. Tight under the mountain ledges were houses made out of the stone, cut deep into the mountain, like cliff dwellings with small holes for windows. These and the ruins of monasteries, castles and fortresses called to mind a dark wild world of proud mountaineers and peasants whose ways and past are unknown to Western civilization.

We stopped at a little village for lunch and had shashlik, a native Caucasian meat dish cooked in small pieces on sticks before an open fire. The toilet here was a hole in the ground with a pail underneath!

On our way again, with only one blowout, we ascended higher—the mountains magnificent and forbidding. The air was cold in the lungs, almost like breathing in crystal spring water—7,700 feet high we were. There was little sign of the new order in these sections. Occasionally a young Communist pioneer camp, a picture of Lenin or Stalin, a new building or modern house, the hammer and sickle, but on the whole the region looked dark, isolated—the people proud, primitive.

As we came close to Tiflis the scenery was not so frightening, the huge masses of rock gave way to high mountains covered with woods. We stopped and drank a little Narzan from the river that flowed down the mountains and trickled under our car wheels. The famous sparkling mineral water comes from this source.

As we neared Tiflis I saw a strange study in contrasts. On top of the mountain was a glittering golden dome and the ruins of an ancient monastery. Underneath this was an enormous picture of Lenin and behind him a gigantic water power plant. The inference was very impressive.

The city of a half-million people is set in a valley between high, bare, tawny-coloured mountains, with ridges and corrugations in them like a mountain relief map, and by the side of a river whose source is in the Caucasus and whose end in the Caspian Sea. The city was formerly divided into three sections, Persian, Armenian, and Georgian, each with its own culture, populations and customs, each an economic and social entity, bound by walls and fortresses. Now all this is changed and the populations mingle freely, though they keep their languages, religions, customs as of old. The city dates from the fifth century and is most curiously beautiful. Twenty different nationalities live in Tiflis and it is the crossroads of the East and West.

The men and women are especially striking-looking in this section of Russia, with dark, finely and strongly cut faces, and black burning eyes; the men are dressed in white blouses and brilliant many-coloured little caps on their dark hair, and the women with veils over their faces because of the heat. During the days I was there the temperature stayed around 113 degrees and I myself wore a chiffon veil over my face. The sun was scorching and prickly, as if millions of small burning needles were piercing the skin.

There are occasional signs of Soviet progress here—new schools and museums, technological institutes, power plants, and hospitals, but the look of the city is still ancient, though prosperous and clean. We drove up to a high hill outside the city and saw Tiflis lying quietly between the golden mountains, still, lifeless, burning in the soft inhuman haze of heat. The sun shone and shimmered on the gold and silver domes scattered throughout the city, the river was a winding shining thread of quicksilver.

We walked through Tiflis and saw the Persian bazaars, the Armenian section, the strange oriental balconies looking out over the river, the bizarre and gaudy churches, drank Narzan at street corners, rested in a cool green park.

A few nights later we took the night train for Batoum. The moon was a luminous soft bright veil flung over wild, golden coloured mountains. We sped across the stirring Russian earth towards the Black Sea.

In Batoum, an almost sub-tropical town but much cooler because of the sea-breeze, beautifully located, we visited the botanical garden and an oil refinery works. The Russian oil is transported through underground pipes from Baku on the Caspian Sea to Batoum where it is exported. This apparently languid jewel-coloured town was the centre of great export and import activity. The view of the sea, from the botanical garden, with the Anatolian mountains in the background—the gateway of Asia—challenges anything I have seen on the Riviera.

The boats in the harbour looked like enormous painted toys set up on a sparkling artificial sea. We boarded our steamer at night, along with many peasants heavily loaded with their goods. I had a lovely cabin with only a few cockroaches. Before going to bed I took one last look at the enormous glowing moon with a black cloud floating in its radiant path, the sea dark and endless under its light. There were glittering little lights, necklace-strung, on the shore, and the friendly sound of a southern port, the busy shouting dock-workers, and the chattering of peasants.

We had two or three days on the boat. It was crowded; all the room space from top to bottom, and the deck space as well, littered with peasants and workers who slept wherever they could find an inch of space. The scenery all along the bright calm blue sea was magnificent: tall, heavily-wooded mountains; tropical foliage in the port towns; gleaming beaches where men and women bathed nude, gleaming in their dark copper-coloured skin.

We stopped for the loading and unloading of cargo outside of Gagri, a small sub-tropical town on the Black Sea. Many boats came from the town to meet our steamer. The sea was a bit rough, the boat swaying heavily, black clouds lay heavily on the horizon, sharp gleaming knives of lightning tearing through them, and a space of glittering stars above us. Enormous swinging spirals of black smoke burst from the smoke-stack in a conflagration of small red sparks—like fireworks seen in a nightmare. The wind changed and the smoke blew in black clouds on each side of the boat. Below us, through the flame and smoke, were the moving twisting bodies of the workers unloading, rowing back and forth, roaring and shouting and standing up. It was like a living scene from the *Inferno*, wild, dark, impressive.

The mountains at night were like huge soft black animals crouching, the lights of the cities sparkling underneath. It was one of the most exciting trips I had taken and I could well understand how the Black Sea got its name from the fierce churning storms in the winter.

The evidence of socialism was plentiful along the Black Sea coast. In almost every city one could see new buildings and factories, docks under construction, the life active, cheerful, reawakened, constructive. We passed by the green, bear-shaped mountain where the great Pushkin lived.

Finally, we arrived in Jalta, one of the loveliest cities in Russia, a summer resort set in gem-green mountains by the sapphire sea. Here formerly, and in its environs, were the magnificent palaces of the Czar, dazzling white structures against the burning blue sky, partly hidden by luxuriant foliage. They were now all, without exception, rest homes and sanatoria for the workers and peasants.

I bathed a lot on the pebble beaches, visited one nude-bathing beach, rode in a droshky out to the Crimean Tartar towns, saw strange and beautiful types of men and women, slim bronze-black bodies of children with gleaming silver hair. At night the moon streamed over the Black Sea; men and women promenaded by the water, the rose ends of cigarettes like captive fireflies in the hands of the smokers.

On the way to Sebastopol, outside of Jalta, we stopped for a moment at the house of Chekov, an attractive white cottage in a valley cup near tall green mountains, where the great writer lived while he was sick with tuberculosis. This beautiful region of the Crimean coast provides ideal rest homes and cures for long diseases—it is high, dry, and warm, and near fresh sea breezes. As such it is used now by the Soviets —there is no industrialization here, only farming, vineyard cultivation, innumerable sanatoria where peasants and workers from all over the Union spend two weeks to a month in the summer. The Caucasus section is also thickly strewn with sanatoria and rest homes, where the regimen is strict, organized according to the best and newest scientific discoveries. The drive along the coast under the shadow of the brilliant green mountains studded with glistening white palaces—the Black Sea Riviera—is strikingly lovely.

We stopped for a day at Sebastopol, near the site of the Charge of the Light Brigade, a sizzling, odoriferous, disagreeable town, and then took the steamer for Odessa. I was rather exhausted by the heat and the strenuous programme I had been following the past month so I took it easy the last few days of the trip. From Odessa, an ideally located town on the sea, thriving and prosperous-looking, we took the train for Kiev, the capital of the vast and rich Ukraine region so hungered for by the Germans. Here again were innumerable signs of Soviet construction work—industrialization of backward areas, hospitalization for workers, parks and entertainment facilities, better housing conditions. In Kiev is the marvellous ancient monastery, now a museum, which once owned and exploited 56,000 serfs—the land now successfully collectivized. The incomparable Sofia Cathedral was being repaired when I was there, though I was able to see it. The pillars were covered with old and mellowed frescoes, the church full of priceless and carefully preserved icons, the domes a marvel of gold and green, starred, criss-crossed and bespangled. Inside one cupola I saw an enormous madonna in gold mosaics, a dream of golden splendour and endless patient exquisite work, partially hidden with scaffolding where the Soviets were cleaning and repairing it.

Since papers took long to arrive in southern Russia, and I could not read the native ones, I heard only indirectly from friends of Dollfuss's murder and then, a little later, of Hindenburg's death. In view of the recent bloody days I had witnessed before I left Berlin and the general subsequent unrest, I felt that international and internal conditions must be rather critical. There was no way of knowing how the Austrians and

Italians might retaliate at this time; there was no way of knowing the repercussions that might come from the death of Germany's "Wooden Titan."

5

I hated to leave Russia but my time was up there, and things were brewing "at home." I had finally seen, and seen rather thoroughly, and certainly to the satisfaction of my own curiosity, the country constantly compared to Nazi Germany by outsiders, constantly reviled, passionately feared and detested by the Nazis themselves. I had come to several important conclusions for myself.

One: Russia was almost like a democratic country in spirit and in plans, and though poverty and dictatorship methods were still apparent, the people seemed to be getting a squarer deal, on a progressively better standard of living, than the Germans. For instance, statistics showed that wages were going down or remaining static in Germany while the cost of living was ever higher, while in Russia the wages were slowly being raised and the cost of living lowered. When I went back several years later there were no bread cards anywhere, bread and food were piled plentifully in all the stores, people were wearing better clothes and shoes, and more supplies of all sorts of goods were available for everybody. As time went on in Germany food cards became compulsory in the winter, supplies of meat, butter, eggs, were stringently limited, the price of clothing and other necessities of life—which by the way were being supplied from substitute elements and materials—was much higher. These are simple observations on the working-out of different economic systems, but just as telling, nevertheless.

Two: I saw in Russia no indication whatsoever of racial discrimination, either against the Jews or against any other group or national minorities.

Three: Though religious attendance in Russia had been greatly diminished, churches were still open for those who wanted to help pay for a priest, and science everywhere was being substituted. In Germany, religion was being liquidated without the reason the Russians had originally. The German church, Protestant and Catholic, never exploited the masses and joined hands with a corrupt state to bleed them to death as did the Russian Orthodox church, one of the most decadent institutions the modern world has known. And the Germans, far from substituting science and a better life, were offering Thor for God, Valhalla for heaven, ancient barbaric Germanic heroes for Christian saints.

Four: the Russians were a definitely going concern, proving the success of socialism within one country and offering a threat to Nazi Germany whose people had always been socialistic and who were the dupes of a fake socialism Hitler and his associates had cooked up to get into power. No wonder there was hysterical fear among the deceivers of the German people.

Five: Though there was a powerful Red Army in Russia, there were no signs of its arrogance or militarism. There was no permeation of army propaganda in the Russian masses as far as one could see, while in Germany every day, and in every town, city, or country scene, one could see the insolence of army groups—the Reichswehr, the S.S., the S.A., the Goering Police, the regular police, and innumerable other branches whipping the psychology of the masses into imperialistic ambitions and persecution manias.

Six: Russia made no threats, either direct or implied, upon other nations, expressed no desire to gobble up either the territory or the people of any other country. The German government, on the other hand, daily made solemn and ugly speeches, either through Hitler or some of his spokesmen, on their *right* to the territories and populations and economic resources of any number of lands. They were snarling at Austria, Czechoslovakia, and the Ukraine; they tried to intimidate, by flattery and dove-like sweetness, the Balkans and the Baltic countries and Poland.

What is even more important than speeches and propaganda, is the ideology underlying the German regime, an ideology which acknowledges Germany's sacred right to all her populations throughout the world, including those in South Africa,

South America, and the United States. In the Nazi way of thinking it is Germany's duty and privilege to seek an outlet for her crowded nation, her right to monopolize and exploit the economic riches of other countries in an attempt to revive her desperate industries and inadequate agricultural produce.

Finally, to know conclusively that there are incontrovertible differences between Socialism and Nazism, one has only to read the literature on the subject. No matter how difficult the names of Marx, Lenin and Stalin might seem to some people, their writings show quite different logic and ideals from those of Hitler, Rosenberg, Goering and Goebbels, the war-lords of German Fascism.

After straightening all this out in my mind and having some personal proof in my observations, I could better understand what prompted German fear and lies in connection with the Soviet Union. I still disliked dictatorship in all its manifestations, and deplored the bureaucracy inherent in it, but I did recognize that there existed many profound differences in these two types of dictatorship.

Outside of the interesting economic system I had just seen in action, I was fascinated by the hugeness of this area of the earth's soil, the hundreds of different races and nationalities living under one control, the strange types of faces, the extremities in climate, customs, dress, religion, and language. Russia was a composite of Europe, of Asia, the Near East, and the farthest Arctic north, both in territory and racial types. It was a sort of Marco Polo voyage of discovery for me, and opened vistas of experience, adventure, and curiosity. I had been by this time in my life in one-third of the world!

After finishing with the tiresome Customs officials of both Russia and Poland and riding through dreary and dreadfully poor sections of Poland, we stopped for an hour in Warsaw, and finally arrived in Berlin. I had been a little sick with dysentery and had lost a few pounds, but I was browner than anyone I had seen in Berlin, healthy and strong. I put on a colourful Caucasian cap and hopped from the train. My parents looked at me askance for a moment and then embraced me. They hadn't for a short second recognized their prodigal and black child, scorched from the Russian sun, with her brilliant Asiatic cap!

They were all eager to know my impressions, and I was plying them with questions about Germany. Revolution didn't seem as imminent as I thought it was. Dollfuss had been brutally murdered by Austrian Nazis instructed from Munich and Berlin, and Italian troops had mobilized on the border. But nothing further happened and all was quiet again.

My father, along with the other diplomats, had been invited to attend the funeral services of Hindenburg. Accompanied, and practically guarded, by two young S.S. men, he rode in a diplomatic train to Tannenburg. He said the young men were amazingly solicitous as to his welfare, practically offered valet services, and scarcely left him alone a moment. Not liking the profuse attentions, he asked them for a little privacy. They retired, quite disappointed—as they and my father later told me—not to hear answers to their subtle and veiled questions. They were no doubt expressly assigned this job—all diplomats were pestered with them—in an attempt, not very clever it seemed to everybody, to find out what the diplomats were privately thinking and feeling about recent events inside and outside of Germany.

The celebration of Tannenburg was one of the most magnificent of Nazi "circuses." Warlike and full of pomp, my father said it resembled more of a military display and threat than it did a funeral. Much of the service dealt with the World War and Hindenburg's part in it, and with a glorification of ancient and modern Nazi Germany. My father was irritated and annoyed by these barbaric ceremonies of splendour, superstition, and chauvinism, and always attended them with real reluctance—when he attended them at all. Quite often he declined on grounds of health—and it was true that sitting for hours upon hours in all kinds of weather, listening and watching the Nazis proclaim their world ambitions, was a physical strain for anyone.

Berlin's social season was somewhat quieter though it never really stopped. Diplomats, after short trips home, would come back and take mansions in the country where they continued

MG

monotonous social affairs even in the hottest and dullest of
seasons. Furthermore, for us there was never real rest from
these obligations since the summer was the season when
Americans chose to visit Europe. We had to be on hand at
least some of the time.

However, my mother was very tired and nervous from
events of the summer, both social and political, so she, my
brother, and I decided to go to southern Germany for a
month's relaxation.

We stayed for a while by a beautiful lake near Munich and
then went on to Oberammergau to see the Passion Play. My
father joined us for a few days and we attended the long sessions of the famous play. It was a bit too "touristy" for my
taste and my father detected subtle Nazi propaganda in the
way they handled the Judas-Christ scenes—an attempt to
recall the Roehm-Hitler fracas! We were amused to see long-
bearded men walking about the streets, in training for their
play, and also I suspect for the tourists. I didn't like the fake
atmosphere of the town, though it was one of the most physically charming ones I have seen in Germany. I tried to imagine
how lovely, simple and exciting it would be in another season
—even in the winter—but for the moment I couldn't over-
come my disappointment in the avaricious natives and the
affectations of the village—dressed up in its Sunday best, in
frills and furbelows for the benefit of foreigners. I was surprised to hear a very intelligent German hotel manager repeat
all the myths about Roehm's treachery and his suddenly discovered immorality. I told him I thought it was ridiculous.
He looked around slyly to see if anyone overheard me, then
pressed my arm and nodded his head, a gleam of warmth and
friendship in his eyes.

My father had to return to his duties in Berlin so the rest
of our family drove on to Vienna, Salzburg and Budapest.
Mother was as thrilled as we had been the year before by
the musical festival and the city, even though it was crowded
beyond capacity. In Budapest, one of the loveliest cities in
Europe, we met an old Hungarian friend who showed us
around. We noticed, in his attitude and in the reports he gave

of Hungarian and European affairs, that the game of Nazi power-politics had definitely been successfully played here. The Hungarians, even this soon after the Nazis were in power, were being persuaded that the fulfilment of their hopes and destiny lay in a Nazi-Hungarian alliance. Their Revisionist League—Fascist in implication, if not more—with its territorial ambitions, felt that Germany would restore part of their soil, then in Czechoslovakia.

Being terribly poor and bankrupted by the war, their nation divided up among her neighbours, their potential anti-Semitism was being driven out of hiding, and you found a ruling class trying desperately to pin the consequences of their exploitation and economic and military failure upon the Jews. More terrified of socialism than of national annihilation, the landed and industrial gentry put their faith in Hitler. In the following years, and up to this moment, the Hungarians, or rather the rulers of the Hungarian people, have come closer and closer to Hitler—though at one time they had the courage to nip in the bud the Nazi putsch said to have been planned by von Neurath's son-in-law. The two countries, amid pomp and circumstance, are continually exchanging visits between their high officials. Recently the Hungarians have found their alliance with Hitler highly profitable and have received a sizeable slice from the now dismembered Czechoslovakia.

But, despite this, I enjoyed my visit there. On the two sides of the muddy Danube river, Buda and Pest have grown up into a flourishing single city. The Hungarians, descended from a Magyar race, speak one of the most difficult tongues in Europe—Finnish, with its Mongolian origin, being the only comparable language. At night, when the impressive government buildings and ancient palaces are illuminated, and the river is glowing from reflected light, it is as fantastic and romantic as you can find among the modern European cities.

We came back to Berlin fresh and renewed, ready for another year packed full of excitement. The steady, infuriatingly boring social events could not lessen our ardour in anticipating world events. Berlin was certainly the increasingly important centre.

Hitler was now all-powerful. He had practically destroyed the influence of the S.A., he had in his incomparable way disposed of all opposition in any direction, left, right or middle, he had taken on Hindenburg's role of President as well as retaining his own as Chancellor. Hindenburg was supposed to have left a will in which he appointed von Papen, or perhaps a Hohenzollern, for whom he always had a hankering and a weakness, as his successor. Von Papen did not get a chance to see the old man until after his death, so he will never know what Hindenburg had intended for his favourite. Hindenburg, the mediocre soldier; the venerable idol of Germany who was far from unimpeachable, though surely venerable; the man who has become a curiously heroic legend; the man who, with the collaboration of von Papen, handed over Germany to Adolph Hitler, was dead and dead at the right moment. Hitler never need worry about him or fear a clumsy over-honest exhortation or revelation from him. He could elaborate on the legend, he could put his own hopes and ambitions, counsel and advice, to the German people through the Old Man's mouth. He need not be jealous of him. Hindenburg was safely dead, and his will in the pocket of the sly, unprincipled, pig-faced von Meissner who was known to have the happy faculty of surviving every Reich, of turning up miraculously and always safe on every fortuitous occasion.

Von Meissner transported the will from Neudeck to Berlin and is supposed to have laid it in the lap of Goebbels. After an embarrassingly long time, the will was made public. The Great Old Man had graciously pointed to Hitler as the saviour of his well-loved country, and Hitler modestly bowed his head and took the noble and unsought-for burden upon his heroic shoulders.

VIII

NAZI PERSONALITIES

I HAD A SPEAKING, or nodding, acquaintance with most of the Nazi leaders and their hangers-on. I saw Hitler in informal surroundings only that one time Hanfstaengl introduced me, but I saw him regularly at military parades, operas, a few social gatherings and every other day at the Olympic Games when I sat in the diplomatic box almost under his nose.

From seeing him and talking to him the first year, watching his picture every few days, in the newspaper and regularly on the screen, I felt I had a pretty accurate picture of him, though I was completely unprepared for the change of his face and bearing at the end of four years. So imperceptibly did the change seem to take place that only by comparing the early photographs and the recent ones does one realize what power and the unscrupulous and brutal wielding of it can do to the human countenance. It is not an ageing process, for Hitler looks no older than when he seized power. In place of the rather slender body, pale, soft, neurotic face, modest bearing, self-conscious social self-effacement, is a figure whose bearing is insolent and arrogant, with shoulders flung back pompously, who walks and marches as though he had made the earth under his feet and the people around him whom he honours with the fantastic taut outstretched arm. His face, at least in public, is harsher, the jaw underslung. His voice has become much harder and firmer, though of course the hysterical and incomprehensible guttural recurs when he is under stress. His doctor, the eminent surgeon Sauerbruch, is supposed to have diagnosed cancer of the throat—it turned out to be a comparatively harmless polyp on the larynx. Hitler may have had fears of cancer and consequently avoided too much straining of his vocal chords. In any case, whether through egotism and a sense of his own rare value or through anxiety, the voice revealed the same type of change as occurred in his features and bearing.

Hitler's haughty and supercilious air of self-confidence and the personal brand of absolute dictatorship he flaunts, make him more impressive, less ridiculous, especially after one becomes immune to the moustache, but infinitely more dangerous to people who watch and observe him. At one time he seemed to be well-loved by the German people; they even broke into spontaneous applause in the cinema when his picture was shown. In the last two years I was in Berlin, the audiences watched attentively and listened carefully, but there was a tense silence when he had finished speaking or marching. Only once or twice in all that time was there a scattered applause. When Mussolini was in Berlin in 1937 his speech and picture were flashed on the screen at the same time as Hitler's. When Mussolini was shown gesticulating wildly, his jaw thrust forward until it looked like that of a mad bull-dog, both ridiculous and maddening, the audiences burst into spontaneous derisive laughter, and I even heard a few muttered irreverent comments. When Hitler's picture appeared on the screen there was again that living silence. Of course, the Berlin-Rome axis was profoundly unpopular with the average German and he may have taken this opportunity to express his displeasure. However, there is no doubt that Hitler's transformation in manner and looks is noticed by everyone.

I don't pretend to know enough medically or psychologically to explain Hitler's personality. There are other books which give interesting medical and psychiatric interpretations and diagnoses of Hitler and his movement, including Schumann's excellent "The Nazi Dictatorship" and John Gunther's "Inside Europe."

My mother several times sat very near to him and observed that in social gatherings he was either glum and wordless or quite charming and informal. On various occasions he was more than cordial to young movie stars who hovered around him. A friend of mine, a rather sensational, sport-loving feminist, had an informal lunch with him in Munich. She said that he talked quite like a normal man for the first third of the lunch, then suddenly got off in a frenzy on a pet subject of his, and continued in a long and impassioned monologue, scarcely touching his meagre vegetable fare but giving his guests an opportunity to eat their food leisurely.

During the Olympic Games which my father only saw the end of, I took his ticket and went to the back of the box and was consequently closer to Hitler. I watched him, of course, as much as I did the field events. He came almost every day during the track meets and watched day by day the marvellous performance of American athletes. The winner of whatever event was on usually went up to his box to be congratulated; however, when Owens or other coloured competitors from America won, he was conveniently out of his box. One day the American flag went up at least five times, almost in succession, and of course everyone in the stadium was forced to rise and remain standing until the National Anthem was finished. Hitler saluted with arm outstretched and with a dour expression on his face. However, if a German would win, his enthusiasm and good humour were boundless and he would spring to his feet with wild and childish joy. In him, in his face and bearing, there was not the slightest indication that he knew what good sportsmanship meant, or had any appreciation or understanding of sport for its own sake. The Olympic Games to him were a Germanic affair, pure and simple, and it was on this basis that he received and encouraged the German winners.

Once Tom Wolfe sat in the diplomatic box. When Owens won a particularly conspicuous victory, Tom let out a warwhoop. Hitler twisted in his seat, looked down, attempting to locate the miscreant, and frowned angrily. It was the Nazi attitude, which I once heard expressed by a supposedly intelligent assistant of von Ribbentrop, to consider Negroes as animals, and utterly unqualified to enter the Games. This young man elaborated his thesis, saying that, of course, if the Germans had had the bad sportsmanship to enter deer or another species of fleet-footed animal, they could have taken the honours from America in the track events. He added that it was an unfair advantage we took when we let non-humans, like Owens and other Negro athletes, compete with fine human Germanic products, and that it should not have been allowed by Olympic officials! I was disgusted at this revelation of vicious stupidity but I reflected that this attitude of theirs, slightly modified, applies to anyone not a member of Aryan Nazidom. There is no argument possible with such people.

If I were to sum up Hitler's character in a few words, I would say that he is one of the most fanatical and nearly-insane men ruling in any country of the modern world. He obviously has his charming and delightful moments, though he has never been known to be either witty, brilliant or wise in his conversations. With his manias, obsessions and fantasies, he seized on a German population bitter in defeat, torn asunder by the squabbles and criminal disunion of its democratic parties, was financed and supported by elements always dissatisfied with democratic rule—the Junkers and landlords, the rich but idle industrialists and the bankers, the conservatives of whatever ilk desiring "safe" government, and even the pathetic liquidated Hohenzollerns. He came to power with a poorly concealed arson trick, backed by irresponsible gangsters whom the World War had displaced in the German social set-up, promised freedom to the working class and prosperity to the bourgeoisie. All these facts are well known historically by now but it is well to remember them as one watches betrayal after betrayal enacted to the peril of European civilization, and it is especially pertinent to those forces of reaction in every country, including our own. The privileged classes, the business men, industrialists and bankers all over the world are taking warning as to what has happened even to them and their class in Nazi Germany. Everyone knows the fate of the rich Jews who once supported and gave huge contributions to the Nazi movement in an attempt to safeguard their fortunes, but apparently there are some wealthy Jews in America who close their eyes to these facts.

It is idle pastime to try to distinguish between the true and false legends about Hitler's private life. He loved his mother, hated his father, had no connection at all with his brothers and sisters—his half-sister, about whom Hitler never speaks, was found as a cook in a Jewish household. A woman cousin killed herself in his apartment. Hanfstaengl's sister, Hanfstaengl's wife, Frau Cosima Wagner, titled aristocrats, actresses—for instance, the talented and sharp-hearted Leni Riefensthal, movie director—were all his friends and admirers —simple and high-born, beautiful and ugly women. Strangely enough, there has been no proof that Hitler has ever slept with a woman. Before the Nazis seized power their enemies were rabidly on the trail for any sort of damaging evidence against him—but they found nothing either unnatural, interesting, or abnormal in his physical relations—except perhaps the abnormality of finding nothing.

It is also unproved that Hitler is homosexual. It is true, however, that many men around him, formerly and at the present time as well, are homosexuals. Talking recently with one of Europe's best psychoanalysts, who knows the European scene thoroughly, I was told that Hitler is suffering from an acute castration complex, which explains both his intense fear and frigidity towards women, and his envy and hatred of the Jews who were once a benighted, weak, and impotent minority— in a position quite comparable, psychologically, with his own earlier frustrated state—and who became powerful and valuable in the economic and cultural life of Germany, to such an extent as to become partially assimilated.

In diplomatic circles, in salon gossip, there was complete bafflement about Hitler's private life. Names fly back and forth, of both men and women, but the association with his name lasts only a few days or weeks. In the spring of 1938 the young Princess Marie of Savoy, the daughter of the King of Italy, was linked in news items with Hitler. But these rumours die from lack of proof of any type. People who have known Hitler for many years say that he will never marry; it is now too late, both from his own utter lack of interest and because of the peculiar and revered position he had as a saintly bachelor.

I believe that Hitler is completely asexual. Psychologically, his sudden frenzy over Roehm and other sexual perverts, his fanatic revulsion, the hunting down and closing of any night club where homosexuals met, might indicate a tortured envy, a vicious revenge against the satisfaction of a desire he could never face in himself.

Most men in the past and present, world leaders, statesmen and soldiers, have had personal and love lives which are open books for the curious to read. Mussolini is noted for his licentious behaviour with women and makes no special effort to conceal it. Stalin has been married twice and seems quite willing to admit it. Mustafa Kemal was not very careful about revealing his love for men and women alike. Chiang Kai-shek has a lovely wife with whom he lives, apparently, in happiness. But Hitler has neither man nor woman lover, neither paramour nor wife, and no clear emotional attachment to men— unless one might question the fanatic and furiously loyal friendship of Hess.

Denied normal sexual and emotional outlets, Hitler, with the passionate, introverted, Catholic background which he betrayed, the thwarted mother complex, and the Jewish obsession, has turned his wrath not upon himself but upon a nation of people and a world at large, where vengeance can be wreaked, his own agony of asceticism expressed in a whirl-wind of rage, in cruelty and sadism scarcely known in the annals of any nation's history. This may account for his ruthless, relentless, and useless persecutions of all elements of the populations, for the fanatic joy in torture itself experienced both actually by Hitler himself and vicariously through the reign of terror he knows to be existing in all of Germany, in her concentration camps and prisons.

One sees the madness, the betrayals, the complete lack of wisdom or intellectuality in Hitler's face, and of course it is impossible to look at him objectively if one knows any of the inner workings either of his own methods or those of his machine. He had shrewd and diabolical advisers, like Neurath, Dieckhoff, and others in the foreign office, who are known to the world to be at least more moderate men than Hitler. But with Hitler, and, of course, with the system he protects, rests the absolute power—a state of affairs that did not exist early in his dictatorship. In his gestures, in his pompous strutting before his troops, in his saluting of wildly cheering crowds which works like a drug on his diseased brain, one recognizes a man in dire necessity of psychiatric treatment, who is now the head of a powerful state, and who menaces, sometimes effectively, sometimes hollowly, the modern world. His dream of power and glory have shaped his face and figure; they must have shaped his mind as well. He himself thinks his will and wisdom irreproachable, peerless, indomitable, because they have worked so many times—one triumph leads to another. Hitler has sometimes the wiliness of a cat, at other times the blundering and brutality of a bull; he constructs the carefully designed plots, deviously and intricately devised, that madmen are known to create; he has the plans of a wishful thinker, a malevolent child. He will seek his Holy Grail of a Nazified Europe and a Hitlerized Nazidom if, in his fevered dreams, he must first wade through the mire, blood, and the war-inferno of a devastated Europe. These things are to be read in his face, still soft and degenerate despite its harsher lines of power, and in the fatal Napoleonic strut. These are facts recognized by every diplomat and student who has observed the German scene from the inside for any length of time. Europe and the world must see that an answer is given before it is too late.

In this brooding tantrum-torn creature, whose model for himself and for his nation he finds in the barbaric dark legends Wagner has put to music, there is a perverse logic and an uncanny power to play upon mass psychology. He cannot be dismissed lightly with the accusations " fanatic," "insane," "psychopathic"—though these threads are woven into the fabric of his mind and emotion. Hitler learned a lot from his enemies within Germany; he learned a lot from Mussolini; he has borrowed technique from innumerable sources to realize his twisted passions for self-aggrandizement and aggrandizement of the Germanic race. Though the overwhelming blame must be laid upon his shoulders and upon those who made possible his seizure of power for the return of Germany to barbarism and Medievalism, the whole story cannot be told without examining the men around him, men whose lives are as distorted and maimed as his own.

2

Hermann Goering, known as Nazi No. 2 (at last counting, Minister President of Prussia, Reich's Minister of Aviation, Chief of the German Air Force, Field Marshal, General of the Prussian State Police, President of the Reichstag, President of the Prussian State Council, Minister of Forestry, Minister of the Hunt—with at least one uniform for each of these offices), has as strange and varied a record as Hitler. Of excellent social background, with wealth and position at his disposal, he entered the War and soon became one of the most sensational air-aces of his time. Next to Richthofen, who had Jewish blood in his veins, Goering shot down more enemy 'planes than anyone in this amazing daredevil squadron. Still in his adolescence, his diet was the blood, horror, murder, and flames of aerial warfare. Slender, blond, handsome, brave, he thrived on the madness of killing; his senses were strangely and powerfully thrilled; his mind twisted, broken, dependent upon the lust of death, upon the excitement and stimulation of cruelty carried out in line of duty towards a vague and sacred Fatherland.

During the war he received a vicious wound. Though some people say he took dope before he was wounded, I am inclined to believe from what I have heard that the drug habit developed later, perhaps in self-protection from the initial horrible pain. In any case, it is a well known fact that he was a dope-fiend for many years and that he and his epileptic wife were denied the right to her child by a former marriage because of his habit and her illness. He was sent to, or voluntarily entered, in 1925, according to records, an asylum for the mentally unbalanced in Sweden where apparently he was cured of his drug addiction.

A journalist friend of mine in Berlin told me that he was convinced that Goering was still a slave of the narcotic habit. This man is quite friendly towards Goering, has entertained

him and seen him on innumerable occasions. He said frequently he had watched him under the influence of cocaine,
and as he came out of it. In public gatherings and celebrations, in the reviewing of parades, in fact at any time when
many hours elapsed without the possibility of escape, the
ebullience and brilliance, the liveliness and energy wore off
into a heavy sodden mood of passivity and depression, the
eyes becoming distant and glazed. However, it is useless to
speculate whether or not Goering still indulges in this
degenerating habit because there is no way to prove it, with
censorship and silence imposed so strictly on such information.
It is interesting nevertheless to know that most people suspect
he does. These facts may seem personal and intimate in the
extreme, but they are important as related to the character
and rash behaviour of one of the most powerful Nazis—and
they throw some additional light on his past, present, and
possible future action.

Goering looks podgy and ridiculous from afar but close up
he is more than that. Of medium height, his once slender
body has been transformed into a huge, paunchy blob of
flesh, lumpy and protruding in places. The once finely cut
face is now lost in rolls of fat; the cheeks like swollen growths
under wide-set blue eyes, which are cold as snakes; the chin
a curious protuberance; all line, beauty or bone structure
vanished in a coarse and florid cushion euphemistically named
a face. One can well understand the bitter irony underlying
the famous joke, told by the German people of a typical Nazi,
in which one must be "as thin as Goering."

After having known Emmy Sonnemann, an actress, for
several years, he was married to her two years ago. This
relationship was the constant source of interesting gossip for
bored and tight-laced diplomats. Hitler disapproved of the
gossip about Goering's illicit relations (first revealed authorita-
tively to me by Jules Sauerwein the first summer I was in
Germany), called a halt to Goering's "affair," and commanded
him either to give her up and live decently or to marry her.

Goering took Emmy on one trip he made to the Balkans
and tried to force the highest society in each of these countries

to accept her, invite her along with him, and give her the homage that would be due to his wife. These royal and diplomatic circles refused to do it and when Goering returned to Berlin he was reprimanded for his presumption, and had his future course of action mapped out for him.

Emmy Sonnemann is a gracious blonde woman, over thirty-five, with coils of golden hair wound around her head, blue eyes and a more than generous figure, a German's idea of a Gretchen grown properly matronly. Her blooming lines and her nice but not intelligent face do not detract from a certain poise and bright cheerfulness she reveals in social gatherings. I remember one tea she gave for a limited number of diplomats, to which my mother and I were invited. We came into the lavishly furnished palace of the Goerings on Leipsiger Platz, and finally found the reception room. Sitting at small tables were the wives and daughters of diplomats and a few German women of high position. Frau Goering was very informal in manner, sat on the arms of the couches and chairs, leaned over her guests and carried on an affectedly naive and delightful conversation, her ruddy face and golden coils of hair very charming. She talked intimately of her husband, calling him by his first name, shyly referring to what he had promised her for Christmas. Frau Goering is the first lady of the land—Hitler being wifeless—and attempts, I suppose, to make her formidable and apparently wildly adored husband more human and understandable to cynical diplomats. She fulfills her role with enough dignity and a fulsome though somewhat monotone of charm.

My mother became rather attached to her—she had to see her quite often, not only at formal affairs, but privately when she took around newly arrived people in our staff or in the corps—and felt that she was a person much superior to Goering.

That same afternoon, Goering himself came in from the office, rotund and breezy, and stood buxomly around greeting the women guests, in his rather badly acted role of naive confusion. The scene was a little too wholesome, homey and cozy for my mother and me. We took another look at the heavy brutal face with the icy merciless eyes, glanced casually again at the Cranachs adorning his living-room walls, stolen from the museum, and went away.

My mother had a story which she told with inimitable humour and with infinite elaborations. She was forced to sit, at one of the innumerable formal concerts given regularly by the Italian Embassy and a source of deep boredom to the entire diplomatic corps, directly behind General Goering and unfortunately very close to him. He was dressed in formal attire—a uniform for the air corps which he is said to have designed himself. The coat of the uniform fits very snugly, open in front and tight as wax in the back, following the outline of the body and leaving the buttocks free in a sort of heart-shaped design. After she had greeted him and passed on to some other group, she turned around and was shocked to see the expanse of tightly clothed flesh, three times the size of an ordinary man. As they sat down to listen to the music she realized with horror that he was in front of her, attempting to place his rear as comfortably and safely as possible on the delicate little gold chairs they have for such occasions. Her account of her uneasiness throughout the concert was delightful —she described her fear that at any moment he might burst through the chair and into her lap. She was so distracted at the sight of the huge portions rolling off the sides and edges of the chair, so perilously near to her, she couldn't remember a single piece that was played!

Another story that caused much amusement in Berlin and, of course, spread rapidly as do all stories detrimental to Nazi leaders, was based on fact, and occurred, if I am not mistaken, when the Lindberghs were visiting Goering. Goering was dressed immaculately in a beautiful white uniform, bedecked with medals and sashes, the perfect host. With heavy swagger he was showing off his prize pet, a lion cub who was getting a little old for playfulness. But Goering had him pressed affectionately to his breast. Suddenly the lion cub forgot himself, and so thoroughly that before Goering could gently release himself (it is not wise to be too abrupt with ageing cubs) he was soaked to the skin. He retired in flaming confusion to change his uniform. Soon after the Berlin Zoo was pleasantly surprised to receive the generous gift of an oldish lion cub from General Goering.

When Goering brought the body of his first wife from Sweden to rest in his estate near Berlin, he was considerate enough to invite the entire diplomatic corps to participate in the ceremony of his grief. They all met at his lodge, were assigned places in open carriages drawn by horses, and were galloped cheerfully all over the estate, being shown the prize animals and enclosures for hunting. Some diplomats could go hunting if they wished, and other kinds of sport were available for the rest. My father was rather chilled from driving in the open and his good taste was deeply offended. However, he stayed a little while, racing over the land with the equally bored Italian Ambassador's wife (pre-Berlin-Rome axis days). Goering, after about an hour of this, having decked himself out in his fetching green hunting costume, dashed back to the lodge to change his uniform. In another and more formal attire he met the diplomats again and took them to the grave of his deeply loved wife, Karin, who died of tuberculosis around 1931. My father left as soon as he could get away, but, according to reports, the affair lasted much longer.

Goering's vanity and egotism are colossal, his mind and emotion as morose and grandiose as those of Hitler himself. He has made a fetish of Karin-worship, which must be very trying to the second Frau Goering. Apparently ideally married to a beautiful and nobly born woman, he seemed unable to recover, either privately or publicly, from Karin's death. He has a portrait of her in his town house before which he keeps a candle burning eternally, and his flagrant ceremonious and public worship of her tomb in Schorf Heide, his country estate, indicate to what extent an unhealthy and morbid imagination can go.

Karin Goering and he remained childless after nine years of marriage—she had borne a son to her former husband. Goering is now the proud possessor of a baby girl by Emmy Goering; it is named Eda, after Mussolini's daughter.

Despite what is known about Goering's career, political and personal, it is distressing to most people who recognize the meaning of this career, to see the amused, almost affectionate, tolerance, with which many Germans regard the antics and egotism of their No. 2 Nazi chief. Goering is vastly more popular than Goebbels—in fact, next to the Leader himself, he comes second in the hearts of the people. They like to laugh at him, they take delight in telling the stories that are malicious in themselves but less so in the hearty telling. That he is more than a conceited clown, and that it is quite possible some of the harmless stories originated from Goering and his office through a perverted desire to be talked about at all costs, seems not to make much difference in the attitudes of Germans themselves.

Hitler is a strange saviour from another world, neither German in his looks nor in his curious ascetic habits. Goering, on the other hand, so the legend goes, is what any German might be. He is greedy, fat, a gourmand and a gourmet. He loves women and has made no secret of it. He takes a rakish old man's delight in ballet girls, who almost invariably adorn any kind of party he gives on a grand scale. He has been happily married, he is now happily married again to the apotheosis of German Fraudom, and is the father of a bouncing girl. Goering is wealthy, aristocratic, brave in the tradition of war heroes. Goering is a soldier, is blond, Aryan, clearly conservative in his political and economic thinking. He is the familiar, trusted, more understandable and human German, the apostle of Hitler's fantastic religion.

Goering is quite the opposite of the picture he tries to draw of himself and which is drawn of him by other people in the Party; he is the most vicious, reckless and dangerous man in Nazi Germany. He has immense power in his hands. As the supreme chief of the air force, (and formerly Secret Police) Prussia (as its President), the Economic Plan, and his own not inconsiderable private police army, he could exercise a control, political, economic, and military—if Hitler were to die or if he were to choose him as chief adviser—as absolute as that of his leader. Ambitious on a grandiose scale, brutal and ruthless, cold and full of vengeance, fanatic and conscienceless, he would lead Germany into possibly further extremities

N6

of misery and bloodshed. It is no wonder that my father said
this man, along with the other two, would never be invited
to the Embassy, through his name, after the 30th of June.

Goering, after five years of power in the Party, equalled
only by Hitler, is considered the potential successor of Hitler.
In this period of time he has made short shrift of his enemies,
people like von Schleicher and von Papen and Schacht and
conservative army generals. He has pursued a relentless policy
of murdering, or eliminating in other ways, all rivals he could
get his hands on. It would be a naive analysis of Nazi politics
that did not give him most of the credit for the entire Roehm-
Schleicher Blood Bath, the Prussian end of which he managed
with surpassing efficiency (from the Nazi point of view). He
has been very shrewd in playing up his conservative social
background, his wealth, his war record, his Germanic qualities,
his belief in the economic status quo, because most people
would be reluctant to believe that such a man would be a
socialist or a radical in any way. Yet Goering is one of the
most reckless extremists in the Nazi party. His swagger and
braggadocio, that seem so harmless and entertaining to so
many people, conceal a will to power as devastating and
unbending as that of Hitler himself.

His pretty obvious role in the Reichstag Fire and the subsequent humiliation in the Trials show what methods he will
use to gain his objective and the objective of the Party to which
he belongs and with which he must rise or fall. He has been
regarded with some contempt and jealousy by the Reichswehr
officers, but the recent shakeup there has helped his case tremendously. One of his deadly enemies was Schacht, who has
stood as a valiant Nazi partisan from the very beginning and
who helped Hitler seize power in the period of confusion in
late 1932 and early '33. But Schacht happened to have different
ideas as to how the economy of the Third Reich should be
handled. Last autumn Schacht was noticeably absent from
cabinet meetings and soon he was, for all intents and purposes,
booted out of his position. The Hermann Goering Eisen-Werke
soon became the dominant factor in the new economic planning, and Goering himself was given the task of supervising

the Four Year Plan (a steal, in name only, from the Soviet economic planning structure; and supposed to be a commentary on what the efficient Germans could do in comparison with the blundering Soviets). This Plan was the final result of Nazi Germany's suicidal economic system. By a tremendously expensive process they were to become an economic self-sufficient nation at the end of four years. The drain upon the economic resources of the nation and the people's wealth is still obvious, and will remain even though rich sections of Czechoslovakia have been added. Schacht warned against this foolhardy project and was dismissed for his pains.

Everything now in Germany is made of substitute materials, from simple household necessities, food and clothes, to more substantial economic goods like rubber, gas, oil and now even iron. The expense involved in the artificial production of these things is colossal, and even with a highly controlled financial system, is uneconomic, dangerous, and, in the end, impossible to maintain.

As one sees in the Fascist assaults upon Spain, China, Ethiopia, Austria, and Czechoslovakia the only temporary solution from the Fascist point of view, for the strain created by autarchical methods applied to these poor countries, is economic imperialism, which again is more of a drain because of the material and money needed for exploitation of foreign lands. Thus the result is a vicious circle, the country being ever worse off than before. Some Nazis like Schacht realize the impasse their policy is leading them into: war or collapse, and it has been seen that all Fascist powers prefer war to their own internal failure.

From a military point of view Goering is more reckless than anyone, including Hitler, in the Third Reich. He considers, so he says, the Nazi air force the most invincible army in the world. There is no question that Germany's air force is a superior organization and that some of the new fast bombing 'planes, like the Messerschmitt, are hard to beat. On the other hand, these 'planes have not been faring too well in Spain, and against 'planes that on the whole were infinitely inferior in number and modern design to the German and Italian.

In the fall of 1938 Charles Lindbergh is reported to have said that Germany's air force is the best in the world. There is no question that the quantity and quality of these 'planes are increasing and perhaps improving. But 'planes, to be effective, must have excellent pilots as well—and the Spanish perform-ance leaves this prerequisite in doubt. When Lindbergh was quoted as saying (and he never denied it) that the Soviet air force was infinitely inferior, the question immediately arose as to how much and what the Russians showed a man they knew to be inimical to their social and military development. Several American military and air attachés whom I have known in Russia held a very high opinion of Russia's air fleet. It is certainly the largest in the world and judging from the Spanish experience, brilliantly effective—even against terrific odds. The Russian pursuit 'planes are said to be, by many authorities, with the exception of Colonel Lindbergh, who has recently received the second highest honour that the Nazis have to give, unmatched anywhere. Of course, the final test is yet to come. It will come on the battlefield.

Though there is certainly food and materials and ammuni-tion stored up in Germany to last for several months after the beginning of a war, a very serious problem would arise after this time. That is why one hears so much of "lightning war-fare"—wishful thinking by which Goering and others may have convinced themselves and the army that a European war would be over in a few months. It is a familiar note in German psychology: Germany, along with many other coun-tries in 1914, believed that the World War would be over in six months. Now, however, other European nations, besides Germany, have a much more pessimistic view and seemed to have learned from horrible and bitter experience that war is not a Sunday picnic, over when the sun goes down.

Goering is the man to be watched in Germany, the one whom next to Hitler the nations of the world consider most headstrong and dangerous, and one whom Hitler no doubt fears and restrains when he feels an encroachment on his own power. It is not too sure he always will be able to. With his conviction of Germany's economic and military invincibility he could persuade Hitler at a crucial moment to strike. He is the one who wanted Germany to enter even more completely with arms and men into the Spanish struggle; he is the one who feared no reprisals from the Austrian invasion. He is the one who surely urged similar treatment of Czechoslovakia. If he should ever take a conservative position in these matters it would be because of necessity, or advantageous to his future role.

3

Goebbels is the so-called brains of the Nazi movement. Sharp, sardonic, unscrupulous, playing first with the right-wing Nazis and then with the left-wing ones, affecting a sort of socialism which fools no one, least of all the simple people, he is, as I have said, the most hated and distrusted man in the Nazi camp. This official Jew-baiter, newspaper editor and mentor of the people in propaganda and public enlightenment, has the rodent's face as well as the rodent's mind.

Personally, despite his clubfoot and small, gnome-like face, he is the most attractive of the men around Hitler. Not much more than five feet tall, slender, limping—as he drags the weight of a deformed foot behind him—gaunt, sallow-faced with a long narrow protruding skull that overhangs his thin neck in the back, large sharp protruding ears—set low and curiously in his skull, a head of lank, longish black hair, a mouth that is both mobile and excessively wide, a coarse unattractively formed nose, Dr. Goebbels is surely one of the most un-German, non-Aryan specimens among all Nazi heroes.

In Nazi eyes anyone who has a clubfoot is unworthy of procreating and indicates by such a deformity that he is the product of mixed breeding. If there were any logic or objectivity in Nazi sterilization laws Dr. Goebbels would have been sterilized quite some time ago. As it is, he is permitted and apparently encouraged to produce as many offspring as his wife can be persuaded to bear. He now has three or four daughters and an adopted son, the child of his wife by another marriage.

Frau Magda Goebbels is a very attractive and worldly woman, formerly raised in a Jewish family. She is blonde, tall (several inches taller than her husband), dresses beautifully, speaks several languages, and has much more real grace, wit, and beauty than Frau Goering of whom she is, of course, a great rival. Frau Goebbels is not a simple or sweet woman; she has the wisdom and intuitive intelligence of a woman quite at ease in any sort of society. Her parties in pre-Nazi days were sophisticated mixed affairs where talk and manners were quite free. Living with a Nazi chief has subdued her considerably, though one still suspects her of being lively and vixenish. However, she has scarcely had enough breathing space between pregnancies to express her own personality.

The first time I saw her she came to a large tea we gave to the Germans and diplomatic corps. At that time, she was one of the most beautiful women I had seen in Germany, though her face didn't have the fresh charm expected of Nazi wives. There was a sophistication, an exquisiteness in dress, a delicate, blasé, and calculated vivacity that was startling in the usual humdrum conventional and heavy manner of most German women. I was intrigued by her who seemed to be more French than German, and I wondered at the time what perverse whim or broken emotional state could have led her to marry Dr. Goebbels. A remark of hers about any woman in Berlin could be so sharp and devastating in its subtle implication that other women less mentally alert were terribly afraid of her. But she won my respect, nevertheless, and on the many occasions when I saw her I was intrigued by her beauty and poise, the sensational, studied, and tasteful dress and manners, the lively wit and intelligence.

Many people who know her intimately say that she leads her husband a lively life and that the Goebbels household trembles with her whims and tempers. But Goebbels himself was passionately and romantically in love with her and wooed her with such persistence and vehemence that she could not resist him.

She used to be carefree, gay, eager for fun wherever she could find it. No doubt unscrupulous, and ambitious, a woman who might have been a brilliant and lovely courtesan in another era, she has, as the wife of No. 3 Nazi, taken a minor role since Emmy's advent. There is still as much rivalry on a social and personal basis between the two blondes as there is between their husbands. Frau Goebbels used to claim Hitler's evening time very often for her musical gatherings, but now she has a rival who seems to have taken advantage of Frau Goebbels' periodic confinements. In any case, though Hitler bounces the Goebbels' daughters on his knee, Magda Goebbels' role has been challenged—it seems she has lost out as favourite of the Leader to the newer Emmy. Emmy's baby girl will perhaps soon be bounced with greater rapture on the Leader's knee.

While Goebbel's friends were in the thick of the War, he himself was disqualified because of his deformity. Not being able to experience the "glory and grandeur" of death and destruction, he determined to make of his mind as effective an instrument as his body was not. He had a long period of university training in which he attended, as was the German custom, many universities in different parts of the country, and received adequate degrees. He longed to be a playwright but the theatres and directors of the time did not put the stamp of approval on his output. His plays were refused production and not until the Nazis had their own theatre in Berlin could he get his plays performed. It is quite possible that at this moment he developed a violent anti-Semitic feeling. No doubt many of the successful playwrights and directors of the German stage were Jewish—and the fact that he was so measurably inferior as a dramatist he unquestionably must have laid to discrimination against him, thus causing resentment and bitterness. He could not admit to himself that his own lack of talent was the reason.

Hitler and his cohorts, with whom Goebbels soon came into contact in the formative years, recognized almost immediately the peculiar and valuable talents of the little Doctor. A place was found for him, a place which has since been enlarged and elaborated, but is essentially the same as in former years. New campaigns, new slogans, new tricks and devices to win over or stir up the people are almost all invented and carried through by Dr. Goebbels. His ideas, perhaps even his actual planning, are realized on a grandiose scale and known throughout the world now as "Nazi circuses." He censors what people read, what they see, what they say, what they hear, and tries even to control what they think and feel.

Propaganda and public enlightenment obviously can cover almost every field of human activity. In Nazi bureaucracy there is much overlapping in each and all of the departments, and you find, for instance, young attachés in the Foreign Office studying in the Propaganda Ministry. Goebbels has his finger in most Nazi pies.

He not only handles all press matters and censorship within Germany, sometimes even being allowed to suppress speeches and statements of his colleagues, but also the foreign press relations. Naturally, he is detested by most journalists and after his periodic blasts and insults which they faithfully report, there is an atmosphere of unconcealed bitterness which does not in any way improve foreign opinion of Nazi Germany. Though he has a rapier mind, his invective is so repellent and vicious that few people respect the intellect he has so carefully cultivated.

There is no question that he is the "mind," the "diabolo," of the Third Reich. But he has done more to make Germany unpopular in the eyes of the world than any other single figure except, perhaps, Hitler himself. He wields great influence and some power in Germany—of that there is no doubt, but his potential dangerousness is lessened by the fact of his unpopularity. He is not only distrusted and disliked by Goering, his immediate rival, but by other colleagues like Rosenberg and Schacht, and by groups like the Reichswehr, the common people, the conservative clique, the aristocrats, and even the intellectuals in whose class and group he has tried so hard to make himself prominent and admired. He has little following in either the S.A. or the S.S. armies, and he has no army or police of his own. His position, except for the place he holds in Hitler's heart, is unenviable. Most Nazis realize he is irreplaceable and that, as far as knowledge of propaganda methods, of the psychology of the masses, of new daring and untried schemes goes, he is unique and cannot be surpassed. For these contributions they give him credit. They believe as well, though they often express a personal desire to have him ousted from his position, that it would be dangerous to have anyone else in his place—the gigantic bubble of Nazi propaganda which he has blown up to Gargantuan proportions might, if touched by any but his deft fingers, collapse on itself, explode in the hot air of its composition.

There is no question that if Hitler should die or be overthrown, Goebbels would be one of the first men to go, no matter what regime came in. He lives and works by the grace of Hitler alone and creates more and more elaborate mechanisms and machinations to realize his dreams of enlightenment and propaganda—knowing full well what would happen to him were Hitler to leave the Nazi scene.

The newspaper Goebbels edits, *Der Angriff*, is on about the same intellectual plane as *Der Stürmer*. It bears screaming headlines; it pursues a relentless, if somewhat more subtle, anti-Semitic policy; it attacks foreign countries and their representatives; it follows in meticulous detail every change in policy, both internal and foreign, of the Nazis, which of course its editor has helped to formulate. Fallacious and full of folly and invective, clever, sharp with a special twisted logic, it serves as a model, along with the official *Voelkischer Beobachter*, for the rest of the German newspapers.

Many diplomats and foreign residents of Berlin think Goebbels is personally the most charming of the Nazi leaders, though on the other hand they distrust his extremism and fanatic chauvinistic mind. I think he has the most charming smile I have ever seen among the Nazis. He laughs a lot, smiles, and affects the role of the gentle lively gracious host with much more dexterity than his rival Goering. Though his body is small and crippled, you forget his deformity and his viciousness when he smiles. His mouth opens widely from ear to ear and the expression of the face assumes an irrepressible and irresistible gaiety. Infectious and delightful, eyes sparkling, voice soft, his speech witty and light, it is difficult to remember his cruelty, his cunning destructive talents. My mother was always intrigued by his *esprit* and enjoyed sitting next to him at the endless diplomatic and governmental parties.

Though my father knew only too well the part that Goebbels played in Nazi politics he, too, often said he was one of the few men with a sense of humour in Germany. They met often at *bier abends*, stag parties, lunches, as well as more formal affairs, and he always reported an amusing exchange of irony between the two of them—Goebbels catching every shadow of meaning and insinuation in my father's humorous sarcasm and returning every quip with light cynicism and effective wit. My father felt that he was a complete opportunist, but that at least in public he could restrain the fierce fanaticism, whether sincere or not, that dominated his speeches, his work, and his writings. Most Germans we met were heavy and ponderous, many of them completely untrained intellectually, too frightened to speak, or so aflame with religious Nazi ardour that it was impossible to carry on any sort of civilized, humorous, or interesting conversation. Goebbels and Schacht were the two astonishing exceptions. Both unscrupulous in character, both confident enough of their positions to allow some lightness and teasing in their conversation, both with shrewd minds which they took delight in using, they were by far the most interesting conversationalists among the Nazi officials. There were several pictures taken of my father and Goebbels and, in each, the two face each other with broad smiles on their faces. Occasionally Goebbels smiles so widely and holds the pose so long that his lips twist at the edge and you have a picture of a snarl. But only the very close observer can catch this.

This is Goebbels' social personality only. But one must give him at least the credit for having mastered the consummate art of seeming what he is not. This talent General Goering does not possess. Goering and Goebbels have the custom of giving annual parties for the diplomatic corps, journalists, government people, stray visitors, and a scattering of Berlin society. And it is usually noticed that neither of them appears at the party of the other. One party that Goebbels gave, after a lavish circus-fair entertainment of his enemy, surpassed anything in elaborateness I had yet attended in Berlin.

Several thousand people were invited to an evening dinner, reception and ballet on an island on one of the beautiful lakes near Berlin. The guests crossed from the mainland on a bridge thrown across the water and held fast by men in boats along the sides. On the island were innumerable lanes through the trees and hills, necklaced overhead with many-coloured little lanterns and lined with young page girls in tights. In an open space, tables were laid and a stage set for the dancing. Overhead were lanterns and, in the huge dark trees were tremendous artificial butterflies lighted from within. The tables were elaborately set with many wine glasses and an endless course dinner which included all the expensive delicacies. Towards the end of the dinner there were fireworks on a grandiose scale—in proportion much more magnificent, as I later observed, than the national French fireworks celebration of their July 14th holiday—ending in a terrific roar and red explosion that called to mind the gigantic bombardment of a war scene. The suggestion was so clear that most of the diplomats at our table commented on it and were deeply offended, believing the whole thing a badly designed threat in the worst sort of taste. Later we were served with ballet girls and a sort of revue. We didn't stay until the end, but took an inconspicuous leave after saying good-bye to the smiling, vivacious, well-pleased host. Goering did not put in his appearance.

There was so much gossip among the simple people of Berlin about the cost of this tremendous festival—with so much bitter comment on their own living conditions and so many questions as to where the money collected through the Winter Hilfe went—the Nazis became somewhat apologetic. A few days later, it was announced that on Sunday the island would be open, with the same decorations, for the German people to visit and disport themselves on.

Goebbels amply proved his genius for propaganda and enlightenment in the management of such stupendous shows as the Nürnberger Partei Tag (Nürnberg Party Day). He unquestionably has the kind of intuitive intelligence, experience, and daring, the knowledge of how mass hysteria can be incited, to make him invaluable to the Nazis who need a never-ending stream of circuses to keep their people entertained.

4

When we first came to Berlin, in fact during the first three years, Dr. Schacht was one of our most constant visitors. He came so often to our house that my mother used to say, "Well, if at the last minute another guest can't come, we can always invite Dr. Schacht." He would come on a day's notice and was one of the intellectual shows of the Embassy.

Tall, sinewy, and wiry, with the ugly clown mask of his face, which was curiously alive and attractive, resembling somewhat the bald tough shrewdness of an old eagle, he was celebrated far and wide in Germany for his wit. He could call Hitler crazy, the Nazis mad, the whole world insane, as he did repeatedly on all occasions, and get by with it. He was interested in our Embassy mainly because he thought my father had enough influence with the American administration to put through some of his schemes for loans and trade agreements. My father consulted him often on other than social occasions, and the two of them were frank in their protestations and exchange of bitter experiences. I think Schacht liked my father personally, and, I have heard, thought highly of his integrity and honesty, wondering at the rare spectacle of an informal and idealistic Ambassador.

Schacht has been called the "wizard of finance" for his manipulations of the mark. It would be a mistake to assume that Schacht was in any way anti-Nazi despite his frequent disparagements of everyone in the government. He helped the Nazis into power, he represented certain powerful financial and industrial interests which needed the Nazis and Dr. Schacht to survive. There is no question, however, that Schacht is a conservative economist in every sense of the word and that many of the Nazi follies and radical absurdities offended him in his hard, clever understanding of economic laws. He is a violent nationalist, and many times has told us sob stories about the plight of Germany's economy, with tears in his eyes, and, I always suspected, tongue in his cheek. In any case, he was for the Nazis as long as his own interests were served and those of the group he represented. That, in some fields, he would like to have seen the same ends accomplished in a slightly slower and more conservative way is also indubitable. He is, as I have said, a vitriolic enemy of Goering and the latter's economic planning ambitions—for personal and official reasons—not to mention the jealousy involved in rival capitalist cliques and schemes.

He has the true capitalist's scorn for an inexperienced novice in the field of economics. He wanted very much to see Germany one of the great European powers, both in military and economic strength. But he wanted to arrive at this success surely and with caution. He couldn't believe that Germany's plunge from the most impoverished economic condition into absolute autarchy could be safely effected without some recourse to modified international trade methods. But he lost out in his fight to keep Germany among the interdependent nations of the world.

He made many enemies among the Nazis and the Reichswehr because, when he was in supreme control of Nazi financial and economic policies, he cut down on the military and the propaganda budget. He told my father and others that it was scandalous, the amount of money Goebbels was using for propaganda, both inside and outside Germany. For this limitation of Goebbels' funds he incurred the everlasting hatred of the little Doctor. With the Reichswehr he had various squabbles on the same score, though on the whole he managed to get on with them. He always allowed them enough from the national budget to keep them fairly well satisfied despite his periodic outbursts that they were draining the resources of the German nation.

Dr. Schacht was at one time a Mason, and it was only recently, under pressure, that he accepted a Nazi medal. This was during the period when all the Nazi cabinet members were forced to take the oath of allegiance to the Fuehrer—all capitulated except Eltz von Rubenach, who resigned rather than compromise himself. We saw Schacht shortly after, when he rather sheepishly wore the Nazi insignia dangling conspicuously near his stomach, and he raised his eyebrows ironically when we congratulated him!

Frau Schacht is a delightful woman with a sharp sense of humour and a critical sense as well. Though she wears, rather tenderly and sentimentally, a Nazi emblem in the form of a pin or pendant between her tremendous breasts, we were never fully convinced that she was as good a Nazi as she seemed. She appeared to have a real hero-worship of Hitler, as many German women of her generation have, but she indicated certain fears of the trends Germany was following. A huge, simple, motherly type of woman with sparkling eyes, she was a comic counterpart to the lean owl-like husband over whom she kept a vigilant watch. In her role as mother she embraced her husband as well as her family.

Schacht was for several years considered the real dictator of Germany, and my father would often tease him about holding the destiny of his country in his hands and surpassing the Leader in potential power. Considered the "bad boy" of Nazi finance, he was nevertheless one of their most solid props. Hitler put absolute trust in him and, as long as he managed German economy and finance, the other nations of the world felt a certain security. When he was ostensibly relieved of his position of power, the foreign nations had a case of jitters. He is (at the time of writing) still President of the Reichsbank, though Goering has apparently superseded him in the economic field.

Dr. Schacht often said that he expected to go under the headsman's axe and many times we heard serious reports of his dangerous position. However, he always managed to weather the storms and, even though for the moment he seems to be under a cloud, one can never tell to what extent he is the power behind the throne. Before we left—some time after he had been excluded from cabinet meetings and after it had been announced that Goering was the chief of Nazi economics —he told my father that he might be looking around for a job as banker or a bank clerk in some American bank!

A mind of excessive alertness, almost a magician's genius of making something out of nothing, Dr. Schacht remains one of the most brilliant masters in his field in the world. He had tremendous success in negotiating trade agreements with European countries, notably the Balkans, though his dealings with America were not so fortunate. One day when my father and Charles R. Crane visited him on his estate several hours from Berlin, as they were walking through the gardens, Schacht said to Crane: "This Ambassador of yours is a nice fellow— he does a lot of talking, but I see nothing but disappointing results when it comes to real commercial action between America and Germany." The remark was, of course, made with humour but underlying it was some bitterness as to the failures he experienced in the trade transactions with the United States.

With a cutting and devastating sense of humour, given to writing sharp sarcastic poems in guest books, providing a sort of show of his own wherever he went, Schacht was, at least, a man with whom you could sharpen your wits, a man whose mental processes gave you a real run for money in attempting to keep up with them. It is quite possible that, if Schacht is not now directing the Four Year Plan behind the front of General Goering, he may be called to do so later when the National Socialists realize the economic drain and danger involved. The enigma of Dr. Schacht will remain—but he is a violent Nationalist and an equally violent and die-hard conservative capitalist who will defend the interests of his group to the last ditch.

5

Alfred Rosenberg, a Balt of Russian origin, is the second most detested Nazi. Loathed by Goebbels, who is his rival even in his own field of propaganda, and by Goering, he enjoys mainly the favour of Hitler, as is the case with Goebbels himself. A Nazi of long standing he has formulated the cultural and racial mythology of the present regime. A mystic, a psychopathic fanatic, he has written the most bombastic book of empty verbiage yet written in its field or in almost any other. "The Myth of the Twentieth Century" is a collection of all the falsities and patently ridiculous theories of Nazi philosophy. However, he is so admired by the Leader that he is the chief of the foreign policy of the Nazi party.

His colossal hatred and fear of the Soviet Union is hardly matched by anyone in the Nazi party. His theory of the *Drang nach Osten* is an accepted tenet in Nazi religion. His one desire in life is to Germanize everyone west of the Russian border and then to overrun the Soviet Union through the annexation of the Ukraine. It is possible that his loathing of Communism came to him when he saw a real revolution in action. In any case, after he left Leningrad in 1919, his brain was already active with its tortured dreams of Teutonic splendour and conquest. He sees, in these nightmares, a vast Germanic Reich extending over the entire continent of Europe and even Asia. Tall, sturdy Germanic heroes, with flowing blond hair, shining armour embossed with a Swastika; barbaric, splendid, pure, worshipping their god of valour, Thor, and visioning their ancestors in a majestic Valhalla, they rush in a gleaming horde over the face of the continent, bringing with them the glory of a new God—Hitler, the soft, flabby, moustached man with the frantic voice and the dark drooping locks, the small gesticulating housepainter.

Besides the dream of the conquest of the East and the revival of the old religion of Germany's pre-civilization, Rosenberg offers a complete extermination of the Jewish people. All of this would seem fit material for a madman to work on—but who is to judge today the mad and the sane in Nazi Germany—if it were not taken so seriously by a good number of Germans. Though Rosenberg is detested by the extremists in his own party as well as by the conservatives, these ideas are being offered daily to the mass of German people and are being accepted by the Nazis among them. The most serious commentary one can make is that Rosenberg is allowed loose in Germany and that he is one of the close and old friends of Adolf Hitler, who has publicly and privately subscribed to all of his theories. Furthermore, it is clear that the Nazis not only follow his lead in racial and religious matters but direct their military offensive in the direction he suggests. It may be pure coincidence that the army declares that its eyes look eastward, that Hitler himself thirsts openly for the Ukraine, that leagues of Germanic Knights exist from the borders of Germany to those of Russia along the Baltic, that propaganda is being poured into these countries in all directions, that army and air bases are growing up swiftly along the Baltic, that even Finland itself possesses islands that the Nazis could use as air bases, and once had the Nazi Baron Mannerheim in high political office—but the fact remains, whether by chance or not, Nazi Germany is following practically what Rosenberg has suggested "ideologically" in propaganda, faith, and organization.

I met this strange phenomenon once at a lunch at the British Embassy. Rosenberg was sitting by the Ambassadress at a formal diplomatic lunch. I was surprised to see that he scarcely opened his mouth except to put food in it. It may have been that he was bitterly remembering the fiasco he made of an ill-timed trip of his to England. As a sort of Ambassador of Propaganda, practically the first thing he did was to lay a Nazi wreath upon the Cenotaph. England turned a cold shoulder and Rosenberg returned considerably dampened and has not since ventured across the border of his adopted Germanic fatherland. Slender, blond, surly to the point of rudeness, he glared morosely around the table and it seemed as if a smile, should it perchance venture on his face, would surely crack up the whole facial structure. With the petulance of a little boy whose stick of candy had been taken away, he was far from the gleaming knight in armour, the splendid giant of Aryan courage and clarity his introverted dreams made of him.

6

Joachim von Ribbentrop, now Minister of Foreign Affairs, came of good background and married into even better. In fact he married the daughter of the largest champagne manufacturer in Germany. He acquired the "von" in his name from an aunt who had no immediate descendants. Considered, I

Oₒ

have heard, something of an upstart by his wife's family, a man of no particular talent or profession, an ambitious wine salesman, Ribbentrop showed no special penchant for anything until Adolf Hitler found him around 1930. Suave, a good linguist (he knew French as well as English), rich and seemingly loyal, he soon came to be depended on by Hitler as a sort of diplomatic bellboy. He did all sorts of errands for the Leader and proved himself absolutely trustworthy. In 1935, he headed the German delegation to England when the Anglo-German naval accord was reached—a great political and military victory for the Nazis. He was appointed, not long after, German Ambassador to London—a reward, I suppose, for his conduct during this mission. His behaviour in London was so conspicuously gauche that I have heard many enemies of Nazi Germany declare the only prayer they had was that Ribbentrop be allowed to stay in London as the Nazi representative. Of course, his worst and most publicized blunder occurred when he was presented to the King—whereupon he Heiled Hitler! The English felt such contempt for him, from all reports in Berlin and in London, they scarcely acknowledged him socially. He was regarded as a *nouveau riche* and a fanatic, and both qualities are notoriously frowned upon by the stiff, reserved, and supposedly aristocratic English.

Some months ago in a general military and diplomatic shakeup he was recalled to Berlin where he took the place of von Neurath. There had always been a profound rivalry between the two Nazis (though von Neurath is not a bead-telling member) and the diplomatic and newspaper corps were prophesying constantly, for several years before the actual events, that he would supersede Neurath. Ribbentrop was regarded as a dangerous and passionate Nazi whose foreign policies would lead Germany to disaster if they became Hitler's guiding ones. Though Neurath was not a loved figure by any means in the German Foreign Office, the prospect of having to deal with Ribbentrop was so infinitely worse that most diplomats pretended to be quite satisfied with Neurath. I remember, for instance, my father saying that if Ribbentrop became Foreign Minister he would have to resign—he could not conceive of dealing with him directly or personally on any subject. Fortunately, my father's resignation took place before this necessity faced him.

The first time I met von Ribbentrop was at a luncheon we gave at the Embassy. He was tall and slender, with a vague blond handsomeness. Outstanding among all the guests, Ribbentrop arrived in Nazi uniform. Most Nazis came to diplomatic functions in ordinary suits unless the affair was extremely formal. His manner of shaking hands was an elaborate ceremony in itself. He held out his hand, then retreated and held your hand at arm's length, lowered his arm stiffly by his side, then raised the arm swiftly in a Nazi salute, just barely missing your nose. All the time he was staring at you with such intensity you were wondering what new sort of mesmerism he thought he was effecting. The whole ritual was performed with such self-conscious dignity and in such silence that hardly a word was whispered while Ribbentrop made his exhibitionistic acquaintance with the guests present. To me the procedure was so ridiculous I could scarcely keep a straight face. However, I wanted to see him perform the last detail of his "act" so I approached him, stepped back, stood silently watching him, eyes pinned on a distant object in back to keep from laughing, and felt that I quite ably sensed the unspoken stage directions! This business he went through at every small party—the pompousness, the maddening leisureliness, the affectation, of course attracted the attention of everyone present—as he no doubt intended.

One evening we were invited several weeks in advance to a formal affair at the Ribbentrops'. We learned on the night of the party that he had been appointed Ambassador to England. As we prepared to go that evening, the newspapers announced the story. Hundreds of people were present and, on the lawns of the suburban mansion, tents had been set up over the tables. We greeted Ribbentrop hastily—and congratulated him —which he took with a sort of pained graciousness, disdain, and bored *savoir faire*. This night he did not have the chance or the time to go through with his ceremony of pontifical Nazi salutation. We found our tables. This was the night when I was told animatedly that there was no difference between Negroes and fleet-footed animals. Later there was dancing, and singing by opera stars. As always we were greatly bored by the gorgeousness of the celebration and figured out that Ribbentrop's wife, a dark, thin snub-nosed woman who looked hard and bitter, had paid the bill. Goering sat by my mother, General Udet was present, and Himmler wove his mincing, quiet, and sinister way through the crowds. It was a magnificent and representative Nazi private party—and served him well, Ribbentrop thought, as a springboard to sophisticated British life.

Von Ribbentrop is a snob, a Nazi, and an extremist. With an inordinate ambition and a pomposity and self-esteem rarely seen so openly proclaimed among Nazis, he bears the mark of acquired wealth upon him, and the brand of a man lost in confusion, seeking his way through the Nazi way of life in conceit and self-consciousness. With no intellectual ability whatsoever, but with the canniness of a cat, he bears now the great responsibility of formulating Nazi foreign policy and has made, in the process of his drive towards power, almost as many contemptuous enemies as Rosenberg himself.

That he was the German signatory of the German-Japanese anti-Comintern pact is well known. It is very possible that he was the "ideological" author of it as well. Out of this pact grew the Berlin-Rome axis. Ribbentrop, among other Nazi officials like Goering and Neurath, certainly had his hand in the formation of this Fascist International that was to extend from the Far East to the West, and which fitted so well into Hitler's original dreams of conquest as expressed in "Mein Kampf."

7

Von Neurath, the portly white-haired diplomat, until recently in power in the Foreign Office, comes of an excellent and well-to-do family. He went through the usual diplomatic schooling and was German Ambassador to London before Hitler called him to direct the Nazi foreign policy. Considered

more moderate and conservative than most of his co-workers—
on a par with Schacht in this regard—trained in the hypocritical verbiage of conventional diplomacy, he was nevertheless considered a lesser evil than Ribbentrop. He gave a polite
and sympathetic ear to protests of foreign missions and just as
politely evaded doing anything about them. Trusted not at all
by the diplomatic corps, a violent Nationalist and anti-Repub-
lican, he was certainly not a Nazi in any obvious fire-eating
sense. Thus Hindenburg wanted him to be a brake on Hitler's
fanaticism. However, as time went on, Hitler found in him
the perfect tool with which to manipulate irate foreign representatives. He looked impressive, he was of the "old school,"
he didn't lose his temper, he deplored Nazi extremities and
fanaticism, he was the ideal "front" for all occasions—official
and personal. There is no doubt, however, that if he did have
a will of his own it was a will to accomplish the ends of
National Socialism. Otherwise he was simply putty in the
Leader's hands, no matter what may have been his indigna-
tions and grievances. In any case, while he was in power the
Nazis neither changed, compromised, nor capitulated on any
point of their pre-designed programme.

Heavy-jowled, tall, with the proportions of a very well-fed,
successful, and retired butter-and-egg man, his face was utterly
expressionless—the proverbial poker-face. Nothing is known
to have seriously ruffled his calm and it must have taken the
good part of a lifetime to develop such complete emotional
and physical apathy. My father once saw him flush deep red
and twist a little in his chair when he presented him with a
strongly worded protest about the wave of slander, smut,
calumny, and hate that flooded the German papers after La
Guardia made his famous commentary on Hitler's place in
the World's Fair. As a rule, however, in addressing him you
got the sensation that you were addressing a stone wall. He
never had an opinion, definitely expressed, about anything,
and the very way he expressed no opinion at all was so ponderous and pompous that everyone was silent as he spoke and
listened for the sound of the weighted word falling through
the air. Phlegmatic is another word used for such men, but

there were some diplomats who spoke more honestly and bluntly of his character.

He wore a bright red sash at formal parties—a banner, I suppose, of honour given by some order, military or otherwise. He stood still usually, like a gigantic owl in face, like a gigantic penguin in shape, while people clustered around him. Occasionally it was necessary for him to move—and he would do so with such dignity and self-importance it was almost like the Sphinx itself deciding to shake its head!

Von Neurath said that he did not want the foreign service to be made the clearing house for propaganda and espionage activities. This may have been because he hated Goebbels and disliked von Bohle. He wanted a set of young men trained in history and diplomacy and the law to go over the world representing Nazi Germany as objectively as possible. How sincere this desire was no one can say. He fought bitterly the schemes of Ribbentrop who was an arch-propagandist rather than a diplomat. Finally, against Neurath's protests, von Bohle's bureau was incorporated into the Foreign Office. This organization, *Auslands Organization,* is clearly an agency for foreign propaganda and espionage all over the world. The excellent book, "The Nazi Conspiracy in Spain," reveals with documentary proof to what extent Bohle interfered in the affairs of a foreign power. When this Bureau was established as an integral part of the German State Department, it was a plain announcement and warning to the world that Embassies, Consulates, agents, and espionage activities were to be directed from the same source wherever Nazi Germany was represented. An official of the Foreign Office told me that as long as Bohle had his activity separate from diplomatic work, he could do little more than complain, but when he, his schemes, and cohorts were unceremoniously grafted on to the State Department there was no longer any use of pretending objectivity, fair play, and diplomatic dignity in German foreign relations. When, to top the climax, Ribbentrop was made Foreign Minister, the German State Department lost all resemblance to similar departments in other countries.

Von Neurath, despite his Nazi leanings and his "stuffed

shirt" manners, to use the phrase of a well-known British
diplomat, was not extreme enough to suit Hitler, and though
his son-in-law Mackensen, from all evidence an extremist and
a former German Minister to Hungary, was in the State
Department working closely with his father-in-law, the atmosphere and structure was not the glorified German propaganda
agency both Hitler and Ribbentrop intended it to be.

8

Von Bülow, who died in the spring after the Nazi re-occupation of the Rhineland, was perhaps the best-loved man in
the Foreign Office. Tall and well-proportioned, with a head of
straight soft white hair, light blue eyes and a handsome and
gentle face, he seemed to recognize more fully than any of his
so-called moderate colleagues the ultimate dangers involved
in Hitler's plans and ambitions. He was a nationalist, too, of
an aristocratic, distinguished, and conservative background,
but his nationalism did not lead him into the mental and
emotional furies it imposed on many Germans. Soft-spoken,
serious, he had a certain severity and dignity of character that
commanded the respect of everyone, including his enemies.
My father and other diplomats preferred always to deal with
him rather than with his colleagues. My mother was especially
fond of him and felt sincere grief when he died—much before
his time.

One felt in his gentleness and frankness that here was a man
who, no matter how reactionary his background might have
been, had a clear perspective of the future and disapproved
for the most part of Nazi inhumanity and destructiveness.
Von Bülow was a gentleman not only by birth but by his
rare quality of intelligence and tolerance towards others. He
may not have been as able a diplomat as Neurath, he certainly
never possessed the impressive stony front of his chief, and he
didn't feel or indicate that dignity and reserve were achievable
only through glumness and pomposity. He was pleasantly
witty, polite, and natural. This luminous quality, this delicacy
and integrity, drew to him a circle of sincere and warm friends.

Before he died he was already in the bad graces of Hitler—
having never been more than tolerable to the Nazis—though
it is said he had capitulated more to Nazi nationalism after
the re-occupation of the Rhine. But, whatever he felt or
decided on in the last months of his life, we all considered
him to be one of the finest representatives of old Germany.

9

Dr. Hans Dieckhoff was long a personal friend of my
father's. In fact, the two of them exchanged visits continuously. He was appointed Ambassador to America, succeeding
the little fat, podgy-faced Hans Luther who was not too
popular either here or in Germany, though I found him
delightful and amusing socially.

One of the first houses we went to among the Germans was
the Dieckhoffs. It was only a few weeks after we arrived and,
as I remember, even before my father had presented his credentials to Hindenburg. They lived in a modest villa in the
suburbs and entertained with disarming informality and grace.
Mrs. Dieckhoff is a lovely slender dark woman whose quiet-
ness and modesty make her appealing to everyone. She took
no active part in Nazi life in any way and seemed satisfied to
devote herself to her husband, family, and children. Dieckhoff
himself was a tall, rather heavy man, with one of the strangest
faces I have seen. Greatly out of proportion to the rest of his
body, his face is almost as round as a full moon, fat and flat;
he has small glistening eyes and a slightly receding forehead
and a pebbly complexion. He looks more like a genial ape-
man than any human I know.

Perpetually polite, almost maddeningly so, he wore a continuous smile on his face like a grimace cemented on the
fleshy expanse. I remember wondering how much his head
weighed in comparison to the rest of his body—as a cynical
critic might estimate the weight of a book rather than its
contents. He spoke English fluently. Dieckhoff was a democrat
and liberal of former days and, unless he had completely
compromised himself, one had to conclude he was at least

partially anti-Nazi. He may have preached moderation to the Nazis—he certainly did if he carried the protests and messages from my father to Nazi officials as he always promised to do (and, of course, as was expected of him). But after July, 1934, he kept the silence of a tomb. During this period he revealed pretty conclusively what he thought personally of the Purge and the dread he had of his own danger. Of course everyone, whether guilty or not, had a case of severe jitters those days, and the years following as well, so his alarm and judgment of the Nazis may have come merely from his hysterical fright.

He was a very subdued Under Secretary of State from that time on, maintaining a cautious and defensive manner. He was as gracious as ever, the smile on his face even broader than ever—like the smile of a man who has been posing too long before a camera—a little stiff as if it might break any moment—and never again had a positive opinion about a controversial matter. He came very often to our dinners and receptions and pretended to be a close and loyal friend of my father's, though my mother, brother, and I never trusted him. He pretended to agree with us on any subject, including the Nazis, and was then just as willing to agree when we assumed an opposite position. These foibles are supposedly notorious with diplomats, but we thought his discretion was a bit too exaggerated even for his professional needs.

There is no doubt that he made a good Ambassador to America.[1] He seems to be a conservative—maybe he is really that politically—not given to Nazi excesses, extremely acceptable socially, never likely to fly off the handle, suave, shrewd, with manners of grace and "breeding." It was a canny choice on the part of the Nazis, and Dieckhoff no doubt attempted to pour oil over the troubled anti-Nazi American waters. He was certainly better than a blustering, smug, crude, and impetuous Nazi fanatic. The officials in Washington have some reassurance that what he does, though meticulously instructed from Berlin and in every essential for the interests

[1] After the unprecedented brutality against the Jews in November, 1938, when President Roosevelt recalled America's Ambassador to Berlin, Dr. Dieckhoff was called home in retaliation.

of the Nazis both as propaganda and as diplomacy, will be done with tact and refinement. Here is a man who belongs to the cultivated, somewhat self-constrained, section of the human race, and that is something for Americans to be grateful for. I personally think there is little difference between Dieckhoff and Ribbentrop—of whom, by the way, he is the brother-in-law (an interesting fact not to be overlooked in one's estimation of him)—either morally or politically speaking. Dieckhoff is a better actor perhaps, and is less ostentatious, more modest, and quiet of demeanour. But these are superficial differences, and whether or not Dieckhoff is a real Nazi is not important since he is serving faithfully to all intents and purposes one of the most ruthless dictators in the history of the world; the sum of his diplomatic record both here and in Germany is of flawless subservience.

10

The amusing Protocol section of the Foreign Office had more trouble retaining appropriate men than almost any other. This department handles the etiquette problems that arise almost every time you turn around in the rigorously formal German diplomatic life. You must consult them about guest lists (for instance, you must never invite the representative of a country that has not recognized the Soviet Union to the same reception where the Russians are to appear), about seating arrangements, about types of dress to be worn, about the endless regulations on every conceivable detail of social behaviour. Every time the German officials give a dinner or reception to the diplomatic corps, the Protocol department must arrange for the affair to progress smoothly. Sometimes Embassies and Ministries have their own native Protocol secretaries. The first year we had ours but my father thought it was a useless expense and a rather ridiculous job for a self-respecting man to devote himself to. So, whenever we were in a quandary about the rules of etiquette which the secretaries of our Embassy had no answers for, we would call up the Foreign Office and get help. We learned shortly after our arrival that a certain Minister in Berlin had refused to speak to the Ambassador of a great power for three years because of a slight the Ambassador had unwittingly made in a seating arrangement—the Minister was one seat lower than his rank entitled him to! At formal affairs, at balls and opera parties, at Olympic Games, at funerals and weddings, at Party Congresses and meetings of any type, the ubiquitous German Protocol secretary is always there.

The first chief I knew in this department was a Herbert von Mumm, of aristocratic and wealthy background, a young and attractive man who spoke many languages, was witty and cosmopolitan, and was no more of a Nazi than I—perhaps less at that time! He was somewhat effeminate and seemed to loathe the job he managed so well. Soon the Nazis realized the presence of the charming, cynical, and intelligent young man was not to their favour and they dismissed him on some disgraceful trumped-up charge of homosexuality. Most of the diplomats were indignant and vociferous in their comments on the treatment of von Mumm, but of course there was nothing to be done. His career was ruined.

Then the diplomatic corps had as its social wet-nurse the middle-aged bachelor Count von Bassewitz, extremely well born if not so prosperous as his predecessor. He took his duties so seriously it was almost painful to watch. There was none of the lighthearted charming cynicism and brilliance of the younger von Mumm. He was deadly in earnest about whether the Colombian or the Argentine Minister was third or fourth in line in the formal two-by-two march towards any specific or general dining-room. In fact, he was so conscientious and perspiringly accurate, he was less proficient than he might have been, his nerves almost giving way at times. I always felt like a sheep being led to slaughter when he flutteringly described a circle around me, and I wanted to duck my head and run from his protection. On the already mentioned occasion of my father's leaving before the Royalty did, he became so nervous and fidgety, perspiring and flushed, I actually felt sorry for him and wanted to help him out. Graf Bassewitz was a nice, pleasant, and pathetic creature who had prominent and slightly crooked eyes, wore a monocle, and was the nearest approach to an old maid I have yet seen among men. I shall never forget his slightly—oh, so slightly and politely—raised eyebrows when he asked me once how I liked Russia and I replied I thought it an extremely interesting country! I have never heard him—and I think my experience is not uncommon—commit himself on any subject. Probably he never heard half of what was being said to him—since his absorption in social matters was final and complete, his ears cocked, his eyes focused on stray bits of conversation, how a Frenchless diplomat was managing with a woman who spoke only French—but what he did hear he thought wisest to have no opinion about one way or another, no doubt remembering the political demise of his predecessor.

In any case, he lasted not much longer than von Mumm, and the corps was again presented with a brooding hen who cluckingly took the diplomatic corps under its wing. This time a Herr von Levetzow was presented to us, a tall lisping man in his late thirties, a relative of the former police president of Berlin and of good lineage. He was a little less excitable and nervous, had a slight sense of humour about the whole thing, and seemed to be rather negatively intelligent. He occasionally ventured a veiled opinion, danced well, seemed more ornamental than Bassewitz but was generally considered as comic and futile as his predecessor. He stayed with us a short time and was then appointed to a German Ministry in South America. The last male Emily Post, who was still in his position when I left, was a young man, short, stumpy, and darkish, who wore spectacles and seemed to be more intelligent though just as fussy as the others. Considering the job these semi-diplomats have to do, I suppose it is not surprising that they were all feminine and somewhat trivial in their types. I always felt very sorry for men in such positions, though I was mainly amused at their antics and concern for meticulous observance of outworn social codes.

The young apprentices in the Foreign Office were very friendly with the diplomatic corps. They danced with the daughters, they sent flowers to the mothers, they escorted the

fathers on trips and were in general the young bloods of
Berlin social life. During the time I was there I saw a whole
batch or two of them trained and disciplined and sent away
to foreign posts. All of them were S.S. men, for instance:
Karl Berger, now in Rome; Hans Otto Meissner (son of
Hitler's secretary) was once in the Embassy in London;
Heinrich Northe in Moscow—lately in Mexico where he acted
as a Nazi spy, according to an article in *Ken*; young Klugquist,
formerly in Spain—each of these suave, attractive youths had
been picked from the S.S. as loyal and well-disciplined Nazis,
worthy to promote their country's interests in the foreign
service. Many of them, at the same time, were being shown
the ins and outs of subtle propagandizing, if nothing more,
and I am sure are able and competent representatives of the
Nazi Reich in a way only severely tested S.S. men could be.
One never thinks of regarding them as intellectually superior
in any way. The Nazis don't expect it and surely the world
doesn't. The S.S. is notoriously an organization of beauty and
brawn—the brain being the least important concern. It is a
pity, however, that young men without training in history,
culture, education, are sent all over the world simply because
they can memorize the tenets of National Socialism and have
proved themselves to be excellent propaganda agents.

II

In Hitler's chancery I knew Hans Thomsen, Fritz Wiedemann—recently famous for his so-called "diplomatic" missions
to England—Lammers, and Meissner. Meissner was formerly
Hindenburg's trusted secretary—he was also a well-known
Social Democrat. Though he pretended to the diplomats that
he greatly disapproved of Hitler's extremes in foreign and
internal policy, he actually offered no resistance whatsoever.
There were many jokes going around about Meissner, mainly
concerning his perfidy and his treacherous ability to survive
every Reich and each time to be, furthermore, in a better
position than before. When Hindenburg died, and of course
before that, during the Purge, Meissner was as nervous as a

cat about his future. He had never been a flag-waving Nazi, had always followed meekly in the footsteps of his chief, the Wooden Titan, who, though he had helped put Hitler into power, resisted him, at times, passively, later. But Hitler apparently sensed or knew Meissner's ability to change face as rapidly as was necessary and the puppet was taken over to Hitler's office after the old Field Marshal's death. Here the now notorious meekness increased rather than diminished. With most of these older men who were not original party fighters and founders, in the first year or two, you found a complete cynicism about Hitler, his movement and the length of time he would endure. In some men the cynicism developed into hatred, with others it solidified into contemptuous resignation; many accepted him completely because of their own personal ambitions—they found both their careers and their fortunes being protected by Hitler and they stuck to him blindly no matter how they had to sacrifice their own submerged principles or the good of their nation. And quite a few actually became converted to Nazism as the best political "philosophy" to effect Germany's world power. Meissner certainly was no Hitlerite to begin with; his attitude began changing before Hindenburg's death—he knew he would be without a job when the old man passed away. He began to understand that his career, if not his financial status, would be guaranteed and improved with Fascism and he observed accurately that Hitler and his movement were not insecure passing phenomena.

By the time we left, Meissner was one of the most obsequious, and at the same time arrogant, Nazis of them all. I shall never forget the bitter disregard he paid to my father's protest and pleas for the life of Helmut Hirsch, a young American Jew accused of plotting the death of Streicher. Backed by vigorous orders from the State Department, my father went to see everyone he could in connection with the case. Meissner avoided a show-down, postponed meetings, evaded the telephone, but finally consented to present the protest to the Leader himself. My father got a curt answer, delivered by special messenger, one evening as we were sitting down to dinner. It said that the Leader did not see fit to grant mercy to an American citizen and that he would be shot at dawn despite the international furore the case had aroused. Meissner signed the letter.

Meissner is a dumpy medium-sized man with proportions somewhat like General Goering's. He has great, fat, blooming cheeks, dark hair that stands up, small dark piggish eyes behind spectacles with magnifying lenses, and a pug nose. His bearing is crass and loud, yet he gives the impression of being a scared rabbit, without courage or real vitality. He is something like the malicious humorous American cartoon of Heinz, the typical German, a fat body, a fat face, a square red neck, and last but not least, a fat brain. Meissner has very few friends among the diplomatic corps and is somewhat contemptuously treated by the "real" Nazis. The last time I saw him he was dancing the Viennese waltz with the fabulously beautiful Italian Ambassadress, Madame Attolico, Meissner bubbling and bobbing up and down like a weighted cork on a heavy sea.

His children came often to my parties. Hans Otto, the young son, was in the Foreign Office at the time, a spoiled, indulged little rascal; his sister was a large, voluptuous dark girl of fifteen precocious years. Meissner's wife was a young and rather pretty faded blonde with a high temper and a sharp tongue.

Lammers, another secretary close to Hitler, was a tall thin man with a bulbous face, bald, with pale weird eyes protruding and looking in opposite directions. Genial, rather gentle and courteous of manner, he was not as frightening as he looked. His wife was a large, dark, motherly person and his daughter was pretty, shy, and charming.

I met Fritz Wiedemann at one of Sigrid Schultz's parties. He was later in the headlines of all papers in connection with his "diplomatic" mission in England; a few weeks before Czechoslovakia's rape. He was supposed to be one of the most powerful men behind Hitler's throne and to enjoy the absolute trust of Hitler. He was the "strong man" in Hitler's closest circle. Tall, dark, muscular, he certainly had great physical brawn and the appearance of bravery. He had known

Hitler in the early days, when they were in the same company in the War. It is hard to know whether at the time he had much respect for Hitler or whether he considered him a hare-brained mystic, as most of his contemporaries in the army felt. In any case, he claimed that he was impressed with him from the start and that he had been loyal to him ever since.

Wiedemann's heavy face, with beetling eyebrows, friendly eyes and an extremely low forehead was rather attractive. But I got the impression of an uncultivated primitive mind, with the shrewdness and cunning of an animal and completely without delicacy or subtlety. When he was sent on various missions to France and England I could hardly believe it could be the same man. There were rumours that he had been put in Hitler's chancery by the Reichswehr to report on the plans and inside moves of the Leader. I think, however, that his reputation as a man of mystery was undeserved. He seemed to be loyal to Hitler, completely so, if not to all others in the Nazi leadership, and he served him as both a body-guard and a political trusty. Certainly Wiedemann was a dangerous man to cross, for despite his social naïveté and beguiling clumsiness he was as ruthless a fighter and schemer as some of his compatriots.

Von Blomberg I saw on many occasions, and several times I went to his house for balls. He was a pleasant, soft, and wordless man. Tall and courtly, with a severe military carriage, and a head of soft white hair, he seemed to be a sort of soldierly nonentity, a man who could execute orders capably but who could never be incited to serious opposition or indignation. Von Blomberg is now out of command in the Reichswehr but I am sure it was not because of any treasonable activity or thoughts on his part. He no doubt displeased Hitler in the very tepidness of his character and perhaps Hitler resented his fine breeding, his faint Royalist sympathies, and his lack of passion.

Blomberg's family was large but several of his daughters married and went away and his former wife died. I knew, consequently, only the youngest daughter and son, both of whom I entertained frequently. The son, a young officer now in the air service, was a delightful boy, gangling, snub-nosed, and humorous, stiff in his manners but amusing in his attitudes and conversation. He was frank and simple and childlike, and danced beautifully. He enjoyed drinking and did so with more abandon than any of the other sons of Nazi leaders— though all of them seemed to find some release from the tense atmosphere of their homes and their country in drinking and in visiting the houses of foreigners where talk and habits were free and informal. His sister was a quiet, brown, mousey girl, whom I liked very much for the quick flashes of her quiet intelligence. She spoke several languages with great ease and had an unpretentious, simple, and charming social personality.

12

One of the most interesting men—in fact, with Prince Louis Ferdinand and Rolf Diels, the third most unusual German I met with any degree of friendly intimacy—was Colonel Ernst Udet. Goering and Richthofen and Udet were the most brilliant and daring aces during the World War. In fact, Udet took over the Richthofen squadron for a period of time and earned the rare and much-cherished medal *Pour la Mérite*. His exploits became legendary in Germany and were later incorporated in a book of memoirs. Feeling intense national loyalty, he entered the War in his early adolescence and fought through to the end. Afterwards, he had various jobs connected with aviation and factories, and finally became a professional stunt pilot. He made trips of exploration and adventure into Africa and the Arctic, flew a glider among the highest Alpine peaks, picked up a handkerchief from the ground with the edge of his wing, and in general enjoyed hanging his life by a thread. He lived by and on thrills—he was an adventurer at heart, romantic, reckless, nerveless, honest, with a sense of humour unmatched by any German I have met on personal, informal terms.

About five feet three or four inches tall, chubby in figure with a pudgy tummy and short little legs and arms, with

Pg

delicate and finely made firm hands, a baldish head, snub nose and thin smiling mouth, his eyes blue and grey, steely and warm, constantly screwed up tight with laughter and framed with the cobwebs of mirth, Udet was rakish, irrepressible—his modest and unassuming figure, posture and manner giving lie to the man he was, to the impression of power and reserve strength one inevitably felt after a few moments.

He was very fond of a little car he had, not much bigger than himself, which he manœuvred in and out of narrow streets, turning around almost on a penny, speeding incredibly on the new German highways. It was a miracle to watch the way he handled his car and one felt intuitively that he could handle any kind of machinery with the same confidence and brilliance of performance. He once told me that his little car could practically drive itself, whereupon he took his hands off the steering gear and it did drive itself almost without error. He handled it lovingly and with joy and some of the most pleasurable and interesting moments I had were in watching him.

In this little man, rather comic-appealing in build, I felt curiously the very spirit and lightness of the air and of the mechanical bird which had dared to challenge its unknown distances and tempers. In his apartment he had a small love-bird which he cherished above all things human or inanimate—except perhaps his 'plane. He would make soft whirring bird noises, chirp and whistle and talk to it as if the bird could well understand. And it seemed that the bird was of the same species as Udet, or vice versa. He flew to his shoulder and obeyed every command, even the command of going into his darkened cage to sleep. Udet rarely took him in his hands and put him to bed—he would spend instead fifteen minutes coaxing and wheedling it in a language the bird seemed to understand, the bird playing and flying away, coming back swervingly and kissing Udet on the face and lips and hair and finally creeping delicately down the wire cage, twirping a little wistfully, and then becoming quiet. It was delightful watching Udet as he trained his bird and very touching to realize how tenderly he felt toward it. This same gentleness he lavished on an old dog he had had for many years.

In his very modest little apartment was a conglomeration of everything that had meant anything to Udet in his life. Pieces of 'planes he had brought down in the War (he was not proud of his record of over sixty 'planes and knew very well the horror the human heart faces when murder must be carried out through cold command), pictures of the air-aces of other nations he had known or met later, medals and awards and mementoes of every shape and material and meaning, pictures of men and women with whom he had been friendly or to whom he felt loyal or grateful, huge albums of pictures of his exploits all over the world, bits of sculpture and souvenirs from Africa, the Arctic, America, and other places he had been. It was an untidy but cosy place, symbolic of the personality which inhabited it. In one room he had a small target at which he shot from the adjoining room. His rifle and pistol shooting had an incredible degree of accuracy and even when he had drunk far too many drinks the accuracy was not even slightly impaired. I always considered this more than remarkable and figured that his nerves must not have existed at all or were so hardened that alcohol could never affect them. I would sit by the hour watching him shoot with his deadly accuracy, listening to the radio which could get every sort of foreign station and to which he also listened with avid interest and turning over the pictures in his fascinating albums.

Shortly after I met him he took me to the airport and showed me his 'plane. He put a cap on my head and told me to get in. He got in, in back of me—it was a single-motored open 'plane—and we rose softly into the blue sky. We must have risen very high because the air was icy and hard to breathe. He shouted to me above the roar of the engine and raised both his arms high into the air. At first I didn't know what had happened but I soon caught the laughing twitch of his eyes as he indicated to me that I should take the controls. I felt very calm and not at all excited—and I had been up at this time only once before—and raised my hands, too. We were soon low over the ground again. He swerved the 'plane over a new road where dedication services were going on, waved lustily, was recognized and cheered as we swung away again.

When we came down I was a little breathless and wobbly on my feet but we had a good stiff *aqua vite* with General Milch, another of the high air chiefs, and a lively conversation. Milch was also a delightful, chubby, short man with glowing ruddy cheeks and bright humorous blue eyes. They discussed the merit of American girls and I learned for the first time that Udet had been desperately in love with an American girl whom he met on a trip over there. His knowledge of American manners and customs, his love for everything American, was something like that of Prince Louis, and I of course felt even more warmly towards them both on account of this. I think Udet would have gladly come to America if he could have without compromising his devotion to his Fatherland.

Udet was a daredevil stunt pilot when the Nazis called him home. His exploits were known all over the world, and wherever men of spirit and courage in any field of sport met, Udet's name was spoken with respect and awe. During the War and the long years afterwards, when he risked his life in some of the most dangerous regions, Udet received only a few minor wounds and had only a few minor accidents. It seemed that his life was charmed and his friends and confrères spoke almost mystically of Udet's luck. Ernst carried dozens of charms which he took up with him every time he flew and he felt humorously superstitious about them.

A year or two after he was called home, Udet was promoted from a simple Captain (he was an enlisted man) to a General and made the supreme chief of the technical work of Germany's air fleet. It had been suggested to him that he live more pretentiously and in the style usually affected by a General. He successfully resisted any attempt to change his mode and habits of life, and when I left was still enjoying his simple little flat and his hobbies.

Though he never admitted it, I thought Udet was miserable the last two years in Germany. He was forced to accept a fanatic nationalism which could never accord with his international spirit—he often said that the air knew no boundaries, had no limited domain. He admired and respected many, people of enemy countries, he was at home in any society in any nation. Though he was a deeply patriotic man, he had a thirst for travel in other countries. His patriotism led him to return to Germany and this same patriotism is the mesh that has ensnared him.

Ernst Udet had a childlike simplicity of character combined with a dreamer's sure vision. His genius, which he had so hoped could be used constructively, is now being put to the evil end of man's intimidation and destruction. No man of his nobility of purpose, brilliance of accomplishment, could be happy in his position though the Nazi world may fawn and flatter and the pangs of patriotic conscience be superficially assuaged. His vivid and sometimes bitter, never-failing sense of humour, his cynical and often sardonic intelligence helped him to endure these years of prison. This delicate little pudgy penguin of a man with his bright bird-like eyes, who once said airplanes should have no propellers, who watched fascinated and envious the flight of a feather or a bird through the air, had had his wings clipped. Chained to a bloody and gigantic machine of war, he saw all plans for experimental aviation for the benefit of mankind which he so deeply cherished shattered under its wheels, probably never to rise again during his lifetime.

IX

DICTATORSHIP THROUGH ESPIONAGE, OPPRESSION, TERROR

I THINK MOST AMERICAN citizens after having read reports from Nazi Germany and about Fascism in general know thoroughly that a system of terror exists there that can hardly be matched in the annals of history. Diels was proud of his network of espionage. Himmler inherited it. Himmler's chief stooge is Heydrich, whom one journalist described to me as the most vicious and perverted man he had ever known or seen. Himmler, according to the Australian author, Roberts, who wrote "The House that Hitler Built," is the man to watch in Germany—he says, in fact, that because of the power Himmler can wield in the Secret Police he is the only logical man to succeed Hitler. Himmler was an unknown schoolteacher with an unsavoury record, whose manipulation of the secret state police has been masterly and ruthless. But anyone who has ever laid eyes on Himmler or who realizes the tremendous unpopularity he enjoys among most people, even in the Nazi party, knows he could never be the Leader's successor. He is short, dark, with a little black moustache and evasive small sharp rodent's eyes behind spectacles. There is nothing interesting, commanding, or even mystic in his face or bearing. Trivial, unscrupulous, and exact, he has his finger constantly pressed against the opposition or hostile pulse of the nation. Certainly he would be used and perhaps might even have a comparable strong behind-the-scenes control in another Nazi's government (assuming, of course, that Hitler could be followed in case of death or accident by another Nazi). But it is hardly conceivable that a nation so terribly oppressed by spies and agents would permit the chief spy to be their leader—and it is difficult to imagine that the other leaders in the party would allow such a man to be in power since he has records and data on every one of them as well. In any case, for the time being Himmler has organized his work so supremely well from his point of view that Hitler leans heavily on him and his information.

The German dictatorship has so encroached upon the life, the culture, the religion of a nation that it will take perhaps generations for the people to put the clock forward again. In a dictatorship as supreme and ruthless as is known in all of history, every human life has in some way been affected. This control has been accomplished by a system of terror and fear before which the Inquisition, in all its methods both subtle and base, would pale. As far as human freedom and the liberty of the individual are concerned, Germany is in the Dark Ages. The German nation and the German people live by the laws of the savage. It is a revival with a vengeance of the creed, *survival of the fittest*. By violence, by fierce destruction, by cruelty, persecution, and oppression unmatched on such a large scale in civilization's history, Germany has been returned to the rule of the jungle where man's most primitive and blood-thirsty instincts have been elevated to the law of the land. The Nazi wolves have devoured a nation.

2

Except for that small number of organized opposition, many of the most civilized and valuable and productive people left Germany long ago. The Nazis came in on a socialistic pro-gramme—the first thing they did was to wipe out the free powerful trade unions of which they could well be afraid. In their stead they gave the workers the National Socialist trade unions which were on an even lower scale of political and economic effectiveness than company unions. The workers, forced to join these unions, had no voice in electing their leaders —Nazi men were appointed arbitrarily by the party. The workers naturally were forbidden to criticize the Nazis, were unable to strike or protest to gain advantages of any sort. They had no voice in the government and they were com-pelled to accept their low wages and long hours without a

wince. Dr. Ley organized a gigantic so-called Labour Front
for which the workers must pay, whose annual holiday trips
they may join if they have enough money and if they are good
enough Nazis. They organize tremendous collective picnics
every year to various parts of Europe near Germany. The
better-paid workers, of course, can afford to attend. For
instance, my maid, after two years of saving her money—
and she belonged to the group of better-paid domestic servants—went on a short trip to Norway by boat. She was very
pleased even though she had to pay for all extras and was
subjected regularly to propaganda. These trips serve as clever
means of propagandizing the hundreds, sometimes thousands,
of picnickers. They learn, as they are taken around Europe
by Labour Front officers, what parts rightfully belong to
Germany and they learn how National Socialism is going to
get them back and why consequently they must support
everything Hitler does.

The workers are given the most careful secret police surveillance. The Nazis know only too well that, if the workers
could organize their discontent and their opposition, there
would be nothing left of Hitler and his set-up. Thousands of
labour leaders of pre-Hitler days were arrested, killed, and sent
to concentration camps. The Nazis succeeded in breaking temporarily the back of the labour movement. Whenever opposition is discovered in these groups, and especially in munition
plants or related industries, it is more ruthlessly stamped out
than in other classes of society. One reads regularly, even in
the Nazi press, of workers who were executed because of
treasonable activities—anything not agreeing with Hitler of
course constitutes treason. This means that the particular
victim's family, relatives, and co-workers, if not arrested or
sent to camps or even quietly killed, are given no further peace
either in their private lives or in their work. With the crippling
of the people's organizations, which to some extent guaranteed,
formerly, their economic and political independence, and with
the tightening web of espionage and secret police agents, the
Nazis believe they have quelled all the stirrings for freedom
so strongly expressed in the German working class before Hitler.

Of course, every Nazi is not only a Nazi in ideology and activity but an agent of the Party as well. It is his duty to report any anti-Nazi feeling or expression wherever he goes and in the homes he visits. It is not uncommon that such espionage is carried on in intimate family circles. One intellectual once told my father that since his young son had joined the Party there was no longer peace in the home. The parents were afraid to express themselves openly in front of him and his friends, and were also fearful for the older friends they entertained who might talk frankly in front of the boy. Naturally, the same spirit exists among friends, both men and women. However, I know of another young Nazi who, before the Third Reich, went often to a home where he met liberals and radicals, Marxists and socialists. Urged to report names and facts of the opposition, past and present, he adamantly refused, declaring that all the friends he had in those days were intellectual and artistic purely and had no interest in politics. I am sure there are many such Nazis whose sense of honour and fair play are repelled by such technique and who have sentimental loyalties to family and friends that no party fanaticism can shake. But these are counterbalanced by the others who sacrifice all human emotions to the prestige they achieve from their knowledge and their betrayals.

Besides the innumerable Nazis who feel in their obligation to the Party to serve as agents, there are in every village, in every countryside, in every city, a network of paid Gestapo agents posing as officials of one sort or another, most of the time posing as secret enemies of Fascism. In one rather small factory town one man, known to be a town official, got the word around among the workers that he was sympathetic to the Loyalist cause in Spain. After a week or so of penetrating into workers' homes and sympathies, he drew up a secret petition for financial aid to the Spanish Government. He got over fifty signatures before someone caught on to him and warned the workers. But these fifty names were off the payroll of the factory and could be found on the concentration camp roll-call.

The number of Gestapo agents increases, of course, wherever there are active hostile groups. For instance, among industrial workers connected with large factories or in the cities, and among the dock workers in port towns, they have efficient *agents provocateurs*. These men not only harass the simple worker about foreign matters, but also try to encourage him to cause labour disputes. If there are any labour leaders already there, they attempt to ferret them and their co-workers out. The *agent provocateur* is perhaps the most vicious type of espionage instrument. The simple employee in a factory, for instance, naturally protests inwardly against his long hours, the low wage, and the increasingly high cost of living, conditions which will always exist under a Fascist economy no matter how many territories full of rich raw materials and natural resources they manage to annex. If a seemingly sincere worker agrees with him and sympathizes, it is natural that he should unburden his thoughts and even describe what he and his fellows propose to do. He is gradually learning however, that such sympathizers are dangerous. But the real tragedy is that the atmosphere of fear and suspicion thus created is so tense that normal human companionship, confidence, and loyalty are destroyed and a psychosis of terror rules the land.

The Gestapo agents are particularly active on voting days. They know if a person in an assigned district, town, or village doesn't go to the polls or if he goes reluctantly. The agent is there to overhear talk near the polls and in the restaurants and beer gardens later. He encourages a man or a group of men to speak openly and, if they do, he sees to it that punishment is accorded as promptly as possible. The culprit is sometimes called before the Nazi local headquarters, sometimes summarily arrested and taken to a camp, often snatched from his home or apartment at night. Naturally, as time goes on, the people who are actively and passively antagonistic in a particular region, are so careful, so continuously on their guard against eavesdroppers, Nazi petty officials, newcomers in their region or in their particular factory, that the Nazis must bestir themselves to find new tactics of detection.

While I was in Germany I heard several instances, told me directly by people who witnessed the vicious procedure, of a

Gestapo agent who went into a town, found out the most insecure people there who were behind in their taxes and in Party assessments, and then went quietly to one poor man and promised him that his taxes would be forgotten and that he would be excused of dues and other financial obligations if he would for a period of a few weeks report the comings and goings of a neighbour. The distressed fellow thought he could tell some superficial and unimportant things about his neighbour which would in no way get his neighbour into trouble with the Secret Police, yet could pretend to the Gestapo agent he was reporting all he knew and could discover. At the end of the agreed period the agent returned to the man, received his reports, told him his taxes were in order and then instructed him to do some other similar job. The man refused saying it was not in the bargain and that he had worked before only under stress which he had been promised would be relieved. If the poor fellow remained adamant the Gestapo agent threatened to reveal him to his village, to denounce him as a Gestapo agent, ruin his small business and his future. This, of course, is only one trick out of an enormous bag of them used against innocent people. When an important section of the government is devoted to uncovering the slightest sign of opposition, is heavily financed by Party funds and employs a huge staff of men, it is not surprising that the net result is several hundred thousand Germans in concentration camps. What does stun the observer is that there is still opposition, organized and unorganized, among different groups and that hundreds of thousands of Germans still dare vote a vigorous and death-shadowed NEIN.

3

Among the upper classes the Gestapo supervision is just as vigorous and ruthless if somewhat more subtle than in the working-class population. But let it be stated very clearly that whenever real opposition is located, no matter where, the technique of the Gestapo is always the same: liquidation. *Agents provocateurs* are even more numerous among the so-called leisure class. I have told how professors, intellectuals, artists, and scientists are able no longer to carry on free and animated conversations. Small business men in the cities and the bourgeoisie in general must be constantly on guard against suspicion and false charges, must be careful not to sell goods to Jews or mix with people not wholeheartedly behind Hitler. Even among the Royalty, old and trusted servants are suspected and new servants watched and distrusted.

Our concern about telephones and dictaphones is an illustration of the complicated and subtle sort of espionage which is always at work even in the diplomatic corps itself. Of our servants there was not one before whom we could speak openly. When we first arrived in Germany, and during the first year, we thought rumours of the Secret Service vastly exaggerated. But as time went on we had more or less direct indications that information was getting out about our private lives that could only be revealed from the home itself. Letters were brazenly opened at the border with the excuse of money control. Some of the letters with a clear Embassy stamp on them and sealed officially were opened and delayed. When my father protested, the German Foreign Office promised to punish the offender and said it was purely accidental. We felt later that it was truly "purely accidental"—since opening of letters has been known to be much more carefully managed. In any case, we never thought for a moment of writing letters, even on our official stationery, of any confidential nature without sending them out through the pouch. But, as I have said, even the pouch was suspect. Our letters usually went on a German boat because of the necessity of speed. My father suggested several times to our State Department that he suspected our pouch of being tampered with and that he strongly advised sending our diplomatic pouch on reliable boats. As far as I know, his suggestion was never acted upon. I heard from a young man in a foreign Embassy of the incident of two young pouch "carriers" on the same route with their important pouches—one was a German, the other a foreigner. When they were at a station together waiting for a train the German suggested that the foreigner get his dinner while he watched both the mails! One time a German woman

asked my mother if she knew how she could get a confidential
letter to a daughter of hers in America. Mother suggested
she try the pouch of some foreign Embassy. The woman
laughed and declined, declaring she wanted "protection!"

The Tiergarten, the beautiful, ancient, and heavily-wooded
park in the heart of Berlin, finally on the black list, was used
not only for fashionable horseback riders, dress-paraders, Sunday walkers, and the exercising of dogs, but also for private
and important talks between diplomats and officials who did
not want to speak within the privacy of their own homes or
offices. My father used to take walks here with other Ambassadors until they suspected that even in this lovely and romantic
setting, they were being followed.

Of course, the Russian and French Embassies were watched
even more carefully than the American and English. I was
told that spies were posted opposite these palaces as well as
within them to report on visitors, the number of their cars and
the length of their visits, among infinitely more important
matters. On several occasions I have been followed on foot
and by car when I left our residence, and I had interesting
experiences leading my "shadow" into all sorts of tedious and
ridiculous spots. In the last year of our residence there I had
a friend quite high among the Nazis. He was secretly not at
all in sympathy with their extreme policies. One night when
he was calling on me he left his car on the street outside our
Embassy residence instead of driving in. When he left, he
found his car had been seriously damaged. I thought of course
that it had been injured in the process of attempted theft. He
was confident that it was a warning to him from the Secret
Police that his visits to the American Embassy—which was by
this time quite unpopular among Nazi Germans—were
unwelcome.

Most of the time my brother and I were serious and tense
enough about this situation. But occasionally our long-lost
sense of humour would break through the strain—and we both
would talk with friends (of course not Germans) in a complicated and menacing-sounding language. We knew that
most of what anyone said was recorded laboriously on discs.

We hoped our conversations would make good "listening" and cause a little more effort. Very undignified procedure, I admit, but it helped relieve the terrific pressure which we could never really accustom ourselves to.

However, to show how really serious the matter was, whenever a friend of mine connected with the Nazi party telephoned, he used another name and we had previously, by word of mouth, arranged a complicated language for meeting at a certain time and place without giving it away over the telephone. We both knew that all Embassies were under suspicion, that particularly the American Embassy, after my father's long and consistent stand against dictatorship, would be under careful surveillance. Even though we were convinced that dictaphones had been installed in our house—perhaps before our lease or perhaps during our absences—we did occasionally talk in the rooms where there was no telephone. I had one friend, however, who refused even to talk in our sun porch which was made entirely of tiles and glass and would have been a difficult job of wiring.

There is no way on earth one can describe in the coldness of words on paper what this espionage can do to the human being. Though we knew we enjoyed the privilege of extra-territoriality, that the Germans could never do us any serious harm no matter what we said, the family's conferences and freedom of speech and action were so circumscribed we lost even the faintest resemblance to a normal American family. Whenever we wanted to talk we had to look around corners and behind doors, watch for the telephone and speak in whispers. A woman friend of mine—a lovely German woman who detested the terror of Nazi Germany—would occasionally mysteriously lead me into our bathroom—also a most difficult place to wire!—and whisper almost inaudibly some new event she had heard about. Such was the life an average American family was subjected to in four years under a dictatorship.

The psychology of fear and terror can penetrate into the consciousness, and unconsciousness for that matter, of the most innocent and even well-guarded people. Our fear was not only for ourselves—because whether rationally or not, we even feared our own safety—but for the people we entertained and for the sources of news we were acquainted with. Most of the people we knew and the opinions we heard expressed were antagonistic only to certain measures of Hitler. When the people were completely inimical to Hitler—and there were few we saw in diplomatic life—they were still inimical in words and were never organized in any sort of opposition movement. So one can well imagine, if this atmosphere existed in the home of the representative of one of the freest countries in the world, what agony and tragedy existed in the home of a liberty-loving German. And now, after months and months away from Germany, the habits of my mind and life are so fixed that I often unconsciously watch for servants and speak in low tones whenever I express a frank opinion. The attitudes of suspicion and caution are so deeply ingrained, the human nervous system so highly keyed, it will take years to forget that racking experience.

4

As a matter of fact there is still a good deal of organized opposition among the people in Germany, which reveals how human courage and belief can survive even through such sacrifice. Parties and organizations representing former labour groups, liberals, pre- and anti-Hitler political alignments, democrats, Centrists (the Catholic party) and Protestants, left democrats and innumerable other groupings opposed to Hitler in 1932 and now, spring up like mushrooms everywhere with their leadership, publications, and propaganda—some disappearing in a few weeks, some lasting for months and years.

Among these are the remnants of the Social Democratic party which has an underground organization within the working class. The Communist Party which polled around six million votes when Hitler took over power has been completely reorganized. Of course, all these six million were not Communists, by any means—nevertheless, they were a strong party. All the leaders who did not escape were shot or imprisoned by Hitler. The old leadership was destroyed and a new one sprang up cautiously. They have nuclei in every factory and in every region in Germany, and remain the most active, well-organized, and militant political opposition, with a definite programme.

One hears frequently of strikes—obviously they are never reported in German papers. Occasionally the strikes are successful—depending on the pressure brought to bear. Sometimes the Nazi labour leaders are forced to accept the workers' demands, oftentimes the strikes are brutally suppressed and all strikers summarily dealt with. The general policy of organized opposition among all political groups now hostile to Nazism is to invade the Nazi ranks, and, if possible, win them over, or to place trained and courageous men in key positions whose allegiance to the opposition has been tested. I know several men in various ministries who are hostile to the National Socialist government. Among the working population the same is true. These men knowingly risk their lives in an effort to overthrow Hitler, to educate their co-workers and to collect information from the inside that will be valuable to their work.

While I was in Germany I heard of at least two different political parties who carried on anti-Nazi work through the dissemination of literature. Some Germans who had received the literature cautiously showed it to me. Speeches of Roosevelt and various statesmen all over the world were reprinted (speeches which are rarely reported in the Nazi papers or, if they are, so badly garbled they are unrecognizable), news of Spain, foreign opinion about Germany and the general European situation, comments about Hitler's policy, and information about labour movements in other countries. These leaflets were not at all incendiary but invaluable newspapers, offering information impossible to get in the German press. The booklets published by the Communist Party deal with much the same material, including, however, articles of Marx, Lenin, and Stalin and reports from Russia and a programme for organization and action, and are passed around among the workers surreptitiously. They have harmless covers, titles of

new Nazi romances or treatises, and contain a few pages of
the original innocuous booklet. Inside, the other printed
matter is in small type. Very small, easy to handle and dispose
of, it is estimated that ten to twenty workers read one copy.
Thousands of these booklets, pamphlets and leaflets circulate
through Germany constantly, many of them poured in through
foreign borders, and many published illegally within Germany. The penalty for owning one is severe, so one can
imagine what courage and passion it takes for the worker to
read and circulate it.

For a year or two an illegal radio was travelling through
Germany. When the Nazis finally found it the whole staff
of operators was executed. Shortly after it was heard again.
It is said that the apparatus was loaded on a truck. The people
of Germany could listen if they wanted to and many of them
did—but the penalty of listening was arrest and prison sentence. Broadcasts from Russia were forbidden for the Germans
and the Nazis tried to cause enough static and interference to
keep it from coming in clearly. However, if you owned a good
enough set you could get it on the short wave most of the
time fairly distinctly. Though it was a great risk, I knew many
Germans, simple and more highly placed, who turned their
dials regularly to Moscow, half out of curiosity and half out
of growing sympathy. Because of the cost of such radio sets
most German workers were unable to get Moscow with their
radios. The German government encouraged the people to
buy, at a reduction, simple sets which were not strong enough
to receive distant stations. However, some German people if
they cannot afford to buy the more expensive sets are beginning to make their own—cheap effective little radios which
bring the outside world to their homes.

There are two other stations, now operating from foreign
countries which come in regularly over the short wave—one
from Barcelona, the other from Switzerland. These stations are
also operated by opposition political parties and furnish interesting information which never leaks into Germany if the
Nazis can prevent it. There is no question that the Germans
who possess good enough radio sets listen in to these stations,

despite the severity of the punishment, particularly to the Barcelona broadcast. The Spanish struggle is one of mystery to most Germans. They suspect, contrary to the information the German press and radio give, that it is not a German and Italian noble crusade against "Communists." Even should a few of them believe such patent absurdity the next question they ask themselves is, "In that case, why, with the combined effort of two great powerful nations, have the Communists been able to hold out for over two years?" Most of the German people who have a glimmering of intelligence can see the obvious loopholes in Nazi logic and wonder at the passionate propaganda necessary to put across contradictory falsehoods. So any bit of news from the outside is a welcome breath of freedom and many will make great sacrifices and take serious chances to obtain inklings of real truth.

The whispering campaign is an old device used on all occasions, since the beginning of Hitler's regime, for the undermining and counteracting of his new policies, both internal and foreign. Sometimes the whispers are in the form of mordantly humorous anecdotes, other times merely stories and facts told soberly in contradiction to Hitler's so-called "truths."

The Berlin-Rome axis from the time of its inception was, as I have said, a highly unpopular alliance in the minds of simple Germans. They could not understand why Hitler should glorify Mussolini and the Italian nation which, first of all, was against them in the World War and which, second, definitely belongs to the inferior races in Hitler's fantastic race-theory. The same applies to the Japanese-Italian-German anti-Comintern Pact. The stories circulated about the latter were both humorous, with a play on the word axis (a creaking, rusty, or broken axis), and serious. Yellow-skinned, pint-sized men did not fit very well into the design of "blond supreme Nordic."

These stories, detrimental to Hitler, disparaging such "charitable" undertakings as the Winter Hilfe, the use of whose funds is not easily traceable, satirizing Goering and Goebbels, grumbling over food shortages and innumerable other economic and political conditions in Germany, are spread quietly from the lowest to the highest class, from man to man and woman to woman, by word of mouth until they cover the country like wild fire. You can hear the same stories and the same complaints in Bavaria and in Prussia, on the Rhine and in the East simultaneously, almost as if a sort of spontaneous combustion of hostility was taking place.

5

In church groups the Nazi persecution is as intense as it is among workers. The Nazis have not only attempted to destroy the Catholic church but they have made inroads on the Protestant church as well. The world famous case of Pastor Niemoeller need only be referred to. Here again the Nazis dared to defy world censure and arrest one of the finest preachers in the land. He was a German with a good War record and was in no way connected with dissident political groups. But by the very fact that he reserved his pulpit for the expression of non-political freedom of opinion was enough for him to be regarded as a traitor to Germany. Despite the fact that Dr. Schacht, several of the more conservative members of the cabinet like Swerin-Crosick, and a few Reichswehr generals attended his church regularly and loyally, he was sacrificed to the Nazi lust for absolute power. The Protestant church then, though it shows extraordinary vitality and possesses some amazingly courageous men, is in the way to be liquidated by Hitler. The Protestant church has never before received such an onslaught aimed at utter extermination of the protestant and religious principles upon which it was founded. In its place the Germans are attempting to substitute the *Deutsche Christen* church founded on the fantastic ceremonies and beliefs of barbaric gods and legends.

With this policy toward the Protestant church so adamantly pursued, it is not surprising to find that the Nazis will be satisfied only when the Catholic church is destroyed or so completely subdued that it can no longer be called Catholic. The Catholics are, from Hitler's point of view, infinitely more

dangerous than the Protestants—not only because over a third
of the German people are born in this faith but also because
the Catholic church is notoriously jealous of the education
of its youth. Consequently, Hitler has forbidden Catholic
schools and has stated categorically, with the chopping block
behind him, that only the State—the Nazi State—has full right
to educate and claim the youth. The hold of the Catholic
church on its youth and its members has gone down in history as a religious marvel. Hitler, himself a Catholic by birth,
is planning to change all this, substituting state education for
the practical and political needs of the people, and a mythical
Thor, Valhalla, and a worship of Germanic heroes and primitive pageantry for their spiritual desires. The Catholic church
must soon end its policy of vacillation—increasingly it becomes
evident that it must take a stand one way or another; capitulation means extermination or a reorganization of the church
agreeable to the Nazis. Surely the majority of simple Catholic
believers cannot be in favour of sacrificing their church and
their faith to Adolf Hitler. But their leaders, the Catholic
hierarchy from the Pope down, are the ones who will be
answerable in history to the survival or death in Germany of
their age-old church.

In the meantime Hitler pursues his ruthless oppression
within the ranks of the church. Bickerings and squabblings
have been the order of the day since the Nazi seizure of power
—with occasionally a blast from Rome or a pastoral letter read
aloud in all German pulpits. But this only enrages Hitler to
further vicious measures. Daily one reads of arrests of priests
—usually with an unprovable accusation that the priests have
been involved in treasonable activities, homosexuality, or
fraudulent money exchanges. Often the foreign press finds
these priests—the objects of Hitler's venom—in concentration
camps or dead by execution. Daily the measures become more
stringent in the limitation of the church's control, even of its
own policies. But among the Catholics, as among the Protestants, there are heroic figures, priests and laymen who proclaim their freedom and their human right to liberty. There
are even secret meetings of Catholic priests and Protestant

preachers, laying out a programme for future action. One seminary forbidden to reopen now holds secret meetings and carries on education of its priests behind locked doors and in the houses of sympathizers—of course, with terrible risk to the lives of everyone involved.

6

Though the Nazis are noted all over the world for their persecution of minority groups, they also have persecuted and oppressed one large majority group. The press has given this oppression little attention or publicity. Women on the whole are not subjected to physical brutality, unless they are Jews or Communists or in some other way enemies of Hitler, but they have been emotionally, morally, and intellectually liquidated. Until Hitler came to power, German women were beginning to escape from the domination of the male to the extent of being self-respecting and productive elements in society. They had leaders and thinkers in all fields and were beginning to unite in an effective feminism that was calm and sure.

They were in youth movements and organizations that were taken over immediately upon Hitler's seizure of power. If real leadership or opposition were discovered, they were immediately and summarily dealt with. The women of Germany, as the women of France and England, to a lesser degree, have the double tragedy of belonging to two generations—one whose ranks of men were decimated by the World War, and the other in which comparatively few children were born. Therefore there were and are not enough men to go around for either generation despite the glorious paradise the Nazis have promised to women who give up their outside activities and retire to the home and the cradle. Certainly the fact that there are men in constant demand accounts partially for German women's weakness in regard to Hitler. They found in him and their loyalty to him, a mystic sublimation for their lonely lives. When this sublimation could promise as well that each and every one of them could have a husband and children, they capitulated.

The young women and girls who had accepted the Nazi faith, joined its various women's organizations and donned the uniforms and marching customs of the nation. They seemed almost abnormally healthy but the absence of spirit and mentality was the obvious result of the extravagant Nazi body-cult. Young girls from the age of ten onwards were taken into organizations where they were taught only two things: to take care of their bodies so they could bear as many children as the State needed and to be loyal to National Socialism. It is not surprising then that one finds a rising generation of women who are as non-intellectual as their men, utterly submissive to them and to the Leader.

Though the Nazis have been forced to recognize, through the lack of men, that not all women can get married even if all German men wanted to—which they don't—huge marriage loans are floated every year whereby the contracting parties can borrow substantial sums from the government to be repaid slowly or to be cancelled entirely upon the birth of enough children. All sorts of reductions in living costs, in income taxes and schooling are offered if the progeny is sufficient. Birth control information is frowned on and practically forbidden.

However, even with all these inducements and restrictions the marriages and births in Germany still do not satisfy Hitler. Though intellectual women are forbidden to be intellectual, careers are closed, feminist leaders abused, sneered at and kept from any activity, there are still millions of women who must work as desperately hard as their husbands to keep themselves alive. They look with the bitterest irony upon Hitler's frantic insistence that they breed more and more children. The financial inducements he offers covers perhaps a few months of the child's care and they must dig deeper and deeper into their empty purses for future costs of food, shelter, and up-bringing.

Women are forced to work at much lower wages than men and are fired or employed arbitrarily as they are needed. Their reproductive functions are glorified by the Nazis to the detriment of all else except their heavy labour, to which they must add it.

Most of the middle class and working women had to continue heavy work after having been promised "womanly work" and were, as well, forced into marriage and parenthood whether they could afford it or not. Nations faced with the imperative need of more soldiers and citizens must make chattels and common breeders of their women. Despite the fact that Hitler and the other Nazis are always ranting about a *Volk ohne Raum*—a people without space—they command their men and women to have more children. It is another proof of course of the basic economic inconsistency in Nazism and indicates only too well to the world that Germany is hell-bent on a campaign of world expansion equal in its grandiose schemes only to the accompanying world persecution.

Hitler and his party friends declare repeatedly, "Liberalism has a large number of points for woman's equality. The Nazi programme has but one: this is the child. While man makes his supreme sacrifice on the field of battle, woman fights her supreme battle for her nation when she gives life to a child," or again, "Woman is entrusted in the life of the nation with the great task, the care of man, soul, body and mind. It is the mission of woman to minister in the home . . . to the needs of life from the first to the last moments of man's existence . . ." and finally, "The new political reality is so constructed that one can say that the German women from now on will live in a state formed and led by the masculine spirit, in a non-parliamentarian and conservative state, on whose being . . . she will not have direct influence as formerly. . . ."

Thus women have been deprived of all rights except that of childbirth and hard labour. They are not permitted to participate in political life—in fact Hitler's plans eventually include the deprivation of the vote; they are refused opportunities of education and self-expression; careers and professions are closed to them; they can call themselves women only if they submit utterly, both intellectually and physically, to the desires and needs of their men. There is not a woman in the world, whether feminist or anti-feminist, who could raise her head proudly under such circumstances. And that is what the Nazis want. Women should be cowed in spirit, atrophied in intellect, emotionally loyal to the party, periodically and "with no foolishness" pregnant, strong and perfect-bodied mothers, slaves and servants in the home and in the state.

The furious sex jealousy that has been unleashed in the German male has destroyed what free spirit there was growing in German women before Hitler. Handmaiden to her man's work and his physical desires, beholden to the state for automatic reproduction, she has truly been thrust back centuries into the time when women were bought and sold like cattle for their healthy bodies and unprotesting submission. It will take many years before the German woman can once again raise her head and face herself as a human being. Surely the "Prussianism," as my father once spoke of it warningly to me, or Nazism, as we call it, of the German man is the darkness that is blotting out woman's dignity, freedom and future.

7

There is nothing left of German art and science, so absolute is the dictatorship and so devastating the terror and enforcement of it. Before Hitler came to power many writers fled with their families, many of them leaving possessions behind them. Later, as I have already described, the others who could not get out, were put in prison, several tortured to death, as for instance the poet Erich Mühsam, or sent to concentration camps. These of course included the writers who were pacifist, liberal, social-democratic, Jewish or Marxist, or in any other way opposed to the reign of the fanatic Hitler. And as it turned out there was not a really good writer left in Germany, with the exception of the rather talented Fallada and the aged Hauptmann. Those who by some quirk escaped Hitler's heavy hand are either silenced by capitulation or must write books censored and approved by the Propaganda Ministry.

The theatre and the cinema, relieved of all brilliant Jewish talent, is a trivial thing compared to its former glory. Naturally, all the actors and actresses must be acceptable to the Nazis, must be Aryan, and must conform to Nazi ideals. They must act in plays that have been passed upon or written, if they are modern, by Nazis, and must be directed by the proper people. Occasionally there are revivals of old plays—German classics written by Aryans and glorifying German history, or Shakespeare. One revival in Berlin was withdrawn after the clamour and applause of the audience during the recitation of a passage extolling human freedom. For the most part the theatre season in Berlin is so dull few people do more than laugh at the appearance of a new play. Once there was a dramatic version of the life of Thomas Paine. It had been so perverted to fit into the Nazi conception of the character that my father left in the middle of the second act. Production and staging jog along in a heavy boring rhythm of mediocrity. None of the brilliance, innovation, and imagination that existed before Hitler and in the Reinhardt days can be found in the contemporary theatre.

In the movies the situation is even worse—if that is possible. German comedy is at best a pathetically heavy-handed slapstick affair. A sense of humour is not a noted German trait and, under Nazism, when the nominal humour the Germans do have must be so restricted, it is especially conspicuous by its absence. The movies of a more serious nature are so dull and so devoted to the extolling of Nazi and national virtues that it is a bore to have to see one. It is a tragic state of affairs when one remembers that the German cinema before Hitler was known over the world for its daring and artistic experimentation. Emil Jannings was perhaps Germany's best actor, but the recent movies he has been forced to appear in are slowly ruining even his reputation.

One would think that the Nazis, realizing the lamentable qualities of their movies and the lack of box-office success, might try to import good foreign pictures. On the contrary, however, the same kind of rules and regulations apply to all movies. Charlie Chaplin is forbidden in Germany because he is Jewish, the same applies to the Marx brothers and many other—both comic and seriously dramatic—American movie stars. Once the Germans were in love with Sylvia Sidney; her pictures were on Kurfürstendamm and her photos in the papers. Unfortunately one day a bright young man found out she was

Jewish and from that time on there was a boycott of Sylvia
Sidney in Germany. Not only is the Jewish boycott considered
in censorship of foreign importations but also the type of picture. If the foreign movies were pacifistic or too flippant or
in other ways failed to meet the standards of pure Aryan
elevation they were not shown. Yet whenever a foreign picture does come to town it usually outlasts the local productions
by weeks and often months.

Since Furtwängler has agreed to knuckle under to the Nazis
(after a few minor squabbles), for which Toscanini branded
him publicly as irresponsible, one can still attend fine concerts
and hear good music. There were other great German conductors and composers who were evicted from Germany or
who left of their own accord. Erich Kleiber, co-conductor of
the Berlin Philharmonic, a conscientious, excellent, and progressive man with fine musical knowledge and restraint, not
specializing in Furtwängler's displays of personality, was
removed from his post and found a place in Vienna
temporarily.

Naturally jazz of any type is loathed and feared by Hitler.
It represents to him the International Marxist-Jewish conspiracy. It is not based solely upon the Germanic rhythms, as
he demands of all music, but rather on rhythms that are deep
in every human being. Consequently, "swing" or any other
variation of jazz is primitive, depraved—in the "sub-human
world spirit" class of music. Only a few night clubs attempt
to play jazz and they are very bad. Hitler allows two or three
such places to stay open in Berlin for the sake of the foreigners
and diplomats living in and visiting the German capital—foreigners who pay heavily into Nazi coffers. The permission is
reluctantly given and may cease at any moment. One never
hears jazz among the true Germanic crowds.

Fritz Kreisler, though not Jewish according to all reports,
a Viennese of world-wide fame, is not allowed to play in
Germany though he resides there with his American wife
He is a gentle, non-political soul, though once he expressed
his fervent admiration for Mussolini. Hitler, however, doesn't
like him. A good friend of Hanfstaengl's, who was always a

welcome guest at their home, one sees him usually at diplomatic homes, among Germans and foreigners not connected
with the government, and hardly ever at a Nazi function of
any sort. Perhaps they have traced a touch of Jewish blood in
his or his wife's veins—I don't know—perhaps he once expressed himself against Hitler, perhaps he is a pacifist, or
perhaps the Nazis think him inferior to their non-existent
musical talent. In any case, Hanfstaengl used to rant at length
about how "when once he got his dear Fuehrer to see or hear
Kreisler," he was sure the Leader would agree to his appear-
ing in Germany. It may be also that Kreisler himself, the fine
and beautiful spirit that he is, would not play, even if he could,
in Nazi Germany.

Many foreign musicians still come to Germany; on the other
hand, there are many who refuse to set their foot in Nazi-land
even though they are not Jewish, as, for instance, Toscanini.
By restricting their native and foreign artists to pure Aryans,
the Nazis have eliminated from the cultural life of their
nation many of the greatest musicians, interpretative and
creative, in the world.

Of course, in the realm of painting, sculpture, and architecture the same conditions of sterility exist. Hitler has announced
both privately and publicly that he will have none of the "new-
fangled notions" in art. In his Munich art show in 1937 he
collected what he and his friends thought were the best examples of German art. The general impression of the exhibit
was one of coloured photography. Among the black list were
many extraordinary and creative talents. If his criticism of art
were applied to foreign art as well, by the logic of his choices
for the Munich Gallery, he would be forced to eliminate artists
like Cézanne, Gauguin, Renoir, Van Gogh, and most of the
great French modern school which represents the only revolution in art in centuries. All of these geniuses he would have to
throw to the dust can. In their stead he would idealize and
glorify to a degree of uncontrolled and passionate approval,
all art that is naturalistic and unimaginative—any tribute to
Germanic culture and Teutonic giants. Most such pictures
would actually be photographs tinted as paintings. His favourite

picture of himself, which caused hilarious amusement all over Germany, except with worshipful and artistically ignorant Nazis, is such an absurd and horrible caricature of painting, it can serve as graphic symbol of Hitler's bad taste.

Hitler's antagonism to modern architecture is as intense as that to modern painting. He disapproves heartily of such structures as Columbus Haus and Shell Haus in Berlin, two stunning and effective examples of steel and glass made into office buildings. It was constantly rumoured that he planned to tear them down. Whenever a new building is constructed its architect and his plans have to pass the rigid censorship of the Nazis. And all new party buildings represent what Hitler believes to be art and they can be seen all over Germany and especially in Munich where a new Nazi city is being constructed, to to speak, on the ashes of the old Munich.

It is obvious that his ideals of art stem from his own frustrated ambitions as a painter and an architect. It is equally obvious that the enforcement of his ideals in this particular line would be as strict and ruthless as other enforcements, especially because he believes he knows this field better than others and because he was formerly denied the right to realize his "genius." Now he can run rampant with no one to stop him, designate the type of art to be produced in Germany, and even design the buildings himself. It is not surprising then that the suppression of artistic talent not in conformance to his vision is drastic. It is more difficult for artists to express in their art any opposition to Hitler than it is for writers. They cannot subtly imply sarcasm in the construction of a building, or paint a picture which, if interpreted in reverse, would reveal a denunciation.

The fashionable sculptor of the moment is a Scandinavian named Thorak whom I saw on many occasions and who was a dear friend of Hanfstaengl's. He has done busts of many of the great and near-great in the world. He has a tremendous, heavy, and heroic style. He is liked by Hitler because no matter what sort of face he does he will instil it with a brute strength, a power and vitality striking to the eye—whether it is there in the face or not. He told me once he thought Hitler's bust—for which he was commissioned—would be a difficult task indeed. He compared it to Mussolini's, and if I am not mistaken Mustafa Kemal's, and deplored the lack of sculptural line in it and the labour necessary to make it appear as compellingly powerful as Hitler wanted it to be. He was commissioned to do the Berlin Exhibit in Paris last summer. In front of the buildings was a group of men and women which took away your breath with its sheer strength and brute force. The heads were the size of enlarged peas and the bodies huge hulking blobs of stone formalized into a synthetic Teutonic beauty. Thorak, a little man somewhat over five feet, with a homely, attractive, and twisted face, has been lashed to the wheel of Nazi art which crushed under its weight all of the delicate, subtle, and genius-torn creations of art and labelled them neurotic, Jewish, Marxist, or sub-human.

The state of German universities is well known throughout the world. The three best historians in Germany were either retired or dismissed at the time my brother was taking his degree in Berlin. There has been a continuous stream of intellectual emigrants to America and England since Hitler came to power. It is exciting to know that we have so profited by the Nazi dictatorship but it is tragic for German youth. There is no university in Germany now that can honourably bear that name. They are all elevated institutions of Nazi propaganda. The number of students has decreased, and especially of women students—who can be at most ten per cent of the matriculated student body—almost to the extent of satisfying Hitler, who believes, perhaps because of his own lack of intellectual ability or training, that young people have had too much education in the past. History, not to mention all the other relevant subjects, must be interpreted from the Nazi racial and historical point of view. The rectors of the universities are, if possible, Nazis, either by membership or by policy, and the professors must take oaths of loyalty to the regime. When they come into the classroom and when they leave, they must Heil Hitler. They cannot say or write anything derogatory to Hitler or to the past of Germany as it has been moulded to Hitler's taste. Of course, contemporary history—that from the World War to the present—must be treated with infinite care. Stresemann and the Weimar Republic, all the statesmen and officials of the Democratic era, are either ignored or calumniated disgracefully. There can be no real research in subjects that impinge upon any of the Nazi theories, and these theories exist in and dominate every field of intellectual life, from anthropology to English literature. Thousands of professors, including naturally some Jews, have emigrated to other countries, hundreds have been retired or dismissed, many have been quietly put away somewhere, and innumerable courageous men must hold their tongues forever or answer with their freedom and safety.

Students are not encouraged to go to universities—there are too many other careers open for young men and women who accept the Nazi tenets of faith. If they do resist going into the army or into the Party work and insist on a university education, they must first go through a year's training in a labour camp. Here they are taught Nazi propaganda and are forced to live as peasants for the period of time they are there. This accords with the Nazi theory of *blut und boden*, the sacredness of Germanic blood and soil, which all good Germans must experience. After this rigorous training, they are allowed to attend a university in restricted numbers which are passed upon, either by the Nazis themselves or their agents in the universities, and must not forget to Heil Hitler and live and think according to Nazi standards. Hitler's plan is that if his education scheme works, from the cradle up, it will not matter what sort of material the student gets his hands on in a university. By that time he will be so conditioned to Nazi theories and ways of life that he will not be influenced by anything else. One only has to read the "Nazi Primer" to see what is in store for young people who may or may not decide to enter the university much later in their lives.

Brawn, not brain, is the ultimate end of university training for both men and women. If a student reveals himself to be proficient at sports and military training, if he can recite the catechism of Nazi faith, if he shows himself to be a disciplined soldier and potential party member, it makes little difference to the Nazis whether he has acquired learning or not. In fact, the intellectual is so sneered at, heaped with such searing contempt and hate, it is better for the student not to reveal intellectual qualities or to show curiosity and objectivity of the sort respected and encouraged in our universities.

If the student wants to be an instructor, he must again be rigorously tested by the Nazis and must prove himself adept in Nazi ideology and present himself as a fine example of Nordic superiority, both physically and mentally.

All branches of practical and theoretical science have been subordinated to war research. The talent and resources they now have left have been concentrated on the perfecting of the war machine, including chemical warfare.

Thus, in art, in science, in the professions, in general intellectual and cultural life, the Nazis have made inroads of destruction which may take generations to repair. For the glory of the past, for the incomparable gifts Germany made to the world, there has been substituted a propaganda and technique of superstition, a perfect organization of sterility, false legends, and sadism upon which every country in the world, except Italy and Japan, looks with horror.

My father was so shocked and sickened at what had happened to the culture and civilization he used to know as a young student in Leipzig, he dreaded even passing through a university town. Several times, before speaking at universities throughout Germany—he thought that by lecturing in his objective, critical, and implicative way he might arouse some sleeping ambitions and ideals in his audience—he made it known as indirectly and subtly as possible that no honorary degree must be offered him. I am sure that nothing would have pleased him more, had conditions been different, than the award of an honorary degree from some of the German universities he used to visit and study in as a young man, but he would have been compelled to refuse a university degree awarded while Hitler was in power.

X

TORTURE

THE DESTRUCTION OF freedom in the German people's private as well as professional life has left Germany a place to be enjoyed only by fanatics and men bent upon the demoralization of the human race. Though much has been written about both the subtle and the more obvious means of accomplishing this end, it seems that the peoples and the leaders of other countries have become criminally inured to the daily horror and brutality existing in Germany. There have been many books written about life in concentration camps, about the liquidation of the Jewish people, about the relentless persecution of everyone not wholeheartedly in sympathy with Hitler. Nevertheless, the human memory is short and we seem to have learned to accept not only the ghastliness of civilian bombings and murderous modern warfare but also the bitter and unbelievable sacrifice of innocent human lives in Germany's bubbling caldron of hate. I can never forget what I know about German concentration camps, for I have been in contact, both in Germany and outside, with people who have suffered untold agony and tortures for periods of months and years in these hellholes. When I read in the papers almost daily of new executions, new arrests, new attacks, new imprisonments, new secret police examinations, I can only feel renewed horror, fresh pain and pity, and an overpowering sense of indignation.

Though it is well known what men and women suffer in concentration camps, many people seem to think those who tell the stories are hate-mongers or sensation seekers. I know these stories to be true and I have spent days with people who have endured their service in purgatory and watched others of their kind do so. Some of them escaped, others were released after the spirit and body had been broken, many

watched their comrades killed or tortured to death. The people
I have talked to have been socialists, artists, or writers who
were completely innocent of any charges made against them.
It must be understood by the reader that what I am repeating
must of necessity be cautiously written, the sources concealed,
because some of these people and their friends and relatives
are still living in Germany.

A young man, now emigrated to a foreign country, whom I
saw in Berlin, and later in Europe, was a promising writer of
rather vicious, sophisticated satire, absolutely harmless from
a political point of view—talented, charming, though I felt
not irreplaceable in the annals of literature. One night his
apartment was raided by the Secret Police and a copy of
"The Brown Book of the Hitler Terror" was found in his
room, left by a friend the night before. He was taken to
Columbia House prison, the worst political prison in Germany.
Here he stayed for several months before he was sent to another
concentration camp. For this offence of which he was innocent
he was brutally knouted on the legs with a stick full of rusty
nails. His legs became swollen, an infection of gangrenous
nature set in, and he barely escaped amputation. Now, two
years later, he walks like a cripple and is periodically laid up,
his legs swelling and filling with pus which he must have
removed before they can heal and he can walk again. While
he was in the first prison he was lined up with the other prisoners
for inspection and abuse from the arrogant guards. He was
asked questions which he attempted to answer calmly. When
he did so, the guards spat in his face. He determined not to
answer them. The result of this "impudence" of silence was
the throwing of lighted cigarettes down his throat. He said
this was a common experience of his fellow prisoners. He said
also he and other inmates were knocked down to a kneeling
position and forced to open their mouths while the guards
urinated in them.

A student, whom I met with his sister the first year I lived
in Berlin and never saw afterwards, was under suspicion, and
was found to have illegal literature on his person. Packed away
to a concentration camp he served the usual sentence of horror

RG

and misery. Beaten daily with rubber truncheons, lead pipes and knotty sticks of wood around the head and body, sometimes until the flesh cleaved open to the bone, he was a mass of wounds whose scars to this day are visible. The Nazis cured him by pouring bottles of iodine into the raw and open wounds. He and the men in his section of the concentration camp, upon arrival and for several weeks after, were awakened every ten minutes during the night, forced to stand to attention while the guard flashed a light in their faces and pretended inspection duty. At the end of this time, they were nervous and physical wrecks, unable to sleep at night and driven to desperately hard labour during the day. One time the guards —usually chosen from the S.S. and selected for their ruthlessness, loyalty to the Party, and cultivated sadism—drew a place on the cell floor and made the student stand, the toes and heels of his shoes outlined by chalk marks, for two or three days. At the end of that time the feet and legs were so swollen he could neither feel nor walk. If he moved from his place he was beaten mercilessly.

A friend of a famous poet, the latter an elderly Jew and a pacifist but completely uninterested in any political party or movement, was in the same prison during the term of the old man. He described the most harrowing scenes of sadistic torture inflicted on this frail, gentle, and aged man. He was forced to strip nude one night before fellow prisoners and the guards. With a burning match they set fire to the bony old form covered profusely with hair. When his screams of pain became too loud they threw a pailful of urine over him to put out the flame. Another night he was stripped nude again and made to dance to a lewd dancehall tune on a table between burning candles and bucketfuls of human manure. Weary and broken, after hours of this humiliating performance, he stumbled and fell forward across the table, upsetting the refuse over him. This courageous man had told a friend that he would endure the torture to the end, that under no circumstances would he succumb to the Nazi desire for his death. If he died, he said, his family and friends could know that the Nazis had killed him. A few months later the shrivelled, beaten and scarred old body was found dead, hanging by a rope in his cell. The Nazis pronounced it suicide. It was the new Germany's answer to race, innocence, ideals, and genius.

Most of the men and women were given the jobs of cleaning out the toilets with their bare hands and told if they wanted their hands clean before eating or retiring, they could lick them. One young anti-Nazi professor was thrust repeatedly against a red-hot stove. Innumerable other experiences either too horrible or nauseating to relate are everyday occurrences in the lives of these prisoners. Ordinary criminals have no such ordeal to go through—it is the political prisoner, so-called, upon whom the cumulative vengeance and sadistic perversion of the nation are wreaked. The several hundred thousand—a conservative estimate—of German men and women who have lived in these concentration camps or who are still "living" in them have not forgotten. Most of them, though they may be physically broken, have not lost their nerve. They fought through the concentration-camp experience—surely one of the most ghastly in man's memory—they still fight there silently and together. And they form an army of people burning with hatred and revenge who will some day have nothing to lose and everything to gain by the accomplishment of their retribution.

Though, as I have said before, I have intentionally avoided underlining this phase of the Nazi terror, I share with the civilized world a sense of outrage made more acute and indelible because of my personal knowledge of some victims and their experiences. The cases I have described happen to be a few I know of directly. I read or heard almost daily of Nazi violence against all forms of opposition including the so-called "Jewish Marxists." Every paper in Europe and America, outside of Germany, carried long and authentic stories of concentration camps, the living death inflicted upon the inmates. People of all races, of all religions and beliefs, were tortured beyond recognition as human beings. Men and women were clubbed to death, shot "while trying to escape," made to commit suicide—both real and fake—subjected to devices and subtleties of torture the human mind finds difficult to believe. Sexual crimes of the most ghastly sort were the order of the day in concentration camps. The basest, most sadistic and destructive instincts of the human being were glorified throughout a land that had lost its right by the advent of Hitler to be a member of the civilized race. I suppose only in the most savage tribes of darkest primitivism and in the worst years of the Inquisition under Torquemada can a parallel be found to Hitler's terror.

XI

GERMAN JEWS

ABOUT A YEAR after my father went to Germany, he had an interview with Hitler in which the leader of millions of human beings shouted in a frenzied and fevered monologue, "I will not be satisfied until there is not a Jew left in Germany." All these years Hitler has been steadily and surely effecting the liquidation of German Jewry. True, they are not all dead, exiles, or refugees; not all of them have been that lucky. Some of them are forced to stay on in Germany, professions closed to them, all privileges and rights as members of the human race denied them, their children taunted and humiliated, their people defiled, their lives in constant danger of violence or starvation. If Hitler is allowed by his own people and by the people and leaders of the world to remain in Germany, I fully believe that eventually there will be no Jews in Germany.

Hitler says in his valuable autobiography that his hatred of the Jews developed when he was in Vienna attempting to be an artist. It is more likely that as a young boy and adolescent he came into contact with anti-Semitism in his own village, even in his own family. He came also to loathe and fear, in his earliest youth, the strength of united class groups. He was "different," a spoiled, neurotic, insignificant *mother's darling* who was heartily disliked by everyone who knew him (except his frustrated, nervous, and ignorant mother), who imagined himself "apart" from other people because of his superior qualities, when actually people disliked him for his "airs" and incompetence. He transferred his frustration in real life and failure with people to his dreams and fantasies. He should do better than others just because he was different. As a member of the petty bourgeoisie he felt himself above the working class and, at the same time, a member of a dispossessed class which unfortunately always identifies itself in its fancies with higher class groups but can never attain their economic or social status. So he saw himself in his dreams and phantasmagoria as a painter, an architect—a member of the creative leisure class. Psychologically, he may have seen his similarity to the Jewish people—a minority group which was disliked or persecuted by those of the majority—downtrodden and frustrated—without opportunity.

Hitler, then, armed with a megalomania because of his failure in life and with people, "different," untalented, classless, not knowing where to turn, unconsciously seeing his own frustration and isolation in a detested and feared people, went to Vienna to become the great artist his sick dreams had led him to think he was. Here again he was booted about, refused by an Academy of Art, forced to live in flophouses, to paint houses and trivial picture postcards. No doubt he saw, during this attempt of his to get along in the arts, many successful and deserving Jewish students or artists, talented Jewish professors or art directors. This must have inflamed his already smouldering hate—that the Jews, the lost and impotent people, who had never been fully accepted economically and socially in Europe and through whom he saw himself, could accomplish things he was unable to accomplish. Already a serious neurotic he could not admit to himself that he was incompetent in his chosen field, inferior in every way to the hated people, so his only other possible conclusion was that the Jews by trickery and bribery, murder and conspiracy, had attained their ends. In addition to this, he fell subject to the influence of a party founded in the last part of the nineteenth century called Kristliebe Sociale Partie Osterreich (Christian Socialist Party of Austria), a violent anti-Semitic organization which reached its prime in 1905 when its leader became Mayor of Vienna. It is interesting to note and revelatory of the impression this group made upon Hitler that the slogans used by this party were later adopted by Hitler in his rise to power.

Finally, unable to realize his ambitions, he was driven to seek work, manual labour, in the building trades. Here again he was regarded askance by a group and class of men far "inferior" to him, he thought. They scorned and ridiculed him, shunned him and sniggered at the diseased fantasies now in fast control of his brain. They tried to force him to join a labour union but he quit rather than subject himself to such "humiliating mass action."

So he began to identify the two groups, the Jews and the working class, and establish in his mind a theory that the working class was Marxist and that its leaders were Jewish. This very neatly took care of both his failures. It became a mania then and has remained one ever since. He elaborated his thesis, found innumerable examples to prove it, indulged in sordid and distorted rationalizations.

It would be interesting to know just exactly when Hitler came upon the "Protocols of the Elders of Zion." I should judge from his conduct and his writing, sometime during the early Vienna days. His political, social, and racial philosophy, if it can be called that, stems surely from the absolute and faithful acceptance of every word of this notoriously fraudulent document. If he had not read these protocols before or heard of them, he surely saw either the 1917 or 1919 edition. With his detestation of the Jews and the Marxists already causing almost unbearable tension, he found the ideal outlet for his passionate sadism in accepting these documents on their face value. It is apparent that in his, and his Party leaders' speeches and books they rely utterly on the authenticity of the Protocols. Ley, Streicher, Rosenberg, Hitler, Goebbels and, less ostentatiously Goering, not to mention all the other minor fanatics, give out statements almost daily that are the results of a belief in this greatest of lies in history. They still acknowledge and accept the Protocols as their Bible of the Devil even though the circumstances and facts of its forgery have long been known throughout the world.

Hitler found in his own anti-Semitism a weapon made to order for his seizure of power. There has always been anti-Semitism in Germany, particularly drawn upon when a scapegoat is needed. After the War, Hitler, his cohorts and his Party stirred up bitterness, wherever they could find it, against the Jews. The Germans had lost the War, there had been desperately hard times economically. They were poor, resentful, many of them longing to find some reason for their humiliations. The Jew was used as the tool. Hitler told people that the Jews, with their stooges the Marxists, had started the War, had caused the revolution, had monopolized industry and finance in an attempt to bankrupt the Aryan German race and establish world control. Some desperate and irresponsible groups of Nazis seized on this legend as a last straw rather than face the much harder and uncompromising economic facts.

After Hitler came to power there was a national boycott and localized pogroms, which have been going on in more or less disguised form ever since. In this way he could satisfy his own lust for blood and his long-postponed revenge as well as those of his Party people. It was something to hold them to their fanaticism—the Jews and the Marxists were to be exterminated. forever from the fair soil of Nazi Germany. Furthermore, it was a sure way of finding jobs for all the Nazis. With every Jewish professional and tradesman, every "Jew-slave" (a term which covered Marxists, liberals, democrats, centrists, and anyone else who didn't agree with Hitler) thrown out of their positions, there were thousands, even hundreds of thousands, of jobs open and waiting for the National Socialist. Finally, if anything went wrong economically, Hitler could, for almost an indefinite period of time, refer to the past work of the Jews and "Jew-slaves" which he said was the cause for all the misery in Germany. If there was discontent with Nazi failures in making good their promises, the Nazis could point to the Jews, excite anti-Semitism, and distract their people with further pogroms and economic violations. Of course, it is a terrible thing to realize that hate and destruction are instincts that lie deep in human nature —but love, idealism, construction are equally deep and strong. Hitler must take the responsibility in history for having attempted to debase one large section of the human race and for having reduced them to the state of sheer primitivism and barbarism, ennobling, to the horror of humanity, man's most vicious drives.

2

Among my own and my parents' circles of friends in Germany I had ample opportunity to experience the immediate impact of innumerable personal tragedies. I knew sons and daughters, fathers and mothers who broke their hearts with grief and despair. I knew a mother who told her daughter to become sterilized rather than bring another victim of Nazi fury into the world. I knew a Jewish woman of middle age, in the trying years of physical change, who was pronounced insane and whose son was forcibly sterilized to prevent procreation of a perfectly healthy line. I have already described what I knew to be true in concentration camps.

The family of one of the most famous statesmen Germany ever produced has been socially ostracized, the busts of the dead man removed from every public building and destroyed, the children (half Jewish only) and widow accorded the same harrowing economic and social treatment given to "untouchables." One son emigrated to America. Another, trained as a lawyer and ready for diplomatic service, extraordinarily talented and productive as a musician and composer, has a position of insignificance in a German bank.

I have seen the doors of German homes close to them. I have seen them all wince with pain at social snubs, not to mention more fundamental restrictions upon their personal lives and property. Even Embassies of foreign countries have taken them off their invitation list rather than incur the irritation of Nazis.

When I have gone out at night with young Jewish men I have felt the sneers of the crowds, the mutterings and under-the-breath insults. At night clubs and restaurants we have been given the worst tables, the most abominable service and sometimes been refused admission. Some former so-called Christian friends through fear avoid their Jewish friends, cross the street rather than speak or chat with them. The son and daughter of one of Germany's wealthiest industrialists were dear friends of mine but they had few others except among Jews. However, many non-Jewish people in Germany have maintained a heroic stand against Nazi prejudice, defended publicly and privately their Jewish friends and their own humanitarian principles. At diplomatic parties to which we always invited our friends, no matter what their race, creed or politics, we would notice how the Nazi Germans refused to mingle with them even on foreign soil and in a mixed gathering.

When I first came to Germany there were still open incidents throughout the country of persecution of the Jews. I have already told of the shocking scene I witnessed in Nürnberg a month or two after I arrived. Since that time one hears of very few such cases in Franconia, the region where Streicher rules, for the simple reason that the Jewish people have either migrated from this section or have been exterminated.

When I came back to Berlin from this first trip I was told that Jews were forbidden to bathe in Wannsee, a popular lake near Berlin. I was shocked and disgusted and could scarcely believe that it was a government edict—as it was. For two years my favourite lake was Gross Glienicke, a beautiful, serene and quiet spot among hills and trees near Berlin. In 1935 I saw the inhuman black notice posted on the edge of the bathing beach: *Jews Not Admitted*. (I never went there again.)

These were minor and comparatively gentle methods—obvious to any stranger visiting Germany—of showing the Jews contempt. Other and more effective ways of eliminating the Jews from German social and economic life were the concentration camps, ostracism, killing, and pillaging.

3

Hitler's ultimate object, as I have said, is to wipe the Jewish people off the map of the Germanic world (which in his grandiose plans includes all of Europe, not to mention Russia and the colonies); in the meantime, he wants to restore the worst conditions of the economic slavery and social hatred of centuries ago by segregating the Jews completely, by confining them to the Ghetto. By these means they will have their own streets, their own schools, their own customs, living in incredible poverty, victims of fear and starvation. Hitler does not want to rid Germany of them immediately; they are too useful to him for the present time. If he can have them marked with the yellow spot, easily accessible and identifiable in their isolated ghettos, he can pounce down on them with bloodthirsty Nazis and conduct pogroms like those of Russia in Czarist days. Thus he can whet and keep whetted the sadistic instinct he has uncovered in his immediate and most fanatic followers; and he can also take the minds of millions of Germans off their needs, hungers, and discontents. Like the degenerate Roman Emperor who kept a small stock of Christians on hand to throw to the hungry lions, Hitler will always retain a few Jews for the amusement and excitement of the restless Nazi crowds. Anyone who can seriously doubt this for a moment has only to read the cruel songs the little German children are taught to love more than their mothers' lullabies, the official rantings and ravings, on paper and by word of mouth, of Streicher and Goebbels, to mention only two. They repeat to the German people, to the infants, and to themselves that they long for the days when murdering a Jew will be the honourable pastime of their nation.[1]

Gradually, after the few remaining Jews—those not killed or suicides, starved to death, or unable to emigrate for financial or other reasons—have been confined to ghettos and forced to mingle only with themselves, more and more rigid laws will be applied to their economic activities and social intercourse. Sterilization, as applied by the Nazis, is looked upon with disgust by any sane German and scientist; it will be the next menacing fact to be faced by the Jews. But not until Hitler feels that pogroms and physical starvation have run their course will he attempt to blot out the Jewish people completely.

[1] The truth of these statements has been only too horribly proved in the first two weeks of November, 1938. Hitler and his friends, drunk with the power Messrs. Chamberlain and Daladier handed to them in Munich, have indulged in a maniacal and frenzied orgy of sadism and destruction that has shaken the world. By utterly disregarding world opinion Hitler has challenged Europe and America to take a stand. If they do not, Hitler's outrages against humanity will know no bounds, will increase and intensify without parallel in the written record of man.

As I said in the earlier chapters of this book, when I first
came to Germany I was no more and no less anti-Semitic than
most gentiles of my background and education. I didn't like
many of what were described to me as their people's charac-
teristics (I fell into that common category of people who said,
"Some of my best friends are Jews, but . . . "), I thought they
were "pushy" and over-intellectual. I had the average gentile's
envy of their brilliance and accomplishment, which was
developed into a vague prejudice. Because their social and
campus activities were circumscribed, I faintly deplored and yet
did not understand their segregation. In Germany for the first
year I was subjected to the most violent and transparent barrage
of propaganda I have ever faced—this propaganda was an
attempt to make me anti-Semitic as well as anti-socialist, anti-
democratic, and anti-intellectual, to force me into emotional
attitudes of hate and anger. I was asked to consider the Jewish
people both subversive and sub-human. As factual and thoughtful literature began to seep in, against the Nazis' will, and
replace the reams of Nazi propaganda, I began to see the
German Jew in his historical role, in his good as well as his
bad light.

There is no question that the Jews had prominent places in
finance, the professions, and the arts. That they dominated
these fields to the exclusion of the Aryans is ridiculous and
untruthful. The Jewish population produced an incredible
number of talented and productive men in proportion to their
population. And one can only consider it creditable to their
people. Being an American, I never had been trained in the
prejudice that only the privileged, those of the moneyed or
familied upper crust, should get to the top. So it did not seem
abnormal to me that there were brilliant scientists, professors, artists, lawyers, and doctors who were Jewish. After
all, the best man wins, or should win according to American
mythology, and I saw no valid reason for excluding talent and
constructive work because of religion or minority groups.

What came as a deep and unforgettable shock to me was
the fact that many of the wealthy Jews among financial and
industrial interests had actually supported Hitler financially

and otherwise. They certainly knew what Hitler had in store for them and their people—he made no secret of it from the earliest days. What then could make them, with open eyes, commit their peoples' suicide? What was more important to them than the fact that they were Jews, in danger of imminent destruction by Hitler? The only answer that made any sense was that their class and their fortunes meant more to them than their own lives and freedom and the human birthright of their children. They would agree smilingly to the extinction of their people and glibly accept a temporary economic amnesty from Adolf Hitler.

These pitiable creatures in the throes of financial ambition and class power paid their penalty in due time. For a year or so Hitler left the wealthiest Jews alone, though he taxed them heavily and in many cases summarily confiscated their financial and agricultural holdings. Now Hitler's constant economic duress has led him to the logical conclusions—he is brazenly taking Jewish property of all types, and the rich Jew who thought he was safe by identifying himself with the capitalist class is under the Nazi axe. A brilliant book was written some years ago describing the wealthy and upper-class participation in Hitler's rise to power. It was printed in Holland and immediately confiscated by the Dutch government and by Royal Dutch Shell, in which the Queen is one of the largest stockholders and whose president, Deterding, is vociferously pro-Nazi. A few copies are extant and tell the tragic story of the Jews who forgot their self-preservation for a now non-existent position as economic royalists. These facts relate not only to German Jewry but also to foreign, especially American, Jewry as well.

4

There are some rich American Jews who either directly or indirectly are supporting Hitler and similar movements—Fascist in implication—in the United States and elsewhere. By using the complicated manipulation of international exchange, they actually contribute to the improvement of German economic conditions, by selling and buying goods and machines, by carrying on profitable business within Germany, having interests there in their own corporations—American and international. In America these same Jews refuse to co-operate in American boycotts, allowing militant anti-Fascists to bear the burden and fight their battles for them. They support financially, morally and personally numerous movements and organizations which are pro-Fascist in implication if not more. Of course there are wealthy Jews who are genuinely anti-Fascist and politically conscious—these people fight directly and often with other groups against Hitler and Nazi persecution and for progressive causes in America. Many Jews of moneyed aristocracy find themselves, ironically enough, on the side of reactionary Republicans and conservatives, unsocial-minded groups, who if they get into power in America, will express themselves, at first in veiled form, through pro-Fascist, anti-Semitic, anti-Labour policies and activities. So when Jews vote conservative, they are voting in a party and group who are bound to turn on the Jews individually and as a minority. As President Roosevelt said in November, 1938, any party that is violently anti-New Deal falls into the category of pro-Fascist ideology. It is a tragic, blind, and self-destructive view for rich American Jewry to take and it comes as a shock to me after having observed how this same class has been persecuted and liquidated by Fascist technique. They hope to save their fortunes temporarily. But these wealthy political reactionaries will not only lose their fortunes; they will forfeit their freedom and possibly their lives as well. They will be forced to live in the Ghetto, to serve as fresh meat, whenever it is needed, to the hungry stomach of Fascism wherever it takes hold.

As a Gentile, I cannot resist saying that any Jew, who, after having had the chance for five years to see Hitler and Fascism in action, supports Hitler, condones his system, no matter where it is or develops, no matter what deceptive new forms it assumes, should not be surprised by the inevitable fate in store for him. The tragedy is that it is not only the pro-Fascist wealthy Jews who will suffer for their lack of foresight, but also the millions of innocent Jews, who because of the criminal betrayal by an irresponsible few of their race, must pay the penalty as well.

The ultimate effect of Hitler's anti-Semitic propaganda is as yet immeasurable. He does not intend his attitudes, his world theory and practice to be effective only in one country, or only in his Germanic world. He expects that other nations—far and near—and other peoples will become acutely conscious of the Jewish problem. He wants to influence the attitudes and actions of governments and citizens in every part of the world still not under his partial or complete domination. This has been fully documented in the book, "The Brown Network." In America, South America, England's Imperial holdings, as well as in countries that have no Jewish populations to speak of, Hitler intends to put "racial" consciousness on the map and incite Jewish prejudice everywhere.

For five years the Jewish people has been receiving daily publicity, such as it has never had before in its history, in the press and on the radio all over the world. No matter what has been the point of view expressed, whether sympathetic or not, the Jews have been prominent in the thoughts and conscience of mankind. The intelligent, wise and foreseeing gentiles are horrified and indignant—they act militantly in many ways to remedy the situation in every country. But this enlightened minority is not large enough, though during Hitler's horrible persecution in November, 1938, we had a stirring proof, in America, of outraged public opinion and a well-timed official challenge. Other gentiles, among society's upper brackets, knowing unconsciously that they are partially responsible for the plight of the Jew, resent the object of their cruel discrimination and want to be rid of the burden. They do not want to be continually faced with the serious economic and moral challenge involved. These gentiles, in all countries, are ready and ripe for the seeds of the anti-Semitism Hitler so viciously plants. They resent Jewish refugees coming in large numbers from Germany and further complicating economic problems. Hitler tells them that the Jews dominate economic and cultural life, that they are responsible for many of the world's evils. They look around them and see Jews prominent in financial and artistic life and they try to convince themselves, though they know better, that the Jews are running the country. As a solution they begin half heartedly to wonder if Hitler's policy of extermination isn't the most effective one. When a political crisis or economic emergency arises many of these gentiles are ready to believe the self-appointed prophets of their particular national brand of Fascism who point their finger at "destructive international Jewry."

Many Jews and many gentiles thought they had found in Zionism an answer to the Jewish sense of homelessness and isolation. They would establish a national home which would mean everything to them religiously, traditionally, and economically. England in the Balfour Declaration made this dream a possibility. But international Fascism not only wants to rid Fascist countries of Jewish populations but also wants the Jews to be homeless everywhere. The Palestinian development has interfered with the progress of imperialist ambitions of Fascist and non-Fascist countries and has proved itself to be a fantasy entirely without basis in bitter economic facts.

Hitler, partially satisfied when the Jews are wanderers, the objects of scorn and ridicule, the victims of hatred and sadism, plays consciously and shrewdly on the growing and implanted anti-Semitism of other countries. Hundreds of thousands of Jews have left Germany in the last five years—they are thrown on the mercy of foreign countries who have willingly opened their doors to them. In America certain reactionary groups begin repeating the old slogan—which of course never had any truth in it—"America for the Americans," "we have too many Jews anyway, we haven't enough jobs for our own American people and we don't like foreigners, especially foreign Jews who clutter up our economic and cultural life." Thus Hitler, diabolically anticipating the latent anti-Semitism in capitalistic countries, manipulates and intensifies it at will.

The effect of this growing anti-Semitism is not only felt by gentiles, and reflected in their political and economic actions which is as Hitler intends, but even more tragically by Jews living in other countries. There are two general reactions, equally devastating to the Jewish people. Some become bitter and vengeful, anxious to have power, and to get what they can through the shrewd, speculative and exploitive methods of their *class*. Others become paralyzed from fear and despair. They isolate themselves and turn inward psychologically and every other way. A cowed group, so conscious of their people and their humiliation, they are handicapped in their fight against their own destruction.

There is only one salvation for the Jew, no matter to which class he belongs. No matter how much courage and self-forgetfulness it takes, he must forever renounce an attitude of defeatism. He must first unite with all other Jewish groups and then join with the militant and forceful gentile groups who really see the racial and economic problems involved. He must by no means isolate himself, on the contrary he must identify himself with the nation and population of which he is a member and fight with every anti-Fascist organization, he can find.

In these desperate and dark times, when for the moment the world looks as if it were terrorized by Hitler, one must remember that five or ten years is a short span in human history and that fundamental economic forces are playing into the hands of democratic and progressive society. In my opinion there will never be world Fascism. The Jews as well as all groups in society should learn this. Though Hitler is persecuting the Jews lately in Germany, Austria and Czecho-slovakia more drastically and ruthlessly than he did in the beginning in his own country, though one of the most brutal and inhuman spectacles in history is being enacted before our eyes—encouraged by such international traitors as Daladier and Chamberlain—Fascism, because of its profound economic contradictions and rivalries, cannot endure. In the meantime the Jews should recognize, once and for all time, that Fascism, no matter what its local colour or brand, is bent on the extermination of their people. They must join, rich and poor alike, in fierce and uncompromising action, against its continued existence and future conquests.

Sa

XII

THE DIPLOMATIC CORPS IN BERLIN

Among our own staff there were men and women who loyally served the American government and refused to capitulate either intellectually or emotionally to Hitler or his system. There were also others who were not so scrupulously faithful to democratic ideals—career men who made no secret of their loathing of President Roosevelt and sympathized with Hitler in his attempt to rescue capitalism from the people's regulation. With the organization of the diplomatic service as it now is, no President can depend upon the devotion of career men. These men, often selected with consideration of family position, money, and nepotism, are supposedly trained in many countries and in all sorts of circumstances, political and otherwise, until real objectivity and unselfish service are attained. Presidents may come and Presidents may go, but the career men go on forever. Most of them with the backgrounds they have—many trained at Harvard and in England— identify themselves with the most privileged groups in society, exploitive and inordinately ambitious. They learn superficially courteous manners and exquisitely boring conversational feats. They seek, in every country they are assigned to, their own brand of conservatism and reaction, their own clique of the social and moneyed superiority.

In most cases they attempt to control Ambassadors who, as a rule, are appointed by each new President, usually as a reward for political or financial service to the party in power. And in most cases, they *do* control them, since these Ambassadors are for the most part untrained in the customs, habits, and formulas of conventional diplomacy. I suppose never before in recent American history have the attitudes of professional diplomats been so clearly delineated. For the first time in a generation we have a President whose policies are uncompromisingly liberal and constructive. These men, then, have taken a strong stand personally. And just as inevitably as they find themselves on the side of the vested interests at home and in foreign countries so do they find themselves bitterly opposed to Roosevelt.

These, the reader will say, are purely personal matters and convictions. Unfortunately, however, personal attitudes cannot be divorced from action and political sympathies elsewhere. They colour a man's entire personality, his evaluation of society, his professional identity. Thus one finds, extraordinarily shocking, and out of place as it is among diplomatic representatives of a democratic power abroad, many men who are either covertly or openly anti-Roosevelt and sympathetic to dictatorship and modified forms of Fascism. The only cure for this situation would be an investigation—with records, orders, letters and official documents made public—of the State Department, in an attempt to uncover the men in America in high-ranking position in this department who are themselves sympathetic to foreign political systems and give their friends, relatives, and subordinates support and encouragement in their work abroad. There are plenty of them, and increasingly the American people realize that the fault lies at home both in the early selective processes and in the known and suspected political attitudes of State Department officials.

It is of great value to know, for instance, that privately and publicly a certain man in the State Department has expressed his belief that the Four Power Pact of Munich marks a new era in international justice, order, and peace. To make this statement, as an official of the neutral United States government, is to condone and encourage Fascist methods. For another official and his family to state that the Loyalists in Spain are Reds and that the heroic Rebels deserve a smashing victory is giving America's moral support to one of the most shameless invasions in history. For a private individual to make such statements openly is one thing, for a government official it is another—especially if that official is instrumental in forming America's foreign policy and is in a department that receives all the confidential telegrams, reports, and general information that come from abroad.

These viewpoints no doubt profoundly influence Ambassadors and other diplomats who feel it their duty not only to express to foreign powers the policy of the American government but to give gratuitous advice to the diplomats of other countries. For instance, one American diplomat made it known, of his own volition, that he considered the Franco-Soviet pact a dangerous thing and advised the French Ambassador to use his influence to defeat it; another announced in private talks that he considered it necessary for the French government to effect a Franco-German alliance and a Four Power pact with England and Italy as the other signatories. Of course, this conduct is inexcusable unless the diplomats in question had specific instructions to act in this way. If they did, America's neutrality is only a cover for a definitely sympathetic attitude toward Fascist powers expressed by certain groups in the State Department. It surely is not Roosevelt's idea to encourage Hitler and Mussolini in their conquests and cruelties—it must then be pressure from irresponsible cliques in the State Department.

After a good deal of shifting about in our own staff, the American Embassy in Berlin finally, after several years, obtained a group of competent and intelligent American service men. Particularly efficient were the Commercial, Treasury, and Agricultural attachés—the first mentioned being one of the most painstaking accurate and objective men in Berlin. In the Embassy staff itself there were several clever and sincere men who had somehow never managed to acquire an Oxford accent, a stick, or a cocktail glass frozen immemorially in their right hand. They worked hard, they used their Embassy offices not as a stopping-off place between golf games, lunches, and tea parties, but as a place in which to write, study, and hold conferences. The other school of diplomats—and they became, in self-defence, a "school of thought" as well—argued that only by being out of the office as much as possible, at every cocktail party, lunch, dinner, and social engagement, could real information be obtained. There could be no happy medium for them. And, when it came to a showdown, it was discovered that the former group of men had heard, seen, and learned somewhat more than those in *professional absentia.*

I shall never forget the amused contempt a Frenchman expressed about the habits of American diplomats. He pointed out that in his Embassy in Berlin, the entire staff had to be in the office at nine in the morning or before, compile a complete survey of the morning press, and be ready at nine-thirty for a conference with the Ambassador who himself was at work at nine. When my father first came to Berlin, long in the habit of regular hours and conscientious work, he went to the office every day at nine o'clock. After a month or two he gave up, because not one of his staff members could be located in the building. He protested to the State Department at the lackadaisical organization of work in the Embassy and shortly after an order was issued from Washington to all American Embassies in Europe that the staffs must be at their desks at nine-thirty. My father kept this regime religiously but he was more of an exception than a rule and was regarded cynically by several of the staff members who even up to the last day we were in Berlin could scarcely manage to drag their work-weary bodies and information-laden minds to their offices before lunch.

All of this seems fault-finding and trivial in itself unless one pauses to consider that diplomacy is a serious profession, supposedly one of the most important services a man can render his government. Germany is not now, and never has been, a vast country club in which American diplomats have chosen to disport themselves, but a country where developments are occurring that menace Europe and the whole world and directly affect the interests and future of the United States. This should be enough to eliminate forever the illusion of career men that diplomacy is a glorified Navy, with the work thrown out and women, wine, and the midnight oil thrown in.

2

There were two men in the Berlin diplomatic corps for whom my father retained sincere respect and friendship as

long as they remained. One was the Spanish Ambassador,
Zuleta, of former Republican Spain who stayed only about a
year after we arrived. He was a tall, thin, humorous, and witty
man, resembling a more wiry and vigorous El Greco type,
whose background had been both democratic and intellectual.
It was a pleasure for our family to entertain him and go to his
parties and a joy to watch the two men together, Zuleta speaking almost as broken a German as my father would have
spoken French. However, they discoursed in German, used
their hands and their eyes, their arms and their laughter and
intuitions to make themselves understood. As a matter of fact,
though Zuleta could not speak German well, he understood
every word that was spoken. He was informal, gracious,
simple, and a bit jerky as a host, but a delight to all of us
with his wit and his gaiety, his earnestness and his competence.
He was the only man for whom my father revealed real
warmth in these years, and his distress and sadness were
apparent when Zuleta was recalled and later when his government was overthrown. Finally, when the Republican spirit
again triumphed in Spain, overthrew the gangster bankers and
the church hierarchy and was almost immediately attacked
by Fascist invaders from without and within, I think my father
understood more completely and felt more profoundly about
the tragic events in Spain than any of his diplomatic confrères.

Zuleta's successor was more kindly accepted by most of the
diplomatic corps. He was a large shortish man, violently pro-
Royalist when there was no Spanish Royalty and equally pro-
Fascist during the reign of Robles and Co. in his country. He
and his wife did more actual curtseying to German Royalty,
and symbolic curtseying to German Nazis, than anyone else
in the corps, except the Italians.

When the Spanish war came, they were held temporarily
in custody in the Embassy on the top floors, while the new
Ambassador from Loyalist Spain lived downstairs. These were
bitter and confused days—part of the Spanish Embassy staff
were on the Loyalist side and returned to their country—
most of them, however, stuck by their native and international
criminals and remained in Berlin in hiding when the new

Ambassador arrived. This new man was shunned completely by the corps, refused recognition by the Nazis and remained virtually an outcast the short time he was there, no diplomat daring to receive or entertain him publicly, or even privately. Many Germans and members of the diplomatic corps made quiet visits of sympathy to the dethroned Royalist representatives residing calmly and safely on the top floor.

Finally, when Germany recognized her puppet state, a new Ambassador was sent as characteristic of the Rebel rule as was Franco himself. He was an old man, I should say around seventy, though he looked and acted eighty or more, behind whose back Hitler and Mussolini joined hands in pulling the strings. He was generally speechless, without vividness of any sort. Always with him, almost like a Faustian diabolo, was a young secretary of the Spanish Embassy, who until the civil war had done nothing but lazily enumerate his women and his wines, recount his erotic conquests, dwell on his fortune, his illustrious name, and the soft beauties and languors of his native land. Before Germany had recognized Franco, when this dark, handsome man suddenly realized he was without fortune, fame and position, he drove desperately about the streets of Berlin, draping his car in black whenever there was a Loyalist victory. I can imagine the panic that must have reigned within him when he realized that he might have to do one solid day's work. In any case, he was the new Ambassador's constant companion, whispering in his ear and guiding his footsteps. We never knew whether the decrepit and aristocratic old general could speak or not, because we never got that close to him, and of course would not, even if we could, have entertained him.

3

Next to the unfortunate Zuleta, my father admired the solid worth and unwavering integrity of the Minister from Holland —a dignified gentleman of the conservative, conventional school, Count Limburg-Stirrum—a name which indicated his impeccably aristocratic background. What drew and held these men together was not their economic and social philosophy but their interpretation of the Nazi scene. Limburg-Stirrum could never be called a radical, not even a progressive democrat, but he was an intelligent, courageous, and stubborn man who saw what Fascism meant, not only to his own little country but to the rest of Europe. Though he and his wife observed socially the most rigid behaviour in Berlin, deviating not a fraction of an inch from accepted Protocol or etiquette customs, a little overwhelming in their stiffness and formality, they nevertheless commanded the respect of everyone. Well trained in diplomacy and history, with kind and wholesome emotions and a mind that could see beyond the end of its figurative nose, Limburg-Stirrum was a cultivated and quaintly charming figure, distinctive among his social-climbing, politically compromising colleagues, a hard worker, a man with true character, and a fighting spirit. He and my father agreed never to attend the Party Congresses in Nürnberg. Neither of them ever did, though their attitude was regarded askance by others in the corps. He was transferred to London and my father resigned, neither having broken his word.

4

The dark portly André François-Ponçet was the dean of the diplomatic corps, having come to Berlin in 1931. He had abnormally sharp eyes, a high forehead, a black waxed moustache whose ends he twirled constantly and expertly, and a monocle. He possessed one of the shrewdest minds in European diplomacy. Long connected with the powerful munitions interests in France, wealthy and aristocratic, he had married a woman whose family were big stockholders in the iron ore mines in Alsace-Lorraine. There was only one man in public life in Germany whose wit could match François-Ponçet's and that was Dr. Schacht. Ponçet, in his mastery of diplomatic verbiage, in his epigrams, his nuances and innuendoes, his sharp elliptical meanings, his fabulously alert mentality, was head and shoulders above anyone else in the diplomatic corps. He used language to conceal rather than reveal meaning. It

was an intellectual exercise to speak fifteen minutes with
Ponçet—so strenuous, vivid, and fascinating, that most people
would leave him exhausted and defeated. He remained calm
and serene, quietly twisting and caressing his moustaches and
adjusting his monocle, ready to take on someone else in this
intriguing pastime.

His manners were exquisite and somewhat condescending
—I have never seen him do anything untimely or indiscreet
(unless it was expressly planned as such). I felt, however, that
he must have been a hard taskmaster, an arbitrary personality
if he were crossed in any way.

François-Ponçet was seemingly, to the end, an interested,
even intimate, friend of my father's. They not only had serious
conferences together—they also teased, joked, and sparred with
each other at every social meeting. My father did not trust
Ponçet, as he did not trust anyone—with the exception of
Zuleta and Limburg-Stirrum—in the diplomatic corps, but he
was always pleased to see him, eager to converse on serious as
well as lighter subjects. I am sure Ponçet trusted my father,
as everyone who ever knew him does, not only because of
my father's personal integrity but because Ponçet knew that
America had no axe to grind, no rapier to thrust in the back
of foreign countries and their representatives. This fact, of
course, made their contact more pleasant and less tense than
contacts Ponçet was accustomed to. Maybe Ponçet was irritated at various times during their friendship—particularly
when my father lectured him on France's policy and pointed
out mistakes both past and current—but he never showed it.
When my father, a year and a half after he came to Berlin,
told Ponçet that Italy was planning to dominate the Mediter-
ranean, Spain, and the colonies of North Africa, and Germany
heading inevitably toward a political and economic control
of southern and eastern Europe, Ponçet is reported to have said
wryly, "These Americans do not have a realistic immediate
view of European affairs—because of their geographical and
potential economic isolation, they see things from too great
a distance, with too long a view, and historians are inclined
to lose sight of the trees for the forest, of the stones for the

blocks." Apparently he saw no reason to advise his government against heavy rearmament, or for an armament conference with Germany early in Hitler's reign, or for firm stands on the Ethiopian situation, the Rhine reoccupation, the Spanish and the Austrian situations. So, now, though my father's perspectives seemed a bit too broad and extensive in outline in those days, Ponçet must think once in a while of these sardonically long-viewed conversations and prophecies of the "historian." As a matter of fact, anyone could have seen the developments of recent years had he really taken seriously the book that Hitler wrote and has tenaciously followed throughout his life in almost every detail. Every statesman and official in Europe knew, if he knew anything, what Hitler was planning to accomplish. That there was no action taken, no block of any sort placed in his way, no sincere or firm effort of anyone to halt him, indicates only too clearly that Hitler worked not only on the war fears of terrified Europe but in collusion with certain of its groups and class interests.

Ponçet belongs to the Radical Socialist party of France—a party which compares with conservative democrats in America. When Léon Blum came to office in France, Ponçet prophesied regularly for several months that the Socialist Premier would not last another month, though, as far as we know, he supported him loyally while he was in power. Ponçet definitely deplored the civil war in Spain and was terribly frightened of the Loyalists, though he could not identify himself with the Rebels openly as long as France officially was neutral or leaned toward the Loyalists.

It has often been said that Ponçet is a Fascist. This I don't believe. Though Ponçet is a Frenchman and an ardent patriot, though he has young sons nearing the age for conscription, one cannot for a moment forget, no matter how brilliant, charming, and kindly he is as a person, that iron ore mines, munitions boards, wealth, family, and political identification present their strong arguments within his personality. I believe that he abhors German Fascism though it seems he has always acted in co-operation with it. Recently he was on a committee composed of Frenchmen and Germans to redraw the map of Czechoslovakia. I am not so sure, if it were Fascism not ultimately directed toward French destruction, or if it were Fascism of a French brand used to control the "unruly" people, to bring "order" to finance and industry, that Fascism would appear disagreeable to him. Certainly, in time, diplomatic history will reveal something of the role François-Ponçet, one of the most important and powerful diplomats in Europe, has played these last five years of German Fascism.

Madame Ponçet was one of the most gracious and lovely women in Berlin. Tall and willowy, with piles upon piles of reddish gold hair, she had the sharp, clear, and spirited beauty of her race. The mother of five or six children, she combined with infinite tact and intelligence the duties of a mother, wife, and impeccable hostess. Living in the most magnificent Embassy in Berlin, dressing modestly, sincerely religious as her husband was not, her character was gentle and passionately partisan when she discussed the future of her young sons. She entertained lavishly, as she no doubt was forced to do—the finest foods, music, champagne, and butlers in Berlin were in her house. Sincerely modest and even shy, her tastes were quiet and delicate, her mind clever and even intellectual, her manners absolutely flawless. Her charity was famous in Berlin and her goodness almost legendary. But her role was not alone that of a mother, an unpretentious and informal hostess, but also that of the wife of her husband, one of Europe's most famous diplomats. And she lived up to her position with ease, charm, and dignity.

5

The representative of Great Britain was Sir Eric Phipps, who came about the same time as my father and left Berlin a year before we did, to go to the one country he loved next to his own: France. He supposedly belonged to the anti-Hitler faction in the British Foreign Office. His brother-in-law was Sir Robert Vansittart.

Sir Eric Phipps was a short man, with thinning hair, a shrewd eye and a monocle. His diplomatic manner was less vivid than François-Ponçet's—but equally suave. You could not tell, from the expressions of his face, what he was thinking, feeling, or even saying. You felt that if suddenly you said, "Your grandmother has just been murdered," his facial muscles would not twitch, would show no sign of having heard your declaration, that he would go on quietly in the clipped, caught-in-the-throat, potato-laden English-well-bred voice, "Yes, yes, you don't say, yes, really, how extraordinarily interesting." He rarely smiled, he rarely quipped, he rarely did anything socially or conversationally except listen intently with owl-like seriousness to everything you said. It was really terribly disconcerting to have to talk to him—you knew that whatever you said would be received with enough ponderous politeness to stumble over. You knew also that whatever you said he would agree to with distressing alacrity. It was, in other words, impossible to carry on a conversation with him.

He was even more glamorously courteous than Ponçet for occasionally Ponçet would unburden himself in passionate and brilliant wordplay. On the other hand, Phipps was sincerely and stubbornly anti-Nazi. If Ribbentrop actually helped to manœuvre Phipps out of Germany, as is reported, he did a great service to Hitler. Phipps genuinely hated Hitler and Nazism; his predilection for France led him to encourage the cementing of Franco-British relations in order to make firm action against Germany possible. To watch him with the Nazis, to overhear his conversation with men it was openly known he despised, was a lesson in the veneer of conventional diplomacy. With these people he was just as laconic, just as unsmilingly earnest, just as agreeable as he was to his friends. But underneath this magnificent stage-play was an intense hatred and contempt for the Nazis and their stooges, whoever they might be and no matter how highly placed. His penetrating knowledge of Nazi leaders and their intentions surpassed those of other foreign diplomats. Even though Phipps was wealthy and titled, with a wife of equal wealth and family distinction, he knew that England and its empire were going to be nailed to the Nazi *hakenkreuz*. As far as it is possible to tell, from his policies and his friend, he kept his integrity unstained and did his brilliant and forceful best to prevent that subsequent humiliating and desperate spectacle. Perhaps he was removed for his efforts or perhaps he insisted on his transfer—in any case, until very recently, he must have found some degree of happiness and ease in France.

Underneath his poker face was a disciplined, thoughtful, and shrewd mind, devoted to the best interests of England as he saw them, sincere under a manner that seemed patently deceitful. My father liked him, consulted often with him, relied to some extent upon his judgment—though most Americans have a way of automatically distrusting the English ruling class. And Phipps often expressed his admiration for my father's unswerving loyalty to democratic ideals and eagerness for Anglo-American friendship on the basis of democratic action, in opposition to capitulation to Fascist bullying.

Perhaps secondary to being anti-Fascist and an effective diplomat, Phipps was a family man. He passionately adored his young wife and his five or six children and was happiest with them. Both of them were quiet, modest, almost embarrassed socially, informal—Lady Phipps with a disarming frankness of manner. But Sir Eric, when he entertained formally, seemed as nervous as a cat, bounced around with his crooked walk—one shoulder hunched up, making one leg seem shorter than the other—his head carried to the side, jerking from one group of his guests to another, emitting almost inaudible "Yes, yes, how interesting" sounds. Lady Phipps stood quietly in one spot, leaving all the introducing and ceremonial formalities to her husband. She was serene, untalkative, a little cold, shy and sweet in manner. Everyone else thought her colourless and arbitrary at the same time. She made no pretensions about liking diplomatic parties. She hated and felt uncomfortable at them. She told my mother she gave as few parties as she could, and tried to meet all her obligations by giving large affairs where she would not have to mingle too intimately with many people. The small parties she reserved for people she really liked and could be natural with.

A short, slender woman, completely without make-up, with a face more beautiful and wholesome than a Madonna's, she was a converted and passionate Catholic. She had borne her deeply loved husband—it seemed to be the only true marriage of love and companionship we found in Berlin—five or six children; she was still bearing them when she was in Berlin. She loved children with all the passion of her nature.

Lady Phipps was one of the most curious combinations of piety and cleverness I have ever known. Her mind was realistic and sharp as a blade, she could make as barbed and witty quips as Ponçet himself. She was extraordinarily honest in her opinions and mental methods. Her judgment of the diplomatic corps, the parties, and the personalities was severe, and extraordinarily funny. Naturally, she had many enemies among snobbish and affected women in Berlin. My mother and I liked her better than any other woman we met in these circles. We trusted her, we did not fear her malice because we knew it existed only for vicious people.

When Lady Phipps was not aroused by hypocrisy or the Nazis who hated her and her church as well, her bitterness and quickness subsided into a gentle, sweet, deeply religious nature. She could be as generous as she was condemning, as gentle as she was hard, as soft as she was sharp. A Catholic convert, a few years before she came to Berlin, her Catholicism became second nature to her.

My mother, whenever she saw Lady Phipps at a social function, came home and said, "I feel so much better, the day is so much more serene and hopeful after having seen that charming woman." I felt, of course, that the two women were drawn to each other because of their similarity, both small, delicate, quiet in manner and classic of feature—though there was perhaps twenty years difference in their ages. Though my mother was never religious in Lady Phipps's sense, she had the same gentleness and sweetness when she knew people were sincere and kind, the same passion, sharpness, and indignation when brutality or injustice faced her.

Many people were heartbroken when the Phippses were sent to Paris. They could command the same quality of loyalty given to Norman Ebbutt. My mother was especially distressed, though many diplomats were almost openly gleeful. Certainly the Nazis breathed a sigh of relief.

6

Sir Nevile Henderson succeeded Sir Eric Phipps. He was in looks a parody of the facetious and suave diplomat. He looked like a younger edition of Mr. Neville Chamberlain upon whose policy it is obvious he based his own. It was said that Henderson was sent expressly to assuage the Nazis' wrath concerning the previous appointment of Phipps. In any case, Henderson played the Nazi game not only subtly but flagrantly. Everyone in the diplomatic corps marvelled and gossiped about the ease and facility with which Henderson was held tight and without protest to the Nazi breast. He made no secret of his fondness for Nazi leaders—in fact in conversation with other diplomats he commended and expressed admiration for their *real politik*, their forceful handling of the European situation. He even expressed, at a party, the view that Austria should be annexed to Germany—long before the plan had been made. The Austrian Minister was so insulted he told his government about it. The Austrian Chancellor sent a protest to the British government, Sir Nevile was called home, severely reprimanded for being so indiscreet, and returned, officially spanked. It did not cure him; it was not intended to cure him. Open sympathizers of the Nazis were shocked at the conduct of Great Britain's representatives—even his staff members talked bitterly against him. But he went on serenely, no doubt specifically instructed by Chamberlain himself, to make up for Phipps's residence and work, preparing the way for Chamberlain's vicious and cowardly sellout of the Western world.

This change in British policy was so brash, brazen and disgusting that the Nazis knew it to be the prophecy of better things to come. It indicated that the English, even in their manners, not to mention their intentions, had lost hold on themselves. The Nazis were proved right when they came to test this assumption.

Sir Nevile Henderson was a man of about forty-five, I should judge, who had had some diplomatic experience in

South America but who apparently knew nothing of modern Europe. On the boat from South America were several high-placed Germans, one or two of them with distinguished titles —all fanatically pro-Hitler. It was a coincidence I suppose that these men were on the boat—but, no matter about that —they made friends with the new Ambassador in short order.

In a few days after his arrival, he was being wined and dined by, and was wining and dining, the most important officials in Germany, enthusiastic as a child, almost becoming, in American terms, a "back-slapper." He went to the Party Congress in September, 1937, almost beside himself with anticipation. That his attitude was adolescent from the start is perhaps not his fault, but that such adolescence was, and is, allowed to represent Great Britain is significant.

Tall, slender, dark, with a gaunt face, slick hair and a little jet-black moustache, he was the Beau Brummel of the corps, convivial, overflowing with good spirits, enthusiasms, and seemingly hearty frankness. It would have been difficult to find a more complete antithesis to the dignified, quiet, and restrained Phipps. Soon a fast friend of Goering, among others, he was to be heard extolling Nazi virtues and political acumen to everyone, including men like my father (who, by this time, was a well-known anti-Fascist).

My father observed his frantic manner, quietly summed him up, commented, and no doubt reported on him, knowing full well that England was doing a pretty undignified act of reversal before the amazed eyes of Berlin. If this was Ribbentrop's choice, it was a good one. Unconventionality is one thing, unconventionality when it is used as a cover for British deterioration is quite another—and that was the way it was regarded by the diplomatic corps and the Nazi potentates.

7

The Ceruttis were the Italian representatives until shortly before the Rome-Berlin axis was conceived by the two dictators, or rather by Hitler. Madame Cerrutti, before she married the diplomat, was a Hungarian opera singer, quite *grande dame* in manner, and a Jewess. Large and dark-haired, sensational in behaviour, she was a passionate devotee of music and started the regular concerts held at the Italian Embassy which ended in boring the diplomatic corps to distraction. She was very sincere about the whole thing—and it was an attempt to interpret Italian music, past and present, to Berlin gatherings, German and foreign. She held them in the afternoon and in the evening—they lasted an hour or two—and then tea or a buffet supper was served. Quite a few diplomats and Germans caught on to the schedule and managed to arrive just in time to hear the last number and get fed!

She made no secret of her intense Hungarian nationalism, and when my father first arrived, sent a package of Hungarian Revisionist propaganda to him. She was equally fervent in her dislike of the Nazis. When her husband was transferred to France she was quite content and left Germany without reluctance. Cerrutti was recalled when France refused to recognize the conquest of Ethiopia by sending a diplomat to Rome. Now, though France has followed the line of reactionary England, or rather the reactionary leadership in England, her policy towards Italy has been reversed. In the meantime, however, Italy has embarked upon an anti-Semitic campaign almost as violent as that of Germany, and Cerrutti's career —because of his marriage to a Jewess—has no doubt been ruined.

Cerrutti himself was a huge, paunchy, important-looking gentleman, a little on the style of von Neurath in manner and in looks. One could never feel intimate or friendly with him, though his manners were impeccable. Teasing, joking, or sparring with him would have been something like tickling an elephant's tail. It was reported that the family life of the Cerruttis was stormy and theatrical. Certainly Madame Cerrutti was as temperamental as one would expect an old-fashioned opera star to be.

One of her most discussed penchants was her habit of cleaning the ashtrays. Living in an Embassy, second only to the French in magnificence, surrounded by servants, Madame

Cerrutti, whenever she gave a large party and the ashtrays began to look overfull, would go around the various reception rooms, pick up two or three at a time and dump the contents into the nearest waste basket.

They were to my mind much nicer people than their successors, for despite their coldness and curious stilted habits, they were sincere and genuinely out of sympathy with the Nazis.

8

The Attolicos came to Berlin after Mussolini and Hitler had decided that both brands of Fascism should pursue the same fundamental policies in Europe. It meant Italy's temporary break with England and France and the orientation of future behaviour around Germany's needs and actions. It seems as though, in the years following, Italy has taken the role of the little puppy dog following timidly in the footsteps of a bullying police dog, which might at any moment turn around and snarl at the little cur. Of course, this is more of a fact than a fiction. Anyone who has watched the rape of Austria, and Germany's economic monopoly of Spain, though Italy has done most of the actual fighting there, can see the truth of the comparison.

The Attolicos were laden with glamour and legend by the time they arrived in Berlin. In the first place, they had just come from Moscow where they had been for several years. Madame Attolico came from a wealthy aristocratic papal family, had brought her chapel with her private priest to Godless Russia, and had been supposedly an intimate of many of Russia's highest political leaders.

She was surely the most glamorously beautiful woman of the diplomatic corps. Her husband, however, was medium height, stumpy and stooped, with a bay window, a face whose features were not only ugly but whose expressions were glum, ungracious, and even surly. His hair was cut in a stubble— like the beer-drinkers of the German middle class—iron grey in colour, and he wore glasses with a magnifying lens which made his eyes prominent and gave them a strange expressionless stare—as often happens to eyes under such glasses. His manners were natural and expressive of his seemingly sour temper. If he had a light, it was surely hid under a bushel, and though one might feel sorry for him in his loneliness and gruffness, this sympathy was not conducive to affection or warmth.

This man was married to the fabulously beautiful Eleanora. Slender, graceful, with a natural rhythm of movement, one could not believe that she had borne four or five children— one of whom was as beautiful as herself and whom she took endless delight in showing off. Her skin was of the purest creamy tone, her hair soft and black, wound in a wonderful braided coronet around her small, elegantly-shaped head. Her nose was finely sculptured, her eyes dark and lively, her forehead wide, her mouth full and red. The perfection of her face and features was so flawless it was breathtaking, and to me, no matter what I thought of her otherwise, whenever I saw her it seemed like seeing a beautiful painting or listening to a haunting phrase of music.

By this time in Berlin, there seemed to have been a reaction to formalism and conventionality in diplomatic manners so complete that Madame Attolico's arrival was like a wave of life over the town. Her absolute naturalness and simplicity of manner captivated everyone, except the jealous wives of other diplomats. She talked frankly about the cost of her servants, about the expense of her dinners, the naughtiness of her children, the ridiculous and boring diplomatic parties. She would put her arms around certain women and kiss them publicly, or make some startling remark about their dress or grooming, she would swing a man's hand, or lightly slap his face, lean down to tie her shoe, chat with the servants, walk to the door with a guest, go shopping and bring home her own purchases—all of these things so unheard of until now in the diplomatic corps that one felt them unbelievably natural and exciting.

Madame Attolico was a consummate diplomat. In a few weeks she was the most popular woman in Berlin, the Nazis having fallen in love with her completely. She was so charming, unconventional, and beautiful that few people even tried to resist her. Several of the former leaders of the corps, women who had been noted for their loveliness and courtesy, were envious and malicious about the lovely Eleanora. They said she was a hypocrite, her manners affected and false. Later, after I came to know her well, I was inclined to believe them, but I still admired and marvelled at the art she had cultivated. She was supposed to have been the bosom friend of Litvinov, not to mention other Soviet officials; in another moment, she was the bosom friend of Hitler, Goebbels, and Goering, not to mention other Nazi officials! It was a remarkable reversal and one to be expected from as shrewd a woman as Madame Attolico. However, the Russians can be quite as wily as was Eleanora.

With her intuitive if untrained mind, she sensed immediately the conquest she was making among the Nazis. One time, however, she was forced to experience the natural consequence of her unconventional behaviour. She had invited an imposing number of guests to lunch, including Ambassadors and Nazi officials. Hanfstaengl was also on the list. She waited for ten minutes, then fifteen, and there was no Putzi. She humorously told her guests that he was a bad boy to keep her waiting but that since she had waited that long she might as well wait a little longer. He would surely come in a moment. Putzi finally arrived a half-hour late, in a roar of fury and apologies, bows, hand kissing, and profusely adoring phrases, and we all went to lunch. She carried it off as best she could, but one could see in her slight flush and petulance that for once the situation had gotten out of hand.

I remember her now, even at this distance and after this period of time, dressed in white, soft folds of material falling around her slender body, with cream-coloured fragrant flowers in her dark hair, in the midst of a group of uniformed Nazis to whom she was animatedly talking and laughing, charming and delighting with her womanliness and her flattering attentions. Whether hypocrite or not, artificial, affected or wily, she was certainly stunning, full of poise, enamoured of success—the perfect diplomat Mussolini no doubt told her to be.

9

The Austrian Minister, Mr. Tauschitz, was a delightful, fat, tall, child-like man who had a shrewdness and humour underneath his deceptive appearance. Always questioned by my father as to when his little country was going to be annexed, he took the teasing earnestness in good grace and answered, sometimes wittily, sometimes seriously. He was a sentimental fellow and loved to dance the waltz, which he did beautifully despite his weight. Of peasant origin, supposedly a friend of the little Dollfuss, he was certainly simple and sincere in manner and appealing in his rough, gay, and child-like behaviour. It is said that through his manœuvring his country was violated by Hitler. It may be true because one never knows what goes on behind diplomatic conduct. I believe, however, that he was no more guilty than was his government, and was as helpless as is any diplomat who carries out official instructions.

10

The Polish Minister, Josef Lipski, also a bachelor, was a sly pasty-looking man of middle age whose prominent pale eyes seemed as deceitful as his manner. I have never seen him without a frozen smile on his face, so frozen and so smiling that it distinguished him even among his other confrères who were proficient frozen-smilers. I once wrote a story, published in a German magazine, about the innocuousness of cocktail parties. Whenever I saw this smiling and quite maddeningly polite gentleman, he would hold my hand and move very close to me and say, "I can well imagine what you are thinking about us now, all of us diplomats and our silly parties." It was supposed to be funny but it was one of those never-to-be-exhausted jokes which I am sure was as infinitely boring to him as it was to me. He very likely heartily agreed with the view he thought I had expressed in the story and probably hated his own mannerisms. However, underneath the seemingly sympathetic view he pretended to hold with me, there was a character as shrewd and intelligent as Berlin possessed, a man to be watched for his manipulation of German-Polish relations, and for his possible future in Poland's political life.

The Soviet Ambassadors—Mr. Chinchuck and Mr. Suritz, now in Paris—having mastered European and diplomatic customs, saw the whole comedy of manners with a hint of wry humour and twinkling sarcasm.

The first two years the Russians were invited to most German and diplomatic functions—except those Embassies and Legations whose countries had not recognized the Soviet Union. Later, however, when the Nazi insults became so personal and unbridled, there was a considerable cooling off in diplomatic relations. The Russians could still be seen at certain places, but few Germans would have anything to do with them. The Russian Embassy parties, once the most popular and eagerly attended events in Berlin, used to include the highest German officials. Now the Germans went so far as to refuse to attend these functions, and at diplomatic parties the Russian Ambassadors, the Embassy, their staff and their wives, would stand grouped together, isolated and disregarded. It was, of course, not their fault but the fault of the Nazified atmosphere in Berlin. The Russians of the Embassy in Berlin were, on the whole, charming people—natural, informal, sprightly and clever.

II

The Ministries representing smaller countries had some of the most interesting and extraordinary people in Berlin's social life. The Scandinavian representatives observed a sort of aloof and frightened distance from National Socialist ideology. They knew too well what was and is in store for them in case Hitler proceeds without being stopped. All of Scandinavia, as well as the Balkan countries, are in the line of Nazi advance.

One of the most amusing couples in Berlin were the Lithuanian Minister and his wife. Mr. Saulys was a silent, tall, hatchet-faced individual, with a florid complexion and strange, glowing, orange-pink hair. He was nice but glum, and I think he didn't open his mouth more than once or twice in his long Berlin term. His wife was a dark, buxom, former opera singer, with a soft, honeyed dramatic voice, a flamboyant and caressing manner. The voluble, dark lady and her speechless partner were quite an extraordinary study in contrasts.

The South American diplomats were, on the whole, intriguing and stimulating. They were lively, intellectually vivacious, unconventional and informal. Their wives were often as clever as their husbands and the Latin sparkle in all of them could not be dimmed by the fanaticism and tension existing in Nazi Berlin atmosphere. They were exceedingly friendly with us and seemed to be trying to make up their minds as to whether their future was with the United States or with Europe. I imagine that their indecision represents exactly the actual policy of their native countries. Many of the South American Republics, to this day, for economic reasons, are lining up with Germany—have even accepted internal and political forms of dictatorship, though they want to respond to America's eager political and economic inducements. In the meantime, these diplomats play off Germany and America against each other with infinite skill. The future of the American continent will depend not only upon European developments but also upon the outcome of Fascist and democratic rivalry in this part of the world.

The Balkan countries were represented usually by very shrewd men. The Roumanian Minister, Mr. Comnène, who is now Minister of Foreign Affairs in his country, was extremely pleasant, if slightly pompous in manner—tall, dark, impressive, with a supposedly anti-Fascist orientation. His wife was a beautiful, artificial blond trying desperately to stay young.

Nervous, animated, full of trembling vitality, and in a constant state of excitement, the Czechoslovakian Minister and his wife were passionately anti-Hitler and equally terrified of him.

Hungary was represented by a sour-faced, disagreeable, pudgy man who was very poor and very snobbish. His wife was strikingly beautiful—a rich, strong, passionate face, a fine head, crowned with magnificent dark red hair. Their daughter was one of the loveliest girls in Berlin. Though scandal haunted their lives, they remained proud, aloof, and pro-Fascist.

The Turkish Ambassador bubbled with energy, vitality and good humour. He was a delightful, natural, solidly intelligent man who pursued the late Mustafa Kemal's policy with great tact and shrewdness. His wife was an oriental-looking woman with a face as solid as the Great Stone Face. One of the most difficult women in Berlin with whom to carry on a conversation, we used to tease my father whenever we knew she was to be his dinner guest—which was quite often. He would attempt half-heartedly to draw her out for a few minutes. After this unsuccessful attempt (it was always the same no matter with whom she was sitting), she would retire to her distant thoughts, sitting, as immovable as a huge stone idol, by my silent father. As a matter of fact, he came to look forward to these evenings with her because it was the one time he could relax completely without feeling rude in so doing.

The Egyptian Minister was one of the gayest bachelors in the corps until the advent of Chamberlain's stooge and the Egyptian's marriage. Heavy, dark and sensual, Hassan Nachât Pasha was both repellent and attractive. He specialized in magnificent parties, red roses, white orchids, delicate and rare wines. Though essentially a fairly good sort, he was spoiled, vain, and indulged beyond comparison. His mind was more realistic and intelligent than one would expect it to be.

The children of these diplomats were for the most part pathetic and unhappy creatures. Shifted about from country to country, from their birth onwards, they had few friends of long standing and little contact with reality. The daughters were on the marriage market wherever they went but many of them never managed to stay long enough in one place to get a husband. They attempted to while away their hours with harmless avocations. One was an amateur actress of no especial talent, one made a study of massage and physical culture, another was absorbed in social service work and another studied sculpture. Their days and nights were filled with the endless, monotonous routine of silly parties and un-interesting social obligations. One dutiful daughter was the social secretary and personal maid for her indolent and selfish mother. The boys were somewhat better since they were sent away to school and came into contact with new attitudes and learned a certain perspective. They knew no other way of life, these children, and most of them, as a result, were mentally sterile, if socially polished. I felt sorry for the young girls and the girls who were no longer young. They were the victims of the kind of life their parents had chosen. And because, on the whole, European women have little economic, social or emotional independence, they knew no alternative but to stay by the side of their parents.

These were the people whom I saw practically every day, sometimes two and three times a day, while I was in Berlin. Some of them were saints, some of them were devils, but for the most part, they were typical representatives of their class and profession. Their parties were almost all the same, following a sort of imperative pattern of conduct and courtesy, and varying scarcely a hair's breadth. Most of them were happy in the artificial lives they led because they had never known anything else—some were miserable, homeless wanderers, conscious of the fact that their social lives represented a sort of emotional and intellectual death. The only way to live such a life and survive was to form a small group of friends and see as much of them as possible—perhaps more. Otherwise, the horrible treadmill of cocktail parties, lunches, dinners and banquets with their accompanying conversations, restricted to inquiries about health, travel, other parties and petty gossip, would have left one desperate and lonely beyond endurance.

XIII

WHAT FASCISM DID TO US

Our last year in Berlin was uncomfortable. By this time the Nazis knew clearly my father's position towards Fascism and its German leader.

When my father first went to Germany he believed he could serve his own country's interests, improve her trade and commercial relations, and perhaps encourage the moderation of Nazi fanaticism. His heart was in his job. He loved Germany and the Germans and he believed them to be the most highly educated, potentially democratic and cultivated people in Europe.

At first his contacts with the Nazi officials and leaders were pleasant if non-productive. And they even liked the modest, unpretentious and scholarly man—as long as they thought he would further their interests. At one time Hanfstaengl told me that Hitler personally felt warm and friendly towards my father! The Leader told Putzi that he could recognize in him a man of complete integrity and simplicity. They well knew his historical attitudes and principles, his knowledge of Woodrow Wilson's policies and his personal friendship with him. But they believed he was unassuming and sufficiently frightened of their power and cruelty to keep silent, acquiesce, or resign.

But a few months after his arrival, my father delivered a speech that must have given the Nazis pause. He compared by indirection and "historic parallels," as the press called it, the regime of Hitler to the brutal Cæsars. Even that didn't disillusion the hopeful Nazis. Because my father attempted to effect better trade relations with Germany, at the specific instruction of the State Department, they felt that he would fall in with their designs. He continued to pursue, during the entire time he was in Berlin, the policy his government had laid down for him. But he had no success despite the foxy

Dr. Schacht who pretended to the last he was in favour of closer commercial relations—needless to say, on his own terms. My father, needless to say also, was as firm on his. So nothing ever came of it—and nothing ever will, unless the State Department, with or without the influence of the present Ambassador, changes its policy and decides to sign trade agreements detrimental to America's business. My father protested regularly to members of the Nazi officialdom and to the Foreign Office on the preferential treatment Germany accorded other nations.

During the first year my father was more bitterly disillusioned about men in German public office than even he thought possible. Though he knew Hitler and Goebbels to be crazy and diabolical long before he went to Germany, he couldn't believe that all the men around them were equally incompetent and dangerous. For a time he thought von Neurath was a conservative, if pompous, man with a sharp intellect and a few principles. But, as he talked more and more intimately with him and Hans Dieckhoff and learned from them that Germany intended to conquer by one means or another the entire Danubian area and that they felt this area was rightfully theirs, he knew they were perfect tools for Hitler's brutal expansion policy. He was not surprised, then, when von Neurath made his southern European trips and his visits with Mussolini. Von Neurath tried also to justify the Italian dictator's conquest of Ethiopia and designs on Egypt, Hitler's and Mussolini's venture in Spain, and Germany's plans in Austria, Czechoslovakia, and the Balkans. Von Neurath may not have always approved of Hitler's method of accomplishing his ends, he may even have advised temporizing and longer delays, but essentially he was in approval of Germanic supremacy. When my father gradually learned these things, he recognized that even the most conservative and intelligent Germans had fallen victims, as Nationalists, if nothing more, to Hitler's blandishments.

There were never, even from the first months, any illusions in our minds about the more conspicuous and brazen Nazi leaders. The few fine men who remained in Germany and were connected in any way with Hitler's government were soon disposed of. The rest stayed and bore upon their faces and revealed in their actions the type of men they were. An American and a democrat, a man of character and honesty, could have but one opinion about them. My father, of course, had to see them and consult with most of them regularly, but the distaste he felt was so strong it had its effect on his nerves and general health.

We suspected that the Nazis got their information about my father's attitude, not only from his public speeches which were carefully veiled and laid in past history, but also from their espionage service which was devoted not only to the telephonic and telegraphic communications but to all phases of our daily lives as well. It is possible that there were certain Germans within the Embassy office itself, appointed in various menial positions, who might have used their knowledge to the advantage of the German government. And, of course, there were many men and women among our guests whom we completely distrusted.

My father made regular trips to the United States and, on several occasions after he had returned to Germany, and quite by coincidence, there was some new hostile speech or measure announced by cabinet members, the Secretary of State, the President, or some branch of the government. Probably the Nazis suspected that my father had had a hand in these matters. When he was in America, reporting to the President, having conferences with committees, and consulting with the Secretary of State, the German Embassy in Washington revealed great curiosity. Germans or those sympathetic to the Nazi regime were surely on his trail, avidly smelling the footprints he left behind. Strangely enough, several confidential messages and letters as well were either sneaked out of the State Department, copied there or read and reported on outside. For on many occasions my father heard repeated to him confidential matter he had given to this Department. One is forced to conclude, therefore, that, either high or low in this Department, there are men close to and friendly with the Fascists; or there are Americans sympathetic enough to dictatorships to reveal this material in an attempt to discredit an

Ambassador hostile to Nazi Germany, though passionately democratic and loyal to his own government.

With these combinations of sources (the American State Department, the German Embassy in Washington, the Nazi espionage system in Berlin and my father's own public announcement of his stand against dictatorships whether they were in Cæsar's time or in the present), the Nazi government, Hitler and his co-gangsters became bitter and avowed enemies of the American Ambassador.

During his assignment in Germany my father offered his resignation several times, but was urged to stay on by various officials in the American government. The second and third year he was in Berlin, he received thousands upon thousands of letters, telegrams, and pleas from America and all over the world congratulating him upon his stand against Fascism and urging him to remain there. Hundreds, if not thousands, of Germans came to his office regularly thanking him for what he had done in the cause of democracy. Most people who held to a militant anti-Fascist position, even in our own governmental circles felt that he could be of service if he remained in Germany—for the simple reason that he stood as a block, moral and intellectual, to Hitler's conquest of the diplomatic corps. As long as my father was there, known to be inimical to Fascism and representing the most powerful country in the world, Hitler could not be too certain of America's attitudes and Roosevelt's direction. If another man were there, in his place, who was in any way sympathetic to the regime, there would be an infinite gain in Nazi prestige. People in the United States and in Europe who stood against Hitler, felt that my father, in his honesty and penetration of issues, would present in his conferences, his telegrams and confidential reports a much more critical and uncompromising picture of Germany than a man whose vision was not so clear and sure and whose historical knowledge and perspective were inadequate. His evaluations of foreign affairs, they said and thought, might influence America into adopting a more positive foreign policy.

So he stayed—studying and analyzing and reporting; doing his best to help what Germans he could in every way he knew how, without, of course, violating international law; describing conditions to those highly placed in American life; urging action at certain fortuitous moments. He would make no compromises of any sort; he would not debase himself to the level of most diplomatic intrigues; he would not play hand in hand with the financial and industrial interests of his country or any other country.

Though most of the diplomatic corps respected him, many of them considered him idealistic and impractical. He did not, as Ponçet did, for instance, have any connections with powerful native industries and corporations who made deals with similar monopolies in Germany; he would not, as did Phipps, assume the hypocritical manner of a diplomat and capitulate if his class were at stake. He was a typical American, of unusual training and brilliant talent, without political, social or family alignments that would affect or influence his objectivity. He was the *enfant terrible* of career diplomats, American and otherwise.

Men on our staff attempted, from the first, to control him, to direct his attitudes and manners, to influence his telegrams and dispatches. My father, on the contrary, paid little attention to men on his staff whom he thought conservative and sympathetic to Nazi Germany, and less to the irresponsible powers-that-be at home. He remained for four and a half years utterly loyal to Roosevelt and the ideals of Secretary of State Hull. With other members of the State Department he was constantly at daggers' point and he fought his battle against nepotism and privilege courageously and unswervingly.

Consequently, the last year we were in Berlin the Nazis gave us a wide berth socially and officially. On several occasions my father was kept waiting for hours before he was permitted to see Nazi officials to whom he wanted to protest or with whom he wanted to consult on some matter. The Nazis seemed to hold him responsible for every new occurrence in America that indicated anti-Nazi feeling. And when the "quarantine" speech of the President was delivered in Chicago, the feeling against the United States in Germany was intense beyond belief. In fact, several times during the last year my father thought it would be wise to post police guards before the Embassy and the residence. At one time Streicher had the audacity to attack my mother, by indirection, in an official speech he made in Berlin. He described the incident which I, not my mother, had witnessed in Nürnberg, and deplored the humanitarian interest a certain prominent diplomat's wife had taken in the way he handled the Jewish problem.

When we gave official receptions most of the high-placed Nazis, with the exception of the Big Three whom my father never invited, declined to attend. After several of such snubs we naturally did not keep them on our invitation list. In return we declined many official affairs given by these same Nazis, though we observed as strictly as possible the rules of courtesy and accepted diplomatic etiquette. I have been told by one or two intimate friends close to Goering and the Leader himself that Nazi officials were forbidden to attend functions at the American Embassy, I remember once or twice a brave friend of ours came to a banquet we gave even though he had been told not to come. He had a genuine affection for my father and mother, loved their friendliness and respected their political position, though as one of the Nazi potentates he was acting against orders. It became to us a matter of amused speculation which families would come and which refuse. We even made accurate guesses as to the excuses they would give.

When Hitler in 1937 gave his official diplomatic function of the year as Chancellor and Reichspresident, all members of the corps were invited to attend, including my own family. In the protocol of German official society my mother was scheduled to sit on the left side of Hitler. She was humorously rehearsing to me what she was going to say. She had a disconcerting habit of asking seemingly innocent but pointed questions. When she spoke in German, her listeners were not sure if it was the stumbling German she used or a sharp and shrewd understanding that went into the content of her acid comments. When the time came to go in to dinner my mother was escorted by, I believe, von Blomberg to her seat—not by the side of Hitler but opposite him! He had placed Emmy

Goering on his left and, of course, Madame Ponçet on his right. There was no excuse, from their point of view, for this official social snub. The reason given later, when my father protested quietly, was that Emmy Goering's husband had just been given a new rank and that the Leader was afraid to offend his Number 2 Nazi by placing his wife in a less honoured position. It was a transparently weak excuse, thought out by God knows how many specialists and with what devious and painful methods. We knew then, and conclusively, that the Nazis not only despised my father politically, but that they intended to make it known whenever they could, publicly before the assembled diplomatic corps and Nazi officialdom.

This same year, the letter my father had written to a few Senators about the opposition to Roosevelt's court reform was published. It was a carefully thought out historical analysis and summary, a devastating attack with factual proof, of what reactionary and unprincipled elements could do towards retarding American progress. It contained, however, one concluding paragraph—which, of course, the press seized upon immediately—describing the willingness on the part of a certain American near-billionaire (in the sense that his financial interests and monopolies amounted to a control of nearly a billion dollars) to finance an American dictator. Though the Nazis did not give this publicity, they considered it a final suggestive attack upon the way they had seized power. It made matters no easier for the family in Berlin. Truth usually hurts.

My father returned to America in the summer of 1937 for a few months of rest and relaxation. Before he left, a Counsellor had been appointed to replace a conservative man we had had for a year or two. It was Prentiss Gilbert,[1] who had been in Geneva for over five years, a blustering, charming, cynical career diplomat. He told us that Sumner Welles had urged his appointment to Berlin. Eager to understand and be close to the Nazis, he believed in pursuing a *real politik*—power politics —in Europe. He was shrewd and naive at the same time, sensitive to flattery and attention. He deplored Fascist ideology

[1] Mr Gilbert died suddenly of heart failure late in February, 1939, at the age of 55.

and I think definitely disliked the Nazis. He lived simply and had an unpretentious and informal manner except for his egotism.

His appointment did not take effect until after my father had left for America. But my father had left instructions that he did not want a Chargé d'Affaires to attend the Nazi Party Congress in Nürnberg. He himself would not have attended, had he been in Berlin. In fact, for three years he had joined with the British and French Ambassadors in a boycott of this most disgraceful of celebrations. We knew, and they knew as well, that they would be forced for several days to listen to unbridled attacks on democracies, to submit to the propaganda that was the life work of the Nazis, and to hear their brutal and poorly disguised plans on their own populations, the Jews, and Europe in general. Refusing to attend was one way of showing Hitler that the democratic powers were, at least, united on one point.

As long as my father was there both Ponçet and Phipps agreed that the three of them could be held to their position, but, if he should leave, it would look conspicuous, and perhaps be ineffective, for only two of the three great democracies to protest. Phipps was recalled and sent to Paris and in his stead came the Beau Brummel representative of Mr. Chamberlain. My father went to America and left, temporarily in his stead, a man who wanted to get along with the Nazis if only, as he put it, to disarm them. So Ponçet was isolated.

Our Chargé consulted with the pro-Hitler Sir Neville, who said he was going to Nürnberg. François-Ponçet told Gilbert that if the British Ambassador was attending, and if America would be represented, he would also have to go. Gilbert knew that the State Department had always left this decision up to my father's discretion, preferring that he take his own stand on the matter. But the new Chargé accepted the Nazi invitation.

In the meantime my father had heard of Gilbert's decision and expressed his indignation. He spoke to the Secretary of State who said that if he had realized the significance of the change in a three-year policy, he would have directed him not

U9

to attend. In any case, it was too late and Gilbert was breaking the precedent of the American Embassy.

My father then wrote a confidential letter to the State Department outlining the reasons he held for never attending this Congress. They involved long precedent in American history when our diplomats refused to attend Party functions and celebrations, and the fact that these Nazi Congresses had consisted mainly in attacks on freedom, vilifications of all political or moral idealism, menacing and vicious threats and designs on the free territory of other nations. My father believed that no democratic representative should dignify by his appearance such disgraceful official behaviour. All of this was written in a private letter. By some confusion this letter was somehow made public, published in the newspapers and widely commented upon. Of course it created a sensation. Hundreds upon hundreds of letters and telegrams deluged my father from all sections of the population, most of them approving his position and congratulating him on his courageous action. But the harm was done, nevertheless.

In the summer before the "fateful September" my father had once again tendered his resignation, giving as reasons his inability to effect any commercial agreements and the damage that was done to his health because of the tense life he was forced to lead. He was urged to stay on.

For perhaps a year or two the German Foreign Office, through its Embassy in Washington, was pressing our State Department and the President as well to recall my father. After his various speeches, his letter about the proposed financial backing of a dictator in America, and a harmless statement he gave out to the press when he first arrived in America in the early summer—a mild statement which he had carefully fully prepared on the ship, indicating his belief that there would be no war and reaffirming his devotion to democratic principles—the pressure from Germany was intensified. Mr. Dieckhoff protested against the prepared statement and said he considered it an insult to his country!

But after the letter on the Nürnberg incident found its way to the press, the Germans had something really to fight about.

My father was again ready to resign and suggested it, but it looked inadvisable to resign under fire. He was told, however, that in March or the early spring there would be a new Ambassador appointed to Germany. When he heard the name of the man proposed, he was distressed and urged against his appointment. This man would have been a fairly competent person in almost any other country, but to be Ambassador to Nazi Germany would have been a disaster. My father's advice was seemingly listened to, and the matter was closed. He was to stay on until March—serving the double purpose of waiting for the appointment of a proper representative to Germany and proving by his return that Roosevelt did not intend to capitulate to the Fascists and recall an Ambassador simply because they wanted it.

While my father was still away, Prentiss Gilbert found himself in a very embarrassing position. When Mussolini came to Berlin the Protocol problem of raising the flag came up. It had never been done before on such occasions and there was no precedent for it. Gilbert, accordingly, called the French Ambassador, who was the chief of the corps, and asked what he intended to do. Ponçet said his Embassy was not going to raise its flag but that other Embassies should decide their own policy. By some misconception, our Chargé took this to mean that he should raise the American flag during that day. Our Embassy, of all the major non-Fascist Embassies in Berlin, was the only one with a flag out on this gala occasion. It caused a sensation and much amused comment in the city. What made the situation even more undignified was that the diplomatic corps was not invited to attend a single function, meeting, or party at which these dictators met. However, the Nazis were overjoyed and soon everyone was talking of the sympathetic attitude of this new Counsellor.

Another unwise procedure occurred when Gilbert decided to protest the German spy activity carried on in America. He went to Goering himself, which is unheard of since all these matters are dealt with by the Foreign Office. Of course, though Goering pretended to be shocked by the reports, calm and forceful in his decisions to do something about it, he was pleased that the American representative would come to him. My father had never done it or thought of doing it in his whole four-year term. He knew too well and from personal experiences that such gestures were futile and in the end humiliating. One can now see what effect this visit had! I think Gilbert wanted anxiously to acquaint himself with the Nazis, and wanted to meet and talk with all of them. He may have, incidentally, thought his personal visit to Goering would accomplish his purpose. I doubt, however, if Gilbert could have hoped for more.

Naturally my father was distressed with the turn of events during his absence from Berlin. He looked well when he came back, rested and relaxed from pressure and tension, even though sensational press stories had annoyed him. Roosevelt had said that he should stay on until March anyway, and my mother and I had gone to a great deal of trouble and expense refurnishing the house.

However, a few weeks after his return he got a peremptory demand from the State Department to return at once, even suggesting a boat two weeks from that date. It was later indicated from various people that Secretary of State Hull did not see the telegram that was signed with his name. In any case, after some insistence, there was a delay allowed until we could pack and make arrangements about our house. Apparently, the German Foreign Office threatened to break off diplomatic relations with America if my father were allowed to stay any longer, and it was also clear that there were men in the State Department as anxious to remove him as were the Nazis.

After some delay in appointing a successor, Hugh Wilson of the State Department and formerly Minister to Geneva was offered the post.

Mr. Wilson, author of the innocuous record of diplomatic experiences, "Education of a Diplomat," was very welcome to the Nazis. According to reports from Geneva, he had been planning to come to Berlin for three or four years—almost from the moment my father was appointed! And personally he made no secret of favouring conservative governments and the "status quo" in Europe. Before his recall in November,

1938, it is said that he embarrassed the Administration considerably by entertaining the Spanish Rebel Ambassador at a reception he gave for Colonel Lindbergh and General Goering. It is well known that America has not recognized Rebel Spain—and it is consequently extremely significant that one representative on his own initiative should choose to recognize this government at such an important and conspicuous function. It will be known soon enough what attitudes Mr. Wilson holds on Fascism, and what directions he follows. He is a career diplomat in any case, well brought up and trained, who may or may not be effective in handling the knotty problem of German-American friendship.

According to Drew Pearson and Bob Allen (editors of that pungent political column, the Merry-Go-Round) Mr. Wilson represents a pro-Fascist clique in our State Department and follows a policy of co-operation with Hitler. It is significant to note that in December, 1938, Sumner Weller, Under-Secretary of State, told the press that he thought Wilson would return to Berlin after his vacation was over. We hope Weller and President Roosevelt do not have the same objectives in American foreign policy.

It is a tragedy to realize there are so few men of high purpose, character, and courage representing America in Europe. Many of the political appointees abroad, not to mention the regular run of career diplomats, are dangerous parodies of American democratic principles—men who fall easily under the influence of foreign political systems and seem to forget their Americanism. The most conspicuous, brilliant and clear-sighted exception is Claude Bowers, now Ambassador to Spain. His record in the last five years has no blot of snobbery, capitulation or confusion upon it. He has been a fighter, a symbol of the finest American qualities of independence and honesty. His representation in Europe has been the happiest instance in our diplomatic selections. If there were more men like Claude Bowers reporting on the European scene, advising the President, our foreign policy would take on a positive and constructive aspect, and we would have less susceptibility to insidious Fascist propaganda abroad.

My father preferred to leave Germany quietly. He had his own opinions about Nazi officials and the activity of the Foreign Office against him, and he had never been a hypocrite. He advised the officials that he wasn't exactly sure when he was going to leave and that he preferred to depart without ceremonies. He, of course, would not hear of paying a farewell call to a man he considered worse than criminal.

There were a few things he could try to do. In Europe, he could attempt to keep the democracies together through personal influence on their representatives. This sounds pretentious as stated. However, such a simple example can be re-emphasized in the case of the Nürnberg spectacles—by acting in cooperation with other diplomats he forced, in a minor way, the Nazis to recognize that there was some opposition. Certainly from the fevered efforts the Germans made to remove him it was obvious that they thought he was doing great harm not only in America but in Berlin. By the time he left, a great many German people knew he stood firmly and adamantly against Hitler's ideology and persecution. This was, to the mute victims of Fascist terror, an attitude infinitely heartening, though, of necessity, passive. He also rendered great service in giving accurate reports and telegrams to the State Department and affected to some degree the foreign policy of America. The vacillating one we have had until recently has altered. Finally, upon incredible provocation, whereby Hitler has challenged humanity, the State Department or, rather, President Roosevelt himself, was forced to recall the present Ambassador in November, 1938.

My father also attempted reforms in the diplomatic service. He believed that the Consulates and the Embassies should work closer together and that a diplomat should have experience in both sections of the service. He deplored the fantastic expenditure in many Embassies, the lazy and extravagant habits of many diplomats, which American taxpayers supported. He thought in many cases that the work was repetitious. He believed career diplomats were valuable only if they were chosen objectively, not for their family, money, or "pull," and if they held securely to democratic principles wherever they were. In fact, his ideals of simplicity and integrity fitted into the common man's hopes and desires and the ancient tradition of Jeffersonian democracy.

He tried to effect, in the first years, a normal profitable trade between the two countries. When he saw this was impossible, he fought tooth and nail against the exploitative methods, the highly profitable deals and manipulations, of certain American business men who unquestionably have a voice in the State Department.

In America, his stand against Nazi Germany no doubt had great influence upon our people. His regular protests; his protection of American citizens; his humanitarian interest in the unfortunate German population, the Jews, intellectuals, workers and Catholics included; his repetition of faith in democracy; even his refusal to go to Nürnberg—all these things made an impression upon the population who knew this was the first diplomat who dared to speak from first-hand information about a country whose leaders he thought a menace to the world.

Thus my father perhaps made more enemies and more friends than anyone else in recent diplomatic history. One almost had to take a positive point of view on his activities and service. He was hated by the fanatic Nazis, the capitalists whose nefarious practices he openly deplored, certain members of his own staff and some diplomats throughout the service. He was loved by most anti-Fascists throughout America and Europe. An Ambassador of such forthrightness—no matter, as I said before, what errors and blunders were made in the process—had not been seen for many years, if ever before, in quite such a situation.

Until the end, he retained the respect and the support of Secretary of State Hull and President Roosevelt.

The conflict and controversy that raged over his head, both openly and *sub rosa*, the devotion, envy, dislike and affection around him took their toll upon his health. By the time he left Germany, he was besieged with terrible headaches and his frail health almost collapsed on several occasions. The tension in the German scene, and his passionate and necessarily reserved expression of hostility were hard to bear. But he was a disciplinarian in his way and he survived an ordeal under which most men, feeling as he did, would have broken. His only respites in these four and a half years were his book and his belief in the principles of liberty which were renewed yearly when he came home to America. During the time he was in Berlin, under almost unendurable pressure from all sides, with innumerable duties, daily work and social obligations swamping him, in a scene which he despised from the depths of his soul, he still managed to impose enough peace and restraint to write the first of four volumes on the "History of the Old South."

2

My father's career as a historian and diplomat would have been only partially accomplished had it not been for my mother's significant role in his life. She was a beautiful woman of southern birth and intellectual training. As a professor's wife she assumed the role of companion, mother, and hostess with grace and simplicity. Fiercely loyal to her closely-knit family, her one ambition in life was to have each of them effective and productive. Naturally, then, when my father was offered the post as Ambassador she urged him to accept, if he thought it would not interfere with his life work. She also believed that it would be a fitting climax to his life of scholarship and unselfish service. She sensed, but did not fully realize, what a burden this appointment would be to her.

From a quiet, modest, intellectual atmosphere, she was thrown into a society bubbling and boiling with intrigue, dishonesty, hatred, and snobbery. She had been regaled in Chicago before she left, in New York, on the boat, and by the Counsellor who met us, with wild stories as to the extravagance and publicity her position would force upon her. I remember the shyness and fear she revealed on the train from Hamburg to Berlin.

However, in a few weeks after she arrived in Berlin, she understood perfectly the obligations ahead of her. She knew she would be forced to live on an almost negligible salary, compared at least to the salaries of other diplomats, completely unaugmented by an outside income.

She found a house which served more than adequately as an Embassy—a beautiful mansion, intimate and informal enough to be a private home, pretentious and large enough to meet the tremendous social demands. She had seven or eight servants, half as many as most Embassies, and paid them the wages they got in every diplomatic household. Her entertainments soon became known throughout Berlin social life as the most charming and interesting there. She chose her guest lists herself and she managed to make her parties stimulating and exciting—a rare feat in diplomatic life.

The people who knew her financial limitations marvelled at her success, those who didn't, never suspected these restrictions. There were actually two reasons for the brilliant mastery of a life pattern she had never known. One was, having lived modestly, she knew something of economic realities and could better face and handle them herself, without the aid of innumerable advisers, social secretaries, and housekeepers. She could save money on things of which most people would never think. The second was her own charm, humour, and intelligence. Her intuition soon made her an experienced hostess, her humour lightened even the heaviest of German gatherings, her intelligence guided her in an amazing selection of interesting and contrasting personalities, her physical charm, gentleness, and simplicity disarmed everyone—even the enemies of my father—and created for them an atmosphere of naturalness, at-homeness, and informality.

In our house, because of my mother and father, people felt more free and human than they did anywhere else in Berlin, except among their most intimate friends and family. Many people have told me that they considered the ease they felt in our house was due to our being Americans. That, of course, is part of it—but I need not say that there are many Americans who fall swiftly into the lap of stiff and stultifying continental society and manners. Their Americanism, so called, vanishes, and their diplomatic parties show it. The tenderness, delicacy, and understanding of my mother's nature were the real sources of the polished and at the same time spontaneous social affairs she gave.

My mother was a small woman, five feet tall, with little hands and feet, a slender frame and delicate bones. Her face was sprightly and soft at the same time. Bright brown eyes sparkled in her naturally highly-coloured face. Her nose was perfectly shaped and her hair was soft and pure white. The qualities that intrigued and conquered me throughout my life were her youth, her sharp and realistic mind, and her sympathy. There was not a sign of cynicism or disillusionment in her character though her heart and mind became hardened to the ruthlessness of Nazi facts. Actually she had more freshness and eagerness for life than any other member of her family.

The help she gave my father was incalculable. She had always been interested in politics and felt it a much more vital subject than scholarship. She had an almost uncanny sense of character. In many cases her analysis of a personality was quicker and more thorough than my father's. She knew the devastating effects ambition and intrigue had upon people's lives and personalities and she could invariably estimate if these drives were working upon a person—man or woman.

Before she went to Germany, my mother was interested in world affairs. But she was critical and penetrating without being entirely informed. In Berlin, however, she read the German, American, and English newspapers carefully every day, she followed new books and magazines dealing with political and economic happenings in Germany and Europe. Her intellectual curiosity seemed whetted by her life in Nazi Germany.

She sensed, as we all did, the inherent openheartedness and honesty of the German people. As she watched the iron heel descend upon and crush these human decencies, she was grieved and indignant. She knew of many cases of misery and fear, told to her by unfortunate German women. She wrung her heart over them and their problems and she tried to help them in every way she could. As time went on, and the horror

increased, her courtesy and graciousness towards the Nazi officials she was forced to meet, entertain, and sit beside, became
so intense a burden she could scarcely bear it. The only way
she managed to preserve her balance and perspective was
through her sense of humour. By making disarming and amusing comment—sharp in their implications—she released her
grief and indignation. But being a woman of soft and gentle
nature, of joyous and brilliant attachment to life, of gaiety
and hope, she suffered more than the rest of us.

With the fear for her family's health and future, the intense
pride and loyalty she felt for them and the anguish over Germany's people and their destiny, she added the incredible task
of being the polite and efficient hostess in a darkening atmosphere, and among people who in the end became hostile even
to her.

As a result of her understanding of the issues involved and
the plasticity of her intellect, she knew more about the trends
of Fascism then other diplomatic wives. My father took her
into his confidence always and always relied upon her judgments. She not only made a home for him, an infinitely understanding mother for his children, an unusual, tactful and beautiful hostess, but she was as well a wise and penetrating friend.

3

My brother was the only member of the family who could
not endure the Nazi scene throughout these years. When he
came to Berlin with us, he was a young and talented student
and teacher of history. Never for a moment did he see the
Nazi picture out of its true proportion. He was like my father
in this respect. He had the unusual advantage of observing
the effects of Fascism at first hand in the university where he
was studying. He was young and vital and courageous. He
did not believe that human freedom could be sullied and
smirched for any length of time by Hitler.

After he took his degree the obvious thing for him to do
was to return to America to find a job. He would have returned anyway because he could not restrain his impulsive

and venomous anti-Fascist feeling. During the time he was there, perhaps because the Nazis knew his honesty and naturalness, he had men and women "planted" on him to find out what confidential attitudes and information he possessed. I imagine he told them all quite openly what he thought of the whole business!

In any case, my brother was young and optimistic enough to survive the most devastating experiences and he quite blithely left Germany loathing the whole outfit and determining to do something about it. For a year he taught history at an American university. Observing what he considered to be Fascist trends in that country, he decided that the classroom was not his battle field. So he joined the staff of the International Peace Campaign and lived abroad for a year, making trips to China, Poland and other parts of Europe in an attempt to stimulate anti-Fascist activity among the youth. Later he worked for an anti-Fascist organization in America until he decided that direct political action was the only solution.

My brother despised diplomatic life, was far more intolerant than anyone I knew of the whole tragi-comedy, but was completely unimpaired by its insidiousness. Bill, however, "grew up" in Germany. Though he was twenty-seven or eight when he went there, he was as immature emotionally as most American men of that age. He sobered down. He was horrified and inflamed by what he saw, heard, and observed. He could barely force himself to stay long enough to get the Doctor of Philosophy degree he wanted. Impatient, enthusiastic, impassioned, Germany deepened and solidified his idealism and plans of action. With the same implacability, courage and integrity of his father, he returned to America two years before we did, armed with his convictions and knowledge.

4

In the winter of 1937 we came home, a family that had remained intact throughout a terrible experience, more trying on the nerves and brain, the heart and health than anything we had ever known. Within four months my mother died, my father retired to his farm in Virginia, my brother entered politics, and I was determined to write an account of this purgatory on earth.

My mother's health had been so seriously affected by the strain and terror of life in Berlin that she never recovered. Within a few weeks, her heart showed the inevitable reactions. She could not stand the sudden relaxing of tension, the easing of the unnatural life she had led. Her nerves and her energy had been so drained in her years abroad, she had no resistance left. Perturbed over the circumstances of my father's resignation, she was furious with the way the world was going, and felt helpless to do anything about it. Indignant, lonely, and full of wrath, she must have realized her own impotence, her inability to take immediate action against the outrages that came so close to her. She died suddenly of heart failure, still youthful and brimming with eagerness and curiosity, in the spring of 1938.

But happily she lived to see my brother active in a Virginia political campaign, my father using his influence against Fascism throughout America, and the beginning of this book. After her death, the family separated and each of us in our own ways, following our own roads, have silently determined to do everything we can within our power to fight Fascism in Europe and prevent its formation in America.

The American scene after almost five years of German dictatorship looked incredibly promising and bright. We could scarcely believe that we were now free to talk, think and write as we pleased. Of course, we immediately availed ourselves of this opportunity.

In the meantime, however, we have had a chance to view the American scene more soberly and to compare it with the prison from which we had just escaped. We met and talked with men and women of the upper-moneyed brackets of society who openly approved Hitler and his methods. We heard remarks to the effect that America needs a strong man who can protect capital and restrain the worker. We have seen university professors who have used their profession to propagandize for Hitler. We have read books, articles, columns, and news by writers who loathe Fascism and yet play into the hands of every anti-labour, pro-Vigilante group in America. We have talked with rich Jews who vote for reactionary Republicans who, not yet daring to be anti-Semitic, still carry in their programmes, all the demagoguery, facile and false promises of the early Hitler. We have seen workers who deplore joining unions and supporting groups for united action. We have listened in amazement to the proponents of isolation for America, when they can see before their eyes the immediate effects of Fascism in commercial relations in growing reactionary movements in America, in Canada, in South America, and in the world in general.

We have witnessed the rape of Austria, the dismemberment of Czechoslovakia, the wholesale and unparalleled murder of the Jews, the vicious and destructive class action by unprincipled if hard-driven Judases like Chamberlain and Daladier. We have seen even America participate inadvertently in the capitulation to Hitler and his war-mongers.

There are two major disasters that could descend upon America. America could remain without a foreign policy and America could succumb to Fascism. If we do not support Roosevelt and his administration as long as he is head of our State; if we do not urge that another democratic and progressive president succeed him, no matter when the time comes; if we do not help united labour and liberal groups everywhere; if we do not fight all forms of suppression and persecution, all signs of anti-Semitism and Red-baiting, we will be opening the door to political and economic dangers that may weaken us sufficiently to fall into Hitler's plot for world domination.

If we do not find out who is holding up progressive and militant action in the State Department; if we do not urge a support of international peace and democracies wherever they remain; if we do not realize that co-operation with England and France can be effected only when Daladier, Chamberlain and their ilk either change their policies or are removed from office; if we do not recognize that the French and English leaders are in desperate straits with their own people because of their betrayal of their nations before, at, and after Munich, we cannot possibly understand their pursuit everywhere and especially in our own powerful democracy for support, and appreciate our potentially constructive influence in remoulding European affairs. If we do not conclude once and for all, as an American nation, that there is no such thing as isolation when the nations of the world are on our doorstep, we will discover too late that we are fighting the destructive international Fascist spirit almost single-handed, aided surely, only by Russia.

For these people, for these positive and immediate policies, as well as for the inestimably important general public whose voice is listened to in America, I have written this book in passion and in hope.